,50

A Daybook
for April
In Yellow Springs, Ohio

A Memoir in Nature

and Handbook for the Month of April,
Being a Personal Narrative and Synthesis of Common
Events in Nature between 1981 and 2017
in Southwestern Ohio,
Including an Almanac with Applications
for the Lower Midwest and Middle Atlantic Region,
with Weather Guidelines
and a Variety of Natural Calendars,
Reflections by the Author
and Seasonal Quotations
from Ancient and Modern Writers

By

Bill Felker

A Daybook for the Year in Yellow Springs, Ohio
Volume 4: April

Cover image from a watercolor by Libby Rudolf

Copyright 2018 by Bill Felker

Published by The Green Thrush Press
P.O. Box 431, Yellow Springs, Ohio

Printed in the United States of America Charleston, SC
March 2018

ISBN-13: 978-1986206167

ISBN-10: 1986206165

For Tat

Bill Felker

No one suspects the days to be gods.

Ralph Waldo Emerson

Bill Felker

Introduction

This memoir is a record of personal experiences I have had with the natural world. It is a diary of everyday walks in fields and woods, a journal of losing myself in finding and watching. The memoir gathers together quotations about time and nature, meteorological commentary made up from my lengthy obsession with tracking the weather, extensive – and often repetitious – notes about common events in nature, syntheses of these events and astronomical information based on my years of writing almanacs. Although I have organized my memoir on a scaffolding of back-yard natural history and observation, I am not a naturalist and have had no training in the natural sciences. All of what is contained in the *Daybook* is the result of my search for myself and for meaning.

This particular aspect of my search began in 1972 with the gift of a barometer. My wife, Jeanie, gave the instrument to me when I was succumbing to graduate school stress in Knoxville, Tennessee, and it became not only an escape from intense academic work, but the first step on the road to a different kind of awareness about the world.

From the start, I was never content just to watch the barometric needle; I had to record its movement, then graph it. I was fascinated by the alchemy of the charts that turned rain and Sun into visible patterns, symbols like notes on a sheet of music, or words on a page.

From my graphs of barometric pressure, I discovered that the number of cold fronts each month is more or less consistent, and that the Earth breathes at an average rate of about once every three to five days in the winter, and once each six to eight days at the peak of summer.

A short apprenticeship told me when important changes would occur and what kind of weather would take place on most any day. That information was expressed in the language of odds and percentages, and it was surprisingly accurate. Taking into consideration the consistency of certain patterns in the past, I could make fairly successful predictions about the likelihood of the repetition of such paradigms in the future. As Yeats says, the seasons "have their fixed returns," and I found points all along the course of the year which appeared to be fixed moments for change. The pulse of the world was steadier than I had ever imagined.

My graphs also allowed me to see the special properties of each season. August's barometric configurations, for example, are slow and gentle like low, rolling hills. Heat waves show up as plateaus. Thunderstorms are sharp, shallow troughs in the gentle waves of the atmospheric landscape. Autumn arrives like the sudden appearance of a pyramid on a broad plain. By the end of September, the fronts are stronger; the high-pressure peaks become taller; the lows are deeper, with almost every valley bringing rain. By December, the systems loom on the horizon of the graph like a range of mountains with violent extremes of altitude, sometimes snowcapped, almost always imposing and sliced by canyons of wind.

From watching the weather, it was an easy step to watching wildflowers. Identifying plants, I saw that flowers were natural allies of my graphs, and that they were parallel measures of the seasons and the passage of time. I kept a list of when each wildflower blossomed and saw how each one consistently opened around a specific day, and that even though a cold year could set blooming back up to two weeks, and unusual warmth accelerate it, average dates were quite useful in establishing sequence of bloom which always showed me exactly where I was in the progress of the year.

In the summer of 1978, Jeanie and I took the family to Yellow Springs, Ohio, a small town just beyond the eastern edge of the Dayton suburbs. We bought a house and planned to stay. I began to write a nature almanac for the local newspaper. To my weather and wildflower notes I added daily sunrise and sunset times, moonrise and moonset, average and record temperatures, comments on foliage changes, bird migration dates, farm and gardening cycles and the rotation of the stars. The more I learned around Yellow Springs, the more I found applicable to the world beyond the village limits. The microclimate in which I immersed myself gradually became a key to the extended environment; the part unlocked the whole. My Yellow Springs gnomon that measured the movement of the Sun also measured my relationship to every other place on earth.

My occasional trips turned into exercises in the

measurement of variations in the landscape. When I drove 500 miles northwest, I not only entered a different space, but often a separate season, and I could mark the differences in degrees of flowers, insects, trees, and the development of the field crops. The most exciting trips were taken south in March; I could travel from Early Spring into Middle Spring and finally into Late Spring and summer along the Gulf Coast.

My engagement with the natural world, which began as an escape from academia, finally turned into a way of getting private bearings and of finding what I loved and believed. It was a process of spiritual as well as physical reorientation. In that way, all the historical statements in this collection of notes are the fruit of a strong desire to define where I am and what happens around me.

The Daybook Format

The format of my notes in this daybook owes more than a little to the almanacs I wrote for the *Yellow Springs News* between 1984 and 2017. The quotations, daily statistics, the weather outlooks, the seasonal calendar and the daybook journal were and still are part of my regular routine of collecting and organizing impressions about the place in which I live.

Setting: The principal habitat described here is that of Glen Helena preserve of woods and glades that lies on the eastern border of the village of Yellow Springs in southwestern Ohio. At its northern edge, the Glen joins with John Bryan State Park to form a corridor about ten miles long, and half a mile wide along the Little Miami River. The north section of the Glen Helen /John Bryan complex is hilly and heavily wooded, and is the best location for spring wildflowers. The southern portion, "South Glen" as it is usually called, is a combination of open fields, wetlands and wooded flatlands. Here I found many flowers and grasses of summer and fall. Together, the two Glens and John Bryan Park provide a remarkable cross section of the fauna and flora of the eastern United States.

Other habitats in the daybook journal include my yard with its several small gardens; the village of Yellow Springs itself, a town of 4,000 at the far eastern border of the Dayton suburbs; the Caesar Creek Reservoir, twenty miles south of Yellow Springs and created by the Corps of Engineers in 1976. My trips away from that environment were principally northeast to Chicago, Madison, Wisconsin and northern Minnesota, east to Washington and New York, southeast to the Carolinas and Florida, southwest to Arkansas, Louisiana, and Texas, and occasionally through the Southwest to California and the Northwest, two excursions to Belize in Central America, several to Italy.

Quotations: The passages from ancient and modern writers (and sometimes from my alter egos) which accompany each day's notations are lessons from my readings, as well as from distant seminary and university training, here put to work in service of the reconstruction of my sense of time and space. They are a collection of reminders, hopes, and promises for me that I find implicit in the seasons. They have also become a kind of a cosmological scrapbook for me, as well as the philosophical underpinning of this narrative.

Astronomical Data: The *Daybook* includes approximate dates for astronomical events, such as star positions, meteor showers, solstice, equinox, perihelion (the Sun's position closest to earth) and aphelion (the Sun's position farthest from Earth).

I have included the sunrise and sunset for Yellow Springs as a general guide to the progression of the year in this location, but those statistics also reflect trends that are world wide, if more rapid in some places and slower in others.

Even though the day's length is almost never exactly the same from one town to the next, a minute gained or lost in Yellow Springs is often a minute lost or gained elsewhere, and the Yellow Springs numbers can be used as a simple way of watching the lengthening or shortening of the days, and, therefore, of watching the turn of the planet. For those who wish to keep track of the Sun themselves in their own location, abundant sources are now available for this information in local and national media.

Average Temperatures: Average temperatures in Yellow Springs are also part of each day's entry. Since the rise and fall of temperatures in other parts of the North America, even though they may start from colder or warmer readings, keep pace with the temperatures herthe highs and lows in Yellow Springs are, like solar statistics, helpful indicators of the steady progress of the year everywhere.

Weather: My daily, weekly and monthly weather summaries have been distilled from over thirty years of observations. They are descriptions of the local weather history I have kept in order to track the gradual change in temperatures, precipitation and cloud cover through the year I have also used them in order to try to identify particular characteristics of each day. They are not meant to be predictions.

Although my interest in the Yellow Springs microclimate at first seemed too narrow to be of use to those who lived outside the area, I began to modify it to meet the needs of a number of regional and national farm publications for which I started writing in the mid 1980s. And so, while the summaries are based on my records in southwestern Ohio, they can be and have been used, with interpretation and interpolation, throughout the Lower Midwest, the Middle Atlantic states and the East.

The Natural Calendar: In this section, I note the progress of foliage and floral changes, farm and garden practices, migration times for common birds and peak periods of insect activity. Some of these notes are second hand; I'm a sky watcher but not an astronomer, and I rely on the government's astronomical data and a few other references for much of my information about the stars and the sun. I am also a complete amateur at bird watching, and most of the migration dates used in the seasonal calendar come from published sources. And even though I keep close track of the farm year, the percentages listed for planting and harvesting are interpretations of averages supplied by the state's weekly crop reports.

At the beginning of each spring and summer month, I have included a floating calendar of blooming dates which lists approximate flowering times for many plants, shrubs and trees in an average Yellow Springs season. The floating chronology describes the relationship between events more than exact dates of these occurrences.

Although the flora of the eastern and central United States is hardly limited to the species mentioned here, the flowers listed are common enough to provide easily recognized landmarks for gauging the advance of the year. I found that a record of my drives south during April complemented the floating calendar and allowed me to see the approximate differences between Yellow Springs and other locations. I also learned that April in the Lower Midwest is more like March in the Southeast and more like May in the Upper Midwest. This daybook and its natural calendar summaries, then, are records of a moveable seasonal feast that shifts not only according to fixed geographical regions but also according to the weather in any particular year.

Daybook Entries: The journal entries in the daybook section provide the raw material from which I wrote the Natural Calendar digests. This section is a collection of observations made from the window of my car and from my walks in Glen Helen, in parks and wildlife areas within a few miles of my home and on occasional trips. It is a record that anyone with a few guidebooks could make, and it includes just a small number of the natural markers that anyone might discover.

When I began to take notes about the world around me, I found that there were few descriptions of actual events in nature available for southwestern Ohio. There was no roadmap for the course of the year. My daily observations, as narrow and incomplete as they were, were especially significant to me since I had found no other narrative of the days, no other depiction of what was actually occurring around me. In time, the world came into focus with each particle I named. I saw concretely that time and space were the sum of their parts.

As my notes for each day accumulated, I could see the wide variation of events that occurred from year to year; at the same time, I saw a unity in this syncopation from which I could identify numerous sub-seasons and with which I could understand better the kind of habitat in which I was living and, consequently, myself. When I paged through the daybook entries for each day, I was drawn back into the space in which they were made. I browsed and imagined, returned to the journey.

Companions: Many friends, acquaintances and family

members have contributed their observations to the daybook, and their participation has taught me that my private seasons are also community seasons, and that all of our experiences together help to lay the foundation for a rich, local consciousness of natural history.

Here are no stories told you of what is to be seen at the other end of the world, but of things at home, in your own Native Countrey, at your own doors, easily examinable with little travel, less cost, and very little hazard. This book doth not shew you a Telescope, but a Mirror, it goes not about to put a delightful cheat upon you, with objects at a great distance, but shews you yourselves.

Joshua Childrey, 1660

Bill Felker

The Month of April
April Averages: 1981 through 2017
Norma April Average Temperature: 51.3

Year	Average
1981	54.9
1982	46.6
1983	46.9
1984	48.6
1985	56.2
1986	54.0
1987	51.3
1988	50.8
1989	50.2
1990	50.7
1991	55.0
1992	50,9
1993	50.0
1994	53.7
1995	50.4
1996	48.6
1997	47.4
1998	52.0
1999	53.6
2000	51.0
2001	55.9
2002	53.5
2003	53.7
2004	50.7
2005	52.5
2006	54.6
2007	49.5
2008	52.5
2009	52.4
2010	57.1
2011	53.8
2012	51.8
2013	52.8
2014	53.9
2015	54.1
2016	51:2
2017	58.0

Bill Felker

April 1st
The 91st Day of the Year

The Snows are thaw'd, now grass new clothes the earth,
And Trees new hair thrust forth.
The Season's chang'd, and Brooks late swoln with rain,
Their proper bankes contain.

Sir Richard Fanshawe, from Ode IV, 7 of Horace

Sunrise/set: 6:20/6:59
Day's Length: 12 hours 39 minutes
Average High/Low: 56/36
Average Temperature: 46
Record High: 79 – 1986/2010
Record Low: 18 - 1923

Weather
There is a ten percent chance for 70s today, 30 percent for 60s, another 30 percent for 50s, and another 30 percent for 40s. Totally overcast conditions occur one day out of two, and there is a 45 percent chance for rain, 45 percent chance for frost. Snow almost never falls on April 1st.

The Weather of the Week Ahead
Two major weather systems, one arriving on the 2nd and another coming in on the 6th, usually dominate the first quarter of April in the Lower Midwest, increasing the chance for precipitation. Snow is most likely to fall on the 3rd, 4th, and 5th. There is a 20 percent chance for a high in the 80s this week, and there is more than a 50 percent chance of an afternoon in the 60s or 70s. Still, the first quarter of the fourth month is its coldest quarter, and daily chances for frost remain steady at an average of 40 percent throughout the period.

The April Outlook
As the month progresses, normal average temperatures rise at the rate of one degree every three days all along the 40th Parallel.

Beginning near 45 in central Ohio on the 1st of April, they reach to the middle 50s four weeks later. Typical highs move from the upper 50s to the upper 60s. Lows advance from 35 to 45. A normal April in the Ohio Valley has two days in the 80s, six days in the 70s, eight days in the 60s, eight days in the 50s, four days in the 40s, and two days in the 30s.

According to my weather history, the warmest days in April(those with better than a 40 percent chance for highs above 70 degrees) are the 21st, 23rd, and the 25th through the 30th. The 26th is the hottest day of all, with a 70 percent chance for 70s or 80s.

The coldest April days, those with a 30 percent chance for highs only in the 30s and 40s: the 1st, 3rd, 4th, 5th, 6th (the 6th is the coldest of all, and the only April day with a 15 percent chance for 20s), and the 9th. After April 22nd, chilly afternoons below 40 degrees occur less than once in a decade. Nightly chances for frost are 40 percent for the first half of the month, but drop to only 20 percent by the 25th. The 26th and the 30th almost never have frost.

An average April brings five completely sunny days, eight partly cloudy days, and 17 totally cloudy days. The brightest days in April (with better than a 70 percent chance for sun) are the 7th, 11th (the sunniest of all with a 90 percent chance), 16th, 18th, 19th, 20th, 24th, 25th, 26th, 27th, and 30th.

Most precipitation usually occurs during the first two weeks of the month. The wettest days are April 3rd, 5th, 14th (both the 5th and 14th bring rain or snow seven years in ten), 29th and 30th. The days most likely to be dry are the 11th, 12th, 24th, 26th, and 27th.

Springcount

Twenty-three major spring cold fronts cross the nation between the middle of February and the last week of May. Three passed through in February, and seven in March – the ten fronts of the subseason, Early Spring. The first six April weather systems belong to the subseason of Middle Spring. The seventh front introduces Late Spring.

April 2: The April 2nd high-pressure system initiates an eleven-day period of unsettled weather, which brings an increased chance of tornadoes in the South and Midwest and spring storms to the North. Rain typically precedes this front, and flurries or even major accumulation of snow follow it, making the 3rd through the 5th some of the wettest and most turbulent days of the month's first half. Although highs above 60 degrees become common in most of the nation during this period, frost continues to strike tender vegetables about one night in four north of the Border States. This cold wave and the next are the last systems to threaten a light freeze in the South. On the other hand, by the time the April 2nd front moves to New England, average air temperatures start to rise one degree every three days instead of ,'s one degree every two days.

April 6: As this front approaches, the chances for frost briefly diminish, and chances for highs in the 70s or 80s increase dramatically across the country. Precipitation, however, often puts a stop to field and garden planting. After the front passes east, the possibility of damage to flowering fruit trees increases in the Appalachians. Early daffodils are sometimes frozen by this front and the next.

April 11: After the April 11 high-pressure system crosses the country, several dry days often follow in its wake. All things being equal, this is the period during which you should try to get in all your Middle-Spring planting. And from now on, the chance of snow below the 40th Parallel rapidly decreases until it becomes only one in 100 by April 20. After the 12th a definite increase in the possibility of warm weather takes place. Afternoons above 60 degrees occur three times more often between the 12th and the 30th than between the 1st and the 11th.

April 16: After this front a major increase in the average daily amount of sunlight occurs: a rise from early April's 50/50 chance for sun or clouds up to a brighter 70 percent chance for clear to partly cloudy conditions. Chances for highs in the 80s continue to climb across the nation's center, reaching the same frequency as in mid-October by April 18th.

April 21: After this weather system passes across the nation, the chances for an afternoon high in the 70s or 80s jump from last week's average of 20 percent way up to 40 percent, and from this point forward, the number of frosts in any given seven days declines by nearly two percent per 24 hours. Chances for snow decline below ten percent in almost the entire country (a notable exception: higher elevations in the West). The steady advance of the year's cold waves slows, and relatively long periods of stable weather encourage the advent of full spring growth. However, the second major tornado period of April begins now, lasting in most years until the 27th.

April 24: After this front passes, chances for frost virtually disappear in the South, become relatively insignificant throughout much of the North. Chances improve for field and garden planting after the April 24th cool front; three days of dry and sunny weather are the rule.

April 28: In advance of this first front of Late Spring, highs in the 90s become possible as far north as Chicago; the chances for a high in the 80s pass the 20 percent mark at lower elevations along the 40th Parallel, and chances for a high above 70s degrees are now 50/50 or better for the first time this year. The warmth, however, comes at the cost of rain five years in ten, and April 29th and 30th are typically some of the wettest days of the fourth month's fourth week. If precipitation spoils planting, at least the odds for frost fall below one in ten in most of the nation.

Notes on the Progress of Spring in April

Average temperatures are very general guides to the weather, and usually they are not effective tools for predictions. Still, they are helpful in mapping the relative progress of the seasons throughout the United States. The *Key* below can be used not only see how cold or warm the weather might be elsewhere, but to imagine what the landscape could be like at different locations.

April temperatures in Indianapolis, Indiana and Columbus, Ohio, cities which lie close to the 40th parallel, rarely go too far from the normal average of 51 degrees (the average of typical highs near 61 and lows near 42). Residents of these areas pretty much know, without consulting any charts or graphs, what April weather is like where they live.

With just a little more knowledge, they can figure out where spring is anywhere in the country. Beginning with February's average of 31 degrees, the average central Ohio/Indiana temperature rises about 10 degrees each month, reaching 40 in March, 51 in April, 62 in May and 71 in June.

Using that average temperature ruler, one can measure the expected temperatures in other places. For example, New York, Pittsburgh, and Des Moines, have about the same averages as Columbus and Indianapolis. The land around them should be about where central Ohio and Indiana cities are in terms of daffodil bloom and wheat growth.

Moving north a little, the April average for Chicago and Detroit, for example, is 46 degrees, so they will usually be approximately two weeks behind Indianapolis or Columbus. Up in Duluth, Minnesota, the average this month is only 37 degrees. That puts them back in the middle of Dayton February.

The April average for St. Louis and Louisville is 56 degrees. Those locations will be about two weeks ahead of spring on the 40th parallel. The April average in Dallas is 65, in Little Rock it's 62, in Atlanta it's 61, meaning that their tree and flower progress has already reached that of May in central Ohio.

And along the Gulf of Mexico, it's summer. The average in New Orleans is 69; the leaves there have just about all come out. In central Florida, averages are well up into the lower 70s, and then it's June for sure.

Even though some years will be warm and others cold, the relationship between averages is usually fairly constant. If spring is late in the Ohio Valley, it will often be late in North Carolina and Georgia. If Chicago is a week or two ahead of average, Minneapolis and Birmingham may be, too.

Key to the Nation's April Weather

Cheyenne WY	-10
Portland, ME	-7
Minneapolis MN	-5
Boston MA	-5
Chicago IL	-4
Des Moines IA	-1

New York NY	-1
AVERAGE ALONG THE 40TH PARALLEL:	51
Washington D.C.	+3
Seattle WA	+4
St. Louis MO	+5
Louisville KY	+7
Los Angeles CA	+9
Atlanta GA	+10
New Orleans LA	+18
Miami FL	+22

April Frostwatch

Between April 1st and June 1st, up to dozen frosts occur at lower elevations along the 40th Parallel during a typical year. Of course, in some years, frosts end with March. Normally, however, the approximate chances for frost follow a regular and steadily declining trajectory through the end of May. Add 10 percent to the figures below for each 100 miles north of the 40th Parallel (or for each 500 feet of elevation above 1000 feet along that parallel). Subtract 10 percent for each 100 miles south of the 40th Parallel.

April 1:	95%
April 5:	90%
April 10:	80%
April 15:	70%
April 20:	50%
April 25:	40%
April 30:	30%

A Floating Sequence
for the Blooming of Shrubs, Trees, Wildflowers and Perennials

The following list is based on my personal observations in southwestern Ohio over a period of 30 years. The dates are approximate, but I have tried to show a relatively true sequence of first blossoming times during an average spring. Although the dates on all flower calendars are somewhat arbitrary (and may vary by up to 60 days between the Canadian border and the South), a "floating calendar" can be used throughout the country by adjusting the dates to fit the climate. For example, if forsythia usually blooms on May 1ˢᵗ in a given location, most of the other plants follow a sequence as listed below.

Day	Flower
March 10:	Mid-Season Crocus
March 11:	Dandelion (taraxacum)
March 12:	Scilla (scilla siberica)
March 15:	Early Daffodils (narcissus)
March 23:	Hepatica (hepatica Americana)
	Dutchman's Britches (dicentra cucullaria)
March 24:	Periwinkle (vinca major)
	Cornus Mas
March 25:	Violet Cress (Cochlearia acaulis)
	Lesser Celandine (ranunculus ficaria)
March 26:	Lungwort (pulmonaria)
March 28:	Bloodroot (sanguinaria canadensis)
	Spicebush (lindera benzoin)
March 29:	Spring Beauty (claytonia)
March 30:	Twinleaf (Jeffersonia diphylla)
March 31:	Virginia Bluebell (mertensia Virginica)
April 1:	Grape Hyacinth (muscari armeniacum)
	Purple deadnettle (lamium purpureum)
	Taxus (taxus)
	Field Peppergrass (lepidium campestre)
April 2:	Ground Ivy (glechoma hederacea)
	Forsythia (forsythia)
	Box Elder (acer negundo)
April 3:	Small-Flowered Buttercup (ranunculus abortivus)
	Creeping Phlox (phlox subulata)
April 4:	Swamp Buttercup (ranunculus septentrionalis)
	Serviceberry (amelanchier)
	Scilla (scilla siberica)
	Shepherd's Purse (capsella pursa-pastoris)
April 5:	Wood Hyacinth (hyacinthoides hispanica)

	Puschkinia (puschkinia libanotica)
April 6:	Dwarf Plum (prunus domestica)
	Red Maple (acer rubrum)
	Wind Flower (anemone nemorosa)
	Rue Anemone (thalictrum thalictroides)
April 7:	Purple Violet (viola papilionacea)
	Toad Trillium (trillium sessile)
	Star Magnolia (magnolia stellate)
April 8	Red-Flowered Quince (chaenomelesspeciosa)
April 9	Early Season Tulip (tulipa)
	Fritillary (fritillaria)
April 10	Cowslip (primula veris)
	Decorative Pear (pyrus calleryana)
	Ash (fraxinus)
	Sugar Maple (acer saccharum)
April 11	Crabapple (malus)
	Cherry (prunus cerasus)
	Peach (prunus persica)
	Bleeding Heart (lamprocapnos spectabilis)
	Blue Cohosh (caulophyllum thalictroides)
April 12	Mid-Season Daffodils (narcissus)
	Bluettes (houstonia caerulea)
April 13	Wisteria (wisteria frutescens)
	Bellwort (uvularia)
	Hawthorn (crataegus monogyna)
	Pink Magnolia (magnolia soulangeana)
April 14	Large-flowered Trillium (trillium grandiflorum)
	Winter Cress (barbarea)
	Jacob's Ladder (polemonium caeruleum)
April 15	Redbud (cercis canadensis)
	Mid-Season Tulip (tulipa)
	Trout Lily (erythronium americanum)
April 16	Domestic Strawberry (fragaria ananassa)
	Pink Magnolia (magnolia liliiflora)
	White Violet (viola Canadensis)
April 17	Buttercup (ranunculus)
	Money Plant (epipremnum aureum)
	Thyme-Leafed Speedwell (veronica serpyllifolia)

April 19	Dogwood (cornus)
	Blue Speedwell (veronica)
	Watercress (nasturtium officinale)
April 20	Lilac (syringa)
	Raspberry (rubus idaeus)
	Ragwort (jacobaea vulgris)
April 21	Snowball Viburnum: (viburnum macrocephalum)
	Azalea (rhododendron indicum)
	Early Meadow Rue (thalictrum dioicum)
	Columbine (aquilegia vulgaris)
April 22	Bridal Wreath Spirea (spirea prunifolia)
	Late-Season Tulips and Daffodils
April 23	Wild Geranium (geranium maculatum)
	Miterwort: (mitella)
	Wild Phlox (phlox divaricate)
	Celandine (stylophorum diphyllum)
April 24	Clematis (clematis x jackmanii)
	Wood Hyacinth (hyacinthoides non-scripta)
	Garlic Mustard (alliaria petiolata)
April 25	Jack-in-the-Pulpit (arisaema triphyllum)
	Wild Ginger (asarum caudatum)
April 26	Meadow Parsnip (haspium trifoliatum Gray)
	Wood Betony (stachys officinalis)
	Honeysuckle (lonicera tatarica L.)
	Buckeye (aesculus glabra)
	Red Horse-Chestnut (aesculus × carnea)
	Nodding Trillium (trillium cernuum)
	Star of Bethlehem (ornithogalum narbonense)
April 27	Early-Season Iris (iridaceae)
	Thyme (thymus vulgaris)
	Horseradish (armoracia rusticana)
	Common Fleabane (erigeron philadelphicus(
April 28	Osage Orange (maclura pomifera)
	Lily-of-the-Valley (convallaria majalis)
April 29	Wild Cherry (prunus avium)
	Spring Cress (cardamine)
April 30	Sweet William (dianthus barbatus)
	Korean Lilac (syringa meyeri)

May 1:
Catchweed (galium aparine)
Larkspur (delphinium carolinianum)
Silver Olive (elaeagnus angustifolia)
Sweet Gum (liquidambar styraciflua)
Comfrey (symphytum officinale)
Spring Sedum (sedum ternatum)

May 2:
Poppy (papaver somniferum)
English Daisy (bellis perennis)

May 3:
White Mulberry (morus alba)
Mountain Maple (acer spicatum)

May 4:
Black Locust (robinia pseudoacacia)
Honey locust (gleditsi triacanthos)
Black Walnut (juglans nigra)
Oaks (quercus)
Wood Sorrel (oxalis acetosella)

May 5:
Painted daisy: Pyrethrum (pyrethrum roseum)
Golden Alexander (zizia aurea)
May Apple (podophyllum peltatum)
Hawthorn (crataegus monogyna)

May 6:
Rhododendron (rhododendron)
Columbine (aquilegia)

May 7:
Sweet Cicely (myrrhis odorata)
Robin's Fleabane (erigeron pulchellus)
English Plantain (plantago lanceolata)

May 8:
Mock Orange (philadelphus coronaries)
Sweet William (dianthus barbatus)
Shooting Star (dodecatheon)

May 9:
Chives (allium schoenoprasum)
Catmint (nepeta)
Waterleaf (talinum fruticosum)
Wild Raspberry (rubus idaeus)

May 10:
Sweet Rocket Dame's Rocket
    (hesperis matronalis)
Dwarf Larkspur (delphinium tricorne)
Tulip Tree (liriodendro)
Yellowwood (cladrastis kentukea)
Snow-on-the-Mountain (euphorbia
    marginata)

May 11:
Elm (ulmus)

	Chamomile (matricaria chamomilla)
May 12:	Clustered Snakeroot (sanicula
	gregaria)
	White Clover (trifolium repens)
	Meadow Goat's Beard (tragopogon
	dubius)
	Red Clover (trifolium pretense)
May 13:	Common Plantain (plantago major)
	Black Medic (medicago lupulina)
	Wild Multiflora Rose (rosa
	multiflora)
	Blue Flag (iris versicolor)
	Wild Daisy (bellis perennis)
May 14:	Wild Mallow (malva sylvestris)
	Spiderwort (tradescantia)
	Scabiosa (scabiosa)
	Lupine (lupines)
	Geum (geum abendsonne)
	Baneberry (actaea)
	Fire Pink (silene virginica)
May 15:	Common Orange Day Lily
	(hemerocallis fulva)
	Stella d'Oro Lily (hemerocallis 'Stella de Oro')

April Estimated Pollen Count

(On a scale of 0 -- 700 grains per cubic meter) Major pollen source: box elders, maples, pussy willows, flowering crabs and cherries

April 1: 10	April 5: 50
April 10: 50	April 15: 100
April 20: 125	April 25: 200
April 30: 400	

April Estimated Mold Count

(On a scale of 0 - 7,000 grains per cubic meter)

April 1: 1300	April 5: 1600
April 10: 1700	April 14: 1800

April 20: 1900   April 25: 2000
April 30: 2100

April Phenology

When nettles are six inches tall, then Middle Spring wildflowers are opening all over the woods.

When the American toad gives its shrill mating, that will be the time to plant corn.

Morel mushrooms appear when May apples push out from the ground, when cowslip buds in the swamp, and when leaves come out on skunk cabbage.

Parsnips in bloom announce that deer are growing their new antlers and all the rest of the garden weeds are coming in.

When the high canopy is budding and greening, wild turkeys are gobbling.

Tulips blooming in the garden parallel the turkey vocalization, and also announce lawn mowing season.

Long grass in the lawn is a sign that opossums and raccoons are giving birth in the woodlots and young goslings are hatching in the ponds and rivers.

When tent caterpillars emerge in the trees and the redbuds start to turn purple, tadpoles will be swimming in the ponds.

Then it won't be long before dogwoods and the crab apples open, and winter grains are almost tall enough to ripple in the wind.

When the pussy willow bushes start to get their leaves, meadowlarks and scarlet tanagers return for summer.

When chicory is almost a foot high, rhubarb should be just about ready for pie, and hops vines will be crawling all over the garden.

When the first strawberry is ripe in Alabama, then peonies are budding in Iowa and privets are getting leaves in Louisville.

As soon as hummingbird moths seek nectar, allergies often intensify as all the trees and grasses come into bloom.

When the great annual dandelion flowering begins, then snakehead mushrooms appear.

When ticks and mosquitoes appear, the morel season is almost over, and the last frost is no more than four weeks away.

When clovers bloom, flea season begins for pets and

livestock, and flies take over the barn.

When wisteria comes into flower, the most fragrant time of year is here. Lilacs, mock orange and honeysuckle follow the wisteria. And that means pheasants are nesting, and warblers move north along their flyways.

When admiral butterflies visit the garden, then buckeye trees will soon be coming into bloom.

And when garlic mustard is flowering in the woods, look for cutworms and sod webworms to start taking over the field and garden. Weevils are showing up in the alfalfa, too.

Natural Calendar

Middle Spring begins at the opening of Field Corn and Sweet Corn Planting Seasons, Lettuce and Spinach and Peas, Carrot, Beet, Turnip, Onion, Collard, Kale, Bussels Sprouts and Potato Planting Seasons, Middle Spring Wildflower Season (violets, bluebells, twinleaf, bloodroot, purple cress, swamp buttercup and hepatica in flower most years).

Oats Planting Season is getting underway. Forsythia Blossom Season and Weeping Cherry Flowering Season color the streets. It's American Toad and Green Frog Song Season, the first week of Duckling and Gosling Hatching Season, the first week of Barn Swallow Season and House Wren Mating Season.

Daffodil Season has started in the dooryards pacing bright blue Squill Season, filling in at the end of Early Spring's Aconite and Snow Crocus Seasons. Throughout the Northern Hemisphere, all these seasons of Middle Spring may occur in different weeks or months, but most often, they appear together.

Daybook

1982: First forsythia flowering.

1983: At the Cascades, hepatica discovered, first bloodroot. Toothwort budding, violet cress full bloom. Buckeyes leafing. Calves noticed in the fields on the way home.

1984: After the coldest March since 1960, the very first forsythia breaks through.

1985: First cherry blossoms seen. Buckeyes leafing.

1986: The first mourning cloak butterfly passes me at Grinnell swamp.

1988: Buckeyes are leafing. Frogs begin to croak at Mrs. Bletzinger's pond.

1989: Crocus are finished for the year. Aconites were gone ten days ago, snowdrops two weeks ago. Japanese knotweed is up two inches. Beggarticks have sprouted by the back door. Pussy willows are losing their catkins today. Peach tree leafing with the apple. Yard full of clumps of old crocus leaves and wild onions. Forsythia full bloom.

1990: Frances Hurie reports that goldfinches at her feeder have gotten half their gold summer color.

1992: Killdeer are suddenly common around Wilberforce.

1993: Small grape hyacinths open now. The mid-season crocuses are still at the height of their bloom. A large clump of small-flowered bittercress opened today at the corner of Wilberforce-Clifton and Brush Row Road. Pastures are bright green. Two possums were hit last night along the way to school. *Cornus mas* full bloom at Antioch.

1994: To Mill Dam, and then down river to the island behind the mill. First hepatica and violet cress of the year found blooming there along the water. Toothwort was very small and spindly, but had buds. Mint was two inches high, snug to the ground, nettles a little stronger, maybe three inches. At home in the north garden, new phlox foliage has been up a couple of days, the first Japanese knotweed pushed up yesterday, lupine foliage is three inches or so, some of the daylilies are up to the top of my boots. There are three daffodils open now in the south garden.

1998: Daffodils wilt in three days of 80 degree heat. Some green in the high canopy. Lettuce and radishes emerge in the garden.

2000: Lil's maple and our front maple in full bloom, and the tree line is greening. Quince red. Toads calling day and night. At the Yellow Spring, I found twinleaf, bloodroot, violet cress, early meadow rue, hepatica, and anemone. Full bloom pears, cherries, serviceberries along Dayton Street. Leaves growing on the forsythia; the flowers will soon be gone. Crocus season has been over for several days.

2001: Hendersonville, North Carolina to Yellow Springs: a cold and windy drive, in and out of rain and sun. Some pears and redbuds in bloom, the latter disappearing as we approached Kentucky. In Hendersonville, most of the pears were waning near the motel. Apples had come and gone. Daffodils gone. One small-flowered buttercup found.

2002: Returning from a trip to Jekyll Island, I noted that Bluefields, Virginia, at an elevation of about 3,000 feet, was as bare of foliage as Yellow Springs.

2007: Peak of serviceberry and pear bloom in town. I noticed that Mateo's taxus tree was blooming in the alley. Green has appeared on the buds of the climbing bittersweet.

2008: Cardinals loud and aggressive this morning when I walked Bella in the alley. A half dozen squills are blooming now, and one daffodil half opened this morning near the peach tree before a cold front moved in. Along the south border of the lawn, Lenten roses – *hellaboris* – are in full bloom, and others seen along Dayton Street. In Wilmington, several white daffodils seen open.

2010: Wytheville, Virginia to Yellow Springs: The landscape season relatively uniform across West Virginia and all the way to Yellow Springs: Full beginning of Middle Spring, marked by daffodils and forsythia. Casey reported spring peepers starting on his property this evening.

2011: Some Asiatic or oriental lilies are up an inch. Monarda foliage is dense in the north garden, leaves about an inch long.

Cardinals and grackles loud through the morning. Periwinkles and primroses are open. The crab apple tree and the pink spirea bushes at home are leafing. Flower buds have appeared on the standard and the Korean lilacs. Puschkinias and squills and daffodils hold.

2012: Judy writes from Goshen, Indiana, 200 miles northwest of Yellow Springs: "Bill and I went wildflowering, and what we saw on April 24 and May 1 last year was already up and running. Henbit, lyre-leaved rock cress, all colors of violets (white particularly abundant), toad trillium, spring beauty (white and pink), cut-leafed toothwort (just about gone), false rue anemone carpeting huge areas, wild blue phlox, white garlic mustard, Dutchman's britches, white trillium (dwarf and regular), some buds on May apples (!) and probably a common buttercup. Today's *Goshen News* noted that temperatures broke records going back 90-some years."

Here in the alley, Mateo's taxis flowers are falling. Yesterday, I saw the first red admiral butterfly - and Rob, the butterfly man, says he saw one, too.

2013: Yellow Springs to Santee-Cooper Reservoir, South Carolina: Drove out before dawn into southeastern Ohio, purple fields of henbit, white patches of bittercress along the roadsides past Chillicothe. Through the mountains of West Virginia, hard rain and wind, a few patches of snow at the highest elevations, then down into sun, fair-weather cumulus, and milder temperatures in North Carolina. Above Statesville, forsythia, plums, daffodils and early pears came into bloom, and spring came on quickly by Charlotte, with redbuds, pink magnolias, the canopy starting to leaf, and pear trees with more leaves than flowers. North of Columbia, South Carolina, bright yellow Jessamine vines fill the undergrowth, weigela in Columbia, then violet wisteria in the trees, black medic in the roadway medians. At Santee – oaks in bloom, dogwoods and azaleas full flower. All this placing southeastern South Carolina one full month ahead of southwestern Ohio, six weeks ahead of Madison, Wisconsin (that still has a foot of snow). Fishing at night, I sat facing north and watched the Big Dipper spinning slowly around Polaris. One small catfish caught after midnight.

2014: Squills gathering momentum in the southwest garden and an entire bed of daffodils in full bloom along Dayton Street. Hellebores so wide open. Yesterday's budded puschkinia has opened all the way. And Jonatha wrote me: "Sunning himself at leisure on my garden path at 10:00 a.m. was a lovely mourning cloak butterfly. He flitted and sunned, and flitted and sunned for the whole 30 minutes that I could spare to watch him!" This afternoon, three daffodils came out while I was working. At the park this evening, crab apple buds showed just a tip of green, and lilac buds were straining to open.

2015: Light frost, no clouds, no wind: I went out with Bella at 5:30 to get a head start on listening to birds, but as soon as I left the house, a cardinal burst into song north near Dayton Street, and all the robins chirped and started their chorus, song sparrows right behind them. I left the doors open today, and the first mosquito of the spring came in and sat on the computer screen. Walking downtown, I saw Don's serviceberry trees with fat, ripe buds. Red maple's buds were almost ready to open. Robin singsong vespers heard a quarter of an hour before sundown.

2016: Tulips about a third in bloom, Mrs. Lawson's (Moya's) old-fashioned yellow tulips coming in, daffodils and forsythia continue full, scillas weakening, some Asiatic and Oriental lilies up three inches, and the first violets blossomed overnight. All pussy willow catkins down. Dock leaves up to eight inches. Driving to the college, I noticed early cowslips blooming across from the Covered Bridge.

2017: Spain: from Sarria on the way to Morgade. Lamium, henbit, hemlock, violets, tall rape, thin leafed bladderwort, wood nettle, blue eyes, dandelions, bright blue five petal borage among the nettles, exotic daffodils like at Gethsemani last year, many small flowered wild flowers, Canadian thistles in early bloom, the hills pale green with early leaves, the pastures deep green, the stone walls rich with heavy moss, plums and apples in bloom, full cherry blossom time in parts of Spain (done in England last week, according to one of the pilgrims we met).

At night I went out into the dark and saw a glimmering star and heard a frog, and nature seemed to say, 'Well, do not these suffice?'

Ralph Waldo Emerson

April 2nd
The 92nd Day of the Year

All that I had dreamed was true, is true.
The earth is fair, more fair
Than I had known or imagined.

Harlan Hubbard

Sunrise/set: 6:18/7:00
Day's Length: 12 hours 42 minutes
Average High/Low: 56/36
Average Temperature: 46
Record High: 81 – 1963/2010
Record Low: 21 - 1961

Weather

This is usually the mildest and sunniest day of first week of April. There is a 25 percent chance of temperatures in the 70s, and 25 percent for the 60s, and another 25 percent for 50s, fifteen percent for 40s, ten percent for 30s. Rain falls a fourth of all the days, snow flurries one day in ten. The sky is partly to mostly sunny two days out of three, and chances for frost are 45 percent.

Natural Calendar

The full blooming of forsythia, glory of the snow, pushkinia, daffodils and grape hyacinths announces the end of Early Spring and the arrival of Middle Spring. This is the time that wildflower season begins with early violet cress, twinleaf, periwinkle, spring beauty, hepatica and small-flowered bittercress. Toad trillium, early meadow rue and May apples are pushing up out of the ground. Cowslip is budding in the swamps, and leaves grow long on the skunk cabbage. Japanese knotweed, columbine, phlox and lupine emerge in the garden.

The first buckeye, apple and peach trees leaf out in the early days of Middle Spring. At dusk, frogs and toads are singing. Gall mites work in the ash trees; pine weevils and moths are eating evergreens. Birch leaf miners and elm bark beetles attack the birches and elms.

Killdeer arrive, and woodcocks call near sunset with a nasal sounding "peent." When barn swallows come to the barns, and the first

29

baby barred owl hatches, when snowdrop and aconite and snow crocus seasons end, then the first of the oats is often in the ground. The first field corn is seeded. Early sweet corn is placed in the furrows, and winter wheat is top-dressed. In town, the lawn is long enough to cut.

Nettles, chicory and leafcup are six to eight inches tall, Asiatic lilies and columbine three to five inches. Ragwort and garlic mustard are forming clumps; some sweet rockets and money plants are getting ready to send out their flower stalks.

Collards, broccoli, and kale are often transplanted to the garden now, new shrubs and trees to the yard, as well. Early head lettuce and sweet corn are being planted, and farmers are band-seeding alfalfa. Most commercial cabbages have been set out in the Ohio Valley, and half the tobacco beds are sprouting in the Border States.

In the flower gardens of the Lower Midwest, the early tulips unfold. Star of Holland comes in beneath the bright forsythia. Buckeyes leaves unravel along the streets. Plums bloom. And just as skunk cabbage starts to produce its foliage in the swamps, the first tremendous mass of wildflowers suddenly opens all at once: inflorescence of periwinkle, hepatica, violet cress, harbinger of spring, bloodroot, Dutchman's britches, bittercress, twinleaf and Virginia bluebell leading now into the endlessly intricate paradise of April.

Daybook

1983: Pears downtown ready to bloom.

1986: Cardinal sings at 5:34 a.m. Catkins have started falling from the pussy willow in the back yard.

1988: Box elder seeds sprouting in the garden mulch. Pussy willow pollen past its prime, a few catkins falling. Insects becoming much more common. Forsythia early full bloom. Sweet pollen smell in the humid warm afternoon. Columbine up two inches in the yard. Cherry buds pushing out, box elder now flowering, mint coming back, Japanese knotweed one inch out of the ground, ferns greening a little, freeway grass half green.

1989: Northern Indiana: forsythia just about to open: about a week behind Yellow Springs: 200 miles northwest, at the rate of three days per 100 miles.

1990: Two opossum road kills last night. Boxwoods leafing out. At the Covered Bridge, red buckeye leaves unraveling. The very first twinleaf, and day-old bluebells and toothwort flowers. Toad trillium full emerged, but not opening yet. Hepatica, henbit, purple deadnettle, and spring beauty blossoming all over. Skunk cabbage leaves three to four inches. Large patches of violet cress in full bloom. Cabbage butterfly and an angel wing.

1993: Garlic mustard and waterleaf have grown enough now to give the woods floor its deep green cloak. New violet leaves have sprouted along the north wall. First clematis leaves have started.

1995: A mild middle March, and everything came out, then cold. The daffodils and forsythia stay in full bloom, some crocus and a few March iris hold. Scilla, puschkinia, glory of the snow are at their best; with the daffodils and the pink wood hyacinths, they make the second season of bulbs after the snow crocus and snowdrops, regular crocus forming a transition between those two seasons. Along Dayton Street, the pears are budding. In the triangle park crab apples bud, too, and silver maple flowers hold. Box elder buds have turned green in the past week. Dogwood buds swell with down. In the east garden, coneflower leaves are up an inch, and veronica has started to grow back.

1998: Redbuds keep emerging, darker purple each day. Box elders full flower. Most fruit and maples leaf. Leaves on lilacs. Dandelions coming in. Bleeding hearts tall and unraveling. Lil's maple full bloom.

1999: First toads called tonight.

2001: Mill habitat: First hepatica, bloodroot, one Dutchman's britches, one spring beauty. Violet cress budded.

2002: In Columbus, some violets blooming, many daffodils, grape hyacinths, glory-of-the-snow, chickweed.

2004: Walking at South Glen with Mike after a week of cool, wet weather: Buckeyes, silver olive and wild roses are leafing, toad trillium emerging, purple cress and Dutchman's britches blooming, euonymus seed hulls falling from the vines that climb the sycamores. Ramps leaves are six or seven inches long – twice the size of the ramps growing at home. In the east garden, forsythia, puschkinia, daffodils, pink hyacinths, and squills are in full bloom.

2005: Blue-eyes seen. Snow-on-the mountain leafing out.

2007: After two weeks of warm weather, Middle Spring continues to unravel so quickly. In Washington D.C., the cherry trees are in full bloom. Here, redbuds are almost flowering, fully flushed. Forsythia is darkening and getting leaves. Some daffodils are already gone. Lil's maple is blooming and the first red tulip is open. Some pink magnolias are in full bloom. In the Glen, many Dutchman's britches and bloodroot have wilted. Rue anemone and the first large-flowered trillium are blossoming. I saw a yellow violet today at John Brian Park. This afternoon, purple violets were coming in by the pond at home.

2008: Snowdrops are fading now in the east garden, and snow crocus are done. Katy's aconites were gone yesterday, probably days earlier. Several yellow daffodils have opened on Dayton Street, and our daffodil is completely unraveled. Mid-season crocus are in full bloom now throughout town. One small red tulip by the pond is open. Snow-on-the-mountain is emerging, its leaves less than an inch long. This is the cusp of the season now, the torturously slow buildup to Middle Spring has finally tipped into fulfillment.

2009: Robins at 5:30 this morning, cardinals and crows before 6:00. Almost all of the pussy willow catkins have fallen now, and the redbud buds are beginning to glow. All the yellow tulips at the south wall are open wide, and the first two orange tulips have just come in. Daffodils gather momentum, grape hyacinth and scilla reaching their best, bleeding hearts up four to six inches, late-planted croci are holding on, red quince buds straining, more winterberry leaves pushing out over the old leaves, all the powder-blue periwinkles suddenly in bloom. Driving to Beavercreek, I saw early patches of dandelions, more weeping cherries, blooming pear trees and even several crab apples flowering. Filled one raised-bed frame with dirt in the 70-degree afternoon.

2010: Inventory on return from a two-week trip to the South: Peonies six to ten inches, one wind flower, one small, red tulip by the pond. Full squills, daffodils, forsythia, puschkinias, hellebores, primroses, grape hyacinths, lungwort, star magnolias, full pollen pussy willows. Early Virginia bluebells. Honeysuckle leaves small, but well along, some green tint to the wood line, some lilac leaves unraveling, cherry tree buds fat and straining, full development of waterleaf. Gold finches full gold. All the crocus, snowdrops and aconites have disappeared.

2011: Cardinals and grackles loud through the morning. Strong robin vespers at sundown, geese flying over a little past 8:00 p.m.

2012: Reports of yellow violets and bellwort. Tat in Madison says her bluebells and daffodils are completely gone (but holding here in Yellow Springs). Along the alley, the Great Violet Bloom parallels, maybe lasts much longer than the Great Dandelion Bloom (which is still going on). A patch of Japanese knotweed is at least four feet tall. In the garden, great ragwort buds are cracking, garlic mustard has budded (Judy says it's blooming in Goshen), sweet rocket is heading up, the New England aster leaves are a couple of inches long, about the same as the white boneset, both late summer and early fall bloomers. The red crab apple by the east side of the house is now fully open, and many other apples and all the pink and the white dogwoods around town are still in full flower. Redbud flowers hold, but leaves are forming around them. The pink quince has started to open just today. The downtown pear trees hold some of their flowers as leaves engulf them. Sweet gums flowering and leafing. Tulips are still at their peak, but Mrs. Lawson's yellow varieties that escaped to Don's yard are ending. When I was weeding this morning, I found a star of Bethlehem budded. A young daddy-longlegs spider was wandering on the pond liner as I worked this afternoon.

Webworms, crawling around in their web that I cut down from our peach tree.

2013: Santee, South Carolina: Most trees with small leaves. Vegetation includes sprawling blackberries, red dock-like ground cover, black medic, sorrel, dandelions, flax-like violet-flowered plant.

2014: Ramps leaves now feathered out, six inches tall, bluebells two inches, tulip foliage full size. Honeysuckle leaf buds opening at the lower branches. Momentum picking up in spite of the cool days and nights. First pink lungwort flowers by the shed. Snow-on-the-mountain leaves have emerged, pacing the waterleaf leaves.

2015: Soft morning in the upper 40s, light wind from the south: The very first robin heard at 5:31, the first cardinal at 5:33. (Compare with this day in 1986 and 2009.) As I jogged through the village, the robins were loud and consistent companions, song sparrows piercing through in several neighborhoods, the cardinals not really joining steadily until 5:45. Crows at 5:49, a blue jay at 5:53. The thin call of an unidentified bird (tee tee with an upsurge, tee tee with a down note) off and on throughout. A deep rose patch of sky about 6:00 disappeared in gray in just a few minutes. Finally a finch came to the feeder today; it was bright yellow. At 8:00 a.m. the first real thunderstorm of the year. This afternoon, I found deadnettle-lamium open by the south wall.

2016: Thin, new lily-of-the-valley stalks are up about two inches in the northwest garden, will be ready to transplant in a week or so. The cherry tree is leafing, and the maples on Stafford Street have sent out small seed wings. Two leaves have come out on the hobble bush. Hard winds and snow this afternoon and evening, gusts past 40 miles an hour.

Looking back over each day's notes, I see my autobiography in the entries. I live again, in this way of nature, my movement both linear and radial, binding together consciousness of years with birdcalls and the length of leaves and the opening of flowers. That narrowest of focus creates continuity, connection with a vague mood of the people and events of my life, omitting all the data of my family and workday resume, but providing feeling and sense of the whole. The myopia does not exclude all the other acts but instead places them almost inconspicuously inside a sprawling, soft and mottled landscape.

2017: Sun and chilly, but gentle with hardly a breeze, to Mercadoiro, Spain: wild large primroses, gurgling streams of runoff from the fields, first large white clover, waysides of violet and gold ground cover bloom, grass so fresh and nothing old or dying, warbling birds all the way. The land of deep middle April, Middle Spring.

> *Spring came on forever,*
> *Spring came on forever,*
> *Said the Chinese nightingale.*

Vachel Lindsay

Bill Felker

April 3rd
The 93rd Day of the Year

The trees are still leafless; indeed the aspect of that valley is not of April -- save where the hepaticas push up out of the bed of leaves; but the delicate fragrance of the blossoms is always faintly manifest and the air is April's with the warm sun slanting down the slope to renew the earth as sight of these delicate flowers struggling forth invariably renews me every spring.

August Derleth

Sunrise/set: 7:16/8:01
Day's Length: 12 hours 45 minutes
Average High/Low: 57/37
Average Temperature: 47
Record High: 83 - 1883
Record Low: 20 - 1965

Weather

Highs in the 70s come 25 percent of the days, 60s twenty percent, 50s ten percent, 40s thirty percent, 30s fifteen percent. Frost occurs 40 percent of the mornings. Rain falls 60 percent of April 3rds, and snow another ten percent. The sun comes out just half the time. The Great Xenia Tornado in southwestern Ohio took place on this day in 1974, and severe weather often threatens on this date.

Natural Calendar

In the Rocky Mountains, moose and elk are moving to their spring feeding grounds. Red-tailed hawks and American bitterns arrive there as white phlox and sagebrush buttercup come into bloom. Night herons and plovers migrate into the Northeast. Wild turkeys gobble all across the South. Monarch butterflies continue their northward migration, reaching as far as North Carolina by the end of the week. Golden poppies, cornflowers, and lupines are still in bloom in Arizona. Indian paintbrush has opened in Nevada. Prickly pear cacti are blossoming in Texas. Spider lilies unravel in the Louisiana lowlands. On the barrier islands of the South Carolina coast, loblolly pines are pollinating, live oaks are shedding and yellow Jessamine climbs through the swamps.

The Stars

In the night sky, the Big Dipper has moved overhead. Below it lies the constellation Leo, with its brightest star, Regulus. To the east, Arcturus leads the Corona Borealis from the horizon. In the far west, Orion is setting, as the Pleiades slide into the northwest.

Daybook

1982: A seven-day cold spell with temperatures as low as ten degrees began today.

1983: Pears blooming in the village. At Jacoby, wild ginger leaves half emerged. Swamp buttercups are blossoming in one stream. Dock ten inches, skunk cabbage leaves seven inches, golden ragwort almost ready to bloom, buckeyes leafing.

1986: Pears on Xenia Avenue burst into bloom overnight. Shepherd's purse open in Wilberforce.

1988: At Wilberforce, my star magnolias are all open. At the Covered Bridge, bluebells must have just come out this morning. Twinleaf is at its peak. Toad trillium is everywhere. Wild ginger leaves are half emerged. One spring beauty seen. A few touch-me-nots have four leaves. Dutchman's britches maybe three days old. Forsythia full bloom. Judy calls from Goshen, Indiana, 100 miles northwest: no forsythia there, but lots of daffodils.

1991: Morning flicker calls increase in length and intensity from a little after 6:00, and on through the day.

1993: Robins awake and singing at 5:15 this morning. Phlox: steady increase in the number of sprouts. Queen Anne's lace and red pyrethrums now up about two inches, coneflowers maybe an inch, asters an inch, peonies six inches, yarrow with many new leaves, crocus declining, some hurt by recent cold in the 20s.

Maple tree buds expanding everywhere, growth on all the foliage of the middle and Late Spring flowers.

1995: Pears starting to open in Xenia. Irmgard says her apricot trees have been flowering for three weeks, ever since the mid-March warm-up. Two groundhogs seen this afternoon, seemed to be adults. At South Glen, leafcups are bushy, about nine inches tall.

1996: The first day in the 70s since October, this cold spring warms a little, bringing out the first daffodil in the yard (only a day behind the other first daffodils seen in town yesterday). On Whiteman Street, lawns full of scilla. In the south garden, aconite season is gone, and most of the spring iris have broken down. Glory-of-the-snow is in full bloom with the puschkinia and crocus and snowdrops. Red maples have been blooming for several days. This evening, just before the moon rose in red total eclipse, birds were singing in the yard, the first time I've noticed the evening birdsong as part of the movement to spring. At Jacoby this afternoon, sky clear, warm wind, the paths bright green, November-Second-Spring green. In the swamp, some skunk cabbage leaves are six to nine inches, touch-me-not sprouts fat and soft. A mourning cloak butterfly came by as I walked. When I got home, Jeanie said she'd seen an orange butterfly in the south garden.

1998: Lawn mowing season begins in town, the smell of cut grass. Forsythia flowers darken with age. Wild geranium has two-inch leaves. Columbine is four inches high. Full bloom of Dutchman's britches, twinleaf, toothwort, violets. Fritillaria is budded. First money plant with purple four-petaled flowers.

1999: Full robin song 5:37 a.m. In the yard, peonies six inches. Still full crocus. Snowdrops done. Early full daffodils, very early forsythia, full *cornus mas*. Bleeding hearts two to three inches, daylilies two to five inches, pink hyacinths in bloom, phlox leaves an inch, lemon verbena an inch, poppies to six inches, apple trees leafing. Toads calling at 9:00 p.m.

2001: First pollen on the east pussy willow. First forsythia opens. Scilla full in the lawns. Puschkinia full in the west garden. First yellow-white bicolor tulip open.

2004: Peonies about six inches, first hosta showing by the east fence, bleeding hearts bushy at about six inches, astilbe unraveling, Korean lilac with purple buds, spiderwort pacing the daylily foliage, purple loosestrife just starting in the pond, lawn clumping – almost ready to cut, apples, the pink quince, and peaches leafing, and the border of honeysuckles begins to fill in.

2005: To the Florida line: Redbuds are just barely open above the full flush of dandelions, forsythia and white magnolias at the Kentucky-Tennessee border. In Knoxville, quince, crab apples and decorative pears are in full bloom. Pears fully open in Hendersonville, North Carolina. Across the divide of the Great Smokies, down toward the middle of South Carolina, the high tree line is gold and orange and pale green with buds and flowers. Yellow Jessamine climbs through the bare branches. Dogwood comes in by Colombia. Tropical red clover grows along the coastal highways. Wisteria and azaleas are at their best in Charleston. Wild cherry trees blossom above Savannah. Monarch butterflies explore the barrier islands. Rhododendrons flower in Jacksonville.

2007: In the yard, the first red tulip is out, and many other tulips seen around town. The redbuds are becoming more obvious; serviceberries and pears continue at their peak. In Clifton Gorge, bluebells are in early full bloom on the high paths. By the water, purple cress is still holding full, but hepatica blossoms are wilting quickly in the heat, bloodroot is just about gone, and Dutchman's britches are disappearing. Miterwort, bellwort, early meadow rue and large-flowered trillium have come in all over the hillsides.

2008: Now five daffodils are blooming in the yard. This evening walking Bella after sundown, I listened to the robins' late chorus.

2009: Loud cardinal at 5:50 this morning in the rain (the first thunderstorm of the year last night). In the alley, the willow tree is in full bloom, a few of its catkins fallen in the wind. In Dayton, all the crab apples appear to be open, the city marked with pale flowers. At home near the corner of High and Limestone Streets, the very first red quince bud unraveled. This evening in a cold, northwest wind, the robins still sang at sundown, the sky gray and gold.

2011: Crows at 6:00 a.m., a subdued frog call at midmorning. Two small fish found dead in the pond, the first visible losses in years. The first yellow tulip has opened.

2012: Winter cress full bloom on the way to Xenia. Redbuds and apples continue full bloom. On the way to the park, the birch catkins hanging down, full bloom. The viburnum at the north side of the house is starting to open, and the Korean lilac buds have fattened up, deep purple. Don's pink magnolia still holding on. Silver olives in full flower near Fairborn. It seems that the relatively mild temperatures - close to normal - are slowly bringing the season back into line. This evening in the park, I stood under the apple trees in full bloom, surrounded by the heavy fragrance of their flowers, the softness of their shelter.

2013: Santee, South Carolina: Light wind, mild temperatures, gathering cirrus throughout the day. Drove to the canal between the Santee-Cooper lakes, fished all afternoon, caught one large channel catfish. The vegetation in the area: sow thistles, black medic, wood sorrel, henbit, small-flowered vetch flowering. One bright tiger swallowtail fluttered downstream. A small cache of webworms was emerging in the shrubs above the still dormant kudzu. At the campsite, white iris late bloom, weigela, dogwood, azaleas dominant. No corn emerged yet in the fields, but wheat was deep green, at least a foot high. Almost all the canopy greening and blossoming.

2014: Hard rains, flooding of the yard. This evening, strong cardinal song and grackles clucking. Privet buds showing a little green, a few lilac buds unraveling .

2015: More rain through the night, pre-dawn temperatures holding in the 50s, very light wind: I went outside at 5:18 to get an early start on the birdsong, but a robin was already chirping as I walked onto the porch. I should have read about this day in 1993 and should have been ready just after 5:00. Almost all snowdrops and aconites in the yard are gone. Snow-on-the-mountain is up and pacing the waterleaf, leaves of one to two inches. The Stafford Street maple is in bloom, shedding onto the street (like it did last year). First puschkinias open near the pond. First small leaves coming out on the lower branches of a few honeysuckles.

2016: The honeysuckle leaves are big enough now to obscure some of the neighbors' yards. Last nights freeze seems to have set the windflowers on their heels, glory of the snow unscathed. Throughout the west gardens, scillas, daffodils and grape hyacinths remain strong and full of color. Just a tad behind the hobble bush, the Annabel hydrangea is starting to leaf.

2017: Spain: to Gonzar, sun and warm, many butterflies: cabbage whites, sulfurs, blues, fritillaries, many in randori, the only day so far with lepidoptera. First chickweed and English plantain in full flower.

The Snows are thaw'd, now grass new clothes the earth,
And Trees new hair thrust forth.
The Season's
Chang'd, and Brooks late swoln with rain,
Their proper bankes contain.

From Horace (Fanshawe) Odes IV, 7

April 4th
The 94th Day of the Year

Every flower marks a different season,
Shows a hidden pattern, time and lesson.

Celtus
(bf)

Sunrise/set: 7:15/8:02
Day's Length: 12 hours 47 minutes
Average High/Low: 57/37
Average Temperature: 47
Record High: 84 - 1883
Record Low: 23 - 1944

Weather

Chilly weather with highs only in the 30s comes 20 percent of the time. Forties occur another 20 percent, 50s thirty percent, 60s twenty percent, 70s five percent, 80s five percent. Skies are overcast half the years, and the clouds bring rain 35 to 40 percent of the years, snow another ten percent. Frost strikes four mornings in ten. Beginning today, the normal average air temperature rises one degree every three days instead of Early Spring's one degree each two days.

Natural Calendar

This is the time that white and pink and violet hepaticas reach their height of bloom in average springs at lower elevations along the 40th Parallel. Spring beauties, violet cress, harbinger of spring, bloodroot, bluebells, twinleaf, small-flowered buttercup, toad trillium, Dutchman's britches, and even toothwort are coming in around them.

Plum trees are full of flowers, and the pears open. Quince, magnolias, crab apples, and cherries blossom, too. The peak period of pussy willow pollen begins, and some of the heavy golden catkins are falling in the wind.

In the waysides, common chickweed, dandelion, purple

deadnettle, henbit, small-flowered bittercress, shepherd's purse, and periwinkles blossom. Daffodils, scilla, puschkinia, anemone, and hyacinths are at their brightest in the lawns and gardens.

Flower producers have finished preparing bedding plants for Mother's Day and Memorial Day. Japanese beetle grubs move to the surface of the ground to feed. New calves and lambs are in the fields. At average elevations along the 40th Parallel, three more weeks of relatively mosquito-free gardening remain, seven weeks before frost-sensitive plants will grow without threat from the cold.

Daybook

1985: Quince foliage coming out by Neysa's window. Comfrey leaves are two inches long.

1986: Quince foliage pushes out. The first redbud is open in town. At the mill, it's the first day for violets, spring cress, and periwinkles. One trillium grandiflorum spotted, and the first yellow trout lily of the year. Henbit in bloom. Comfrey two to three inches. Mulberry buds are greening, peonies getting their first leaves. There are buds on the Jacob's ladder; buds extend on the tree of heaven. A clump of dandelions in bloom at Wilberforce.

1987: High winds and an inch of snow, even some drifting.

1988: Peonies and hops are a foot tall, with leaves starting. Pussy willow catkins fall, loaded with pollen. The first water cress has flowers at Jacoby. Hops vines are at least a foot high under the honeysuckles. Moths are common in the mild evenings now. Spring beauties, hepatica, snow trillium, bloodroot in full bloom along the river. Pears full bloom in a near-record 83 degree afternoon.

1989: To St. Louis: Vegetation similar to Yellow Springs throughout the first part of the trip. Past Terre Haute, leaves developing on a few high trees. At the Botanical Gardens in St. Louis, daffodils full bloom, magnolias, certain cherries, including a weeping variety. Peonies twice as tall as in Yellow Springs. Red oaks leafing. Some azaleas out. In all, maybe a week ahead of home. On the return trip, April 6th, redbud seen, and a clear difference in the roadside green and leafing from St. Louis to Terre Haute, a definite lack of leaves at the approach to Indianapolis.

1991: Flicker calling steadily from early morning. Young phlox budding, mint two inches, leafcup strong, low catchweed spreading, chickweed blooming, bloodroot very early. The undergrowth of honeysuckle is light green now, filling in. First ragwort blooms at the dam. One buzzard circling; they seem scarce this year. Viburnum buds, magnolias full bloom, crabs leafing at Wilberforce. Everything on the brink, but still countable.

1992: First bright yellow finch seen along the north bushes.

1993: Scilla, miniature grape hyacinth, windflower, glory of the snow have replaced almost all the snow drops, the aconites, and crocus. Jonquils seen along Dayton-Yellow Springs road today, and then along Jacoby, old-fashioned daffodils in early full bloom. One of ours on the north side of the sidewalk came about a fourth open this afternoon.

1994: Mill Habitat: I finally found the snow trillium I knew were there along the river; they were simply late coming in, full bloom now. The first toad trillium were up, the first bloodroot, lots of hepatica, a few scattered violet cress. The basal leaves which I saw so early in March and which I thought were snow trillium seem to be turning into trout lily plants. At home, pussy willows have all their pollen, daffodils are maybe a fifth emerged, snow crocus are almost all gone, regular crocus holding in the cool weather, scilla are in full bloom, magnolias are opening in Xenia and in Wilberforce, wood hyacinths have reached their peak, the forsythia buds that survived the below-zero weather are flowering.

1999: Robins sing-songing at 5:21. At 5:54 a.m., the first cardinal call in the yard, close by, piercing clarity, intense and strong. Pussy willows laden with pollen, first catkin falls in the rain.

2000: Leaves overpowering the aging, darkening forsythia flowers now, dandelion season coming on full force, peach tree blossoms past their prime. Daffodils and grape hyacinths still hold.

2002: Full bloom of weeping cherry in Columbus and Yellow Springs. Willows just starting to green up.

2004: Dayton: Pears and pink magnolias are starting to open.

2006: Inventory: Hyacinths, purple and pink open on Dayton Street. Lungwort in the southwest garden has two pink flowers, bluebells there are budded. Forsythia full bloom everywhere, full squills and daffodils, full grape hyacinths. Apples leafing in the park, buds yellow on the climbing hydrangea, purple deadnettle full, small flowered cress eight inches tall. Small red tulips killed by frost. First yellow tulip open. Stella d'oro ten inches, bushy poppies nine inches, pink spirea leafing. Crocus and snowdrop leaves long and floppy, aconite foliage all grown up, lamb's ear coming back, leaves about three inches. Lilac leafing, pink quince buds cracked. Resurrection lilies fifteen inches, honeysuckle and mock orange with one-inch leaves, daylilies eight inches, ramps six inches, euonymus buds pushing out. Catmint and lemon verbena low and bushy. Purple coneflower leaves and purple penstemon leaves two inches. Pollen on the pussy willows. Peonies a foot tall. Motherwort six inches, knotweed three inches. Blue eyes still strong (a fat variety in front of the library in Vevay in southern Indiana, too). Some Asiatic lilies three to five inches, Dutch iris seven inches, Canadian thistles six inches. Purple buds on the Koran lilac. New sweet William leaves, peach buds pink, roses and raspberries leafing. Rhubarb has nine-inch leaves, a fourth of the way to pie. Periwinkles all open. Puschkinia open, hosta have one-inch spears, bleeding hearts are three inches and bushy. Snow on the mountain is spreading low. Chickweed flowering throughout.

2007: Mateo's apple tree noticed in early bloom this morning as I walked Bella in the cold wind. Serviceberry petals coming down the front moves across the village. The pear trees downtown have started to leaf out already, at least a week to ten days ahead of schedule. Snow flurries this evening. I covered the candy lilies in the south garden with plastic tarps.

2008: Two white koi fingerlings have appeared in the pond for the first time since March 7. Scilla early bloom, daffodils gathering momentum. Red maples shedding. Many finches bright gold, some males spiraling in competition for seed. Cowbirds and house finches feeding. Bleeding hearts two inches. Purple deadnettle blooming. Canadian thistle leaves two to three inches, pacing the mallow. Pussy willows fat but no pollen noticed. Puschkinias and small red tulips full bloom. Lilac leaf buds opening. Viburnum buds cracking. Stella d'oro foliage pacing the other daylily leaves. Lungwort with fresh leaves and first buds. Low honeysuckle branches leafing. Cardinals loud throughout the morning. Driving to the Ohio River about four in the afternoon: Just a hint of green to the undergrowth, the roadside grass still dull. In Cincinnati, a sudden change in the honeysuckle and silver olive undergrowth. Roadside daffodils and forsythia bushes were in full bloom.

2009: Cold and sunny today. Robins, grackles and doves accompanied Bella and me on our alley walk. In the west garden, the few pachysandra plants we have are in full bloom. In front of Greg's old house, the first spears of lily-of-the-valley are just starting to emerge. In our east garden, hosta are up an inch or so.

2010: Keeping a notebook of what happens every day in the small world around me, I often think about the cyclical quality of events in nature. The repeating quality of the sky and the landscape, is something similar to what sociologist Charles Taylor describes as "Higher Time" (as opposed to linear, "Secular Time") in his study of the rise of humanism, *A Secular Age.*

In Secular Time, says Taylor, "one thing happens after another, and when something is past, it's past." Higher Time, on the other hand dramatizes cycles like those represented in the Christian liturgical calendar or in the repeating nature of the year. And even though the modern world seems to do business completely in Secular Time, the alternate viewpoint persists and may even be dominant inside memory.

Memory Time is always Higher Time. Not only does memory retain a whole impression of experience, but it also blends, erases, and re-sequences pieces of the past, allowing the feasts of birth and death, love and disappointment to return, mellow or fester, winnowed to their core.

So too with observation of the natural year, the repetition of the seasons within the mind mixes and combines the years, unifies them, reevaluates them, distortions showing the selective power of emotion and insight over linear statistics.

To withdraw from Secular Time is to come home to a centered self where experiences are sifted and unified and made whole to return again. Like a book of days, the mind recollects choices and destinies, showing and combining in the radii of its vortex the higher shadows and auras of repeating suns.

2011: A patch of bloodroot in the library alley in full bloom. Matted areas of blue-eyes in the south garden, full.

2012: More soft, pale green days. Garlic mustard bloomed by the south wall as I was working on the pond yesterday. The toads sang last night, the first time I've heard them since their mid-March orgies. Don's pie cherry is losing more petals, but the crab apples and the redbuds are holding beautifully. Many of the Asiatic lilies are six to eight inches, the wood hyacinth bud stalks are pushing up, ferns are a foot tall.

2014: Heavy rains, standing water in the yard, especially deep around the pond, and most of the snowdrops have been battered and closed by the raindrops, the aconites are flooded, and the snow crocus flowers washed away. One forsythia blossom open, lying on the sidewalk. On Stafford Street, the maples are shedding their spring bloom. Through the afternoon, hard and chilling wind.

2015: Yesterday's rain gone to clear, dark sky, full moon setting with its southern half shadowed in eclipse, light but biting wind, temperature near freezing: First robin whinny at 5:30, waiting until 5:41 to become a singsong chorus; first cardinal at 5:43 with song sparrow nearby, doves at 5:47. At 7:45, Casey called: He had just seen the first red-winged blackbird at the pond on his farm, a bit more than a month later than he has reported them in previous years. In the garden, I transplanted a clump of spiderwort, leaves violet, about two to three inches long.

2016: A walk in the North Glen with Lindy's kindergarten class from the Antioch School, my first walk with so many happy people: skunk cabbage leaves half size, bellwort stalks a foot tall. One ragwort, one wild phlox, two early toad trilliums, many violets, swamp buttercups, bluebells, toothworts, Dutchman's britches and hepaticas in bloom. Maybe a third of the May apples had spread their glossy leaves, and a few trillium grandiflorum were budded. Some late violet cress were holding on. Some touch-me-not sprouts had six leaves. But no bloodroot or twinleaf seen. At the back yard, the first cowbirds – male and female – came to the feeder.

If I ever lose my way,
It will be in April.
Dazzled by the brightness of bloodroot and twinleaf,
I will stumble from the woodland path
To her one, lost, perfect space.

Leon Quel

Bill Felker

April 5th
The 95th Day of the Year

The Sun advances, and the Fogs retire:
The genial Spring unbinds the frozen Earth,
Dawns on Trees and gives the Primrose Birth.

Poor Richard's Almanack, April 1742

Sunrise/set: 7:13/8:03
Day's Length: 12 hours 50 minutes
Average High/Low: 58/37
Average Temperature: 48
Record High: 83 - 1988
Record Low: 21 - 1944

Weather

There is a 70 percent chance for rain, plus a five to ten percent chance for snow, all of this making April 5 one of the wettest days of the month. In spite of the odds for precipitation, however, completely overcast conditions occur only 35 percent of the time. Highs reach the 80s five percent of the years, climb into the 70s fifteen percent, are in the 60s ten percent, 50s thirty-five percent, 40s thirty percent, and 30s five percent. Breezy conditions seem to contribute to the low incidence of frost on the 6th: a light freeze comes just 15 percent of the mornings; this one of the two days in the first half of the month with such low odds.

Natural Calendar

Warming air temperatures and the sun's position higher in the sky brings spring to the rivers and lakes as well as to the field and garden. Local water temperatures reach the upper 40s and low 50s; bluegills, large-mouthed bass, and rock bass are active, as are yellow perch, northern pike, suckers, and catfish. Bullheads start their spawning run. Crappie fishing usually peaks, then continues steady through the first week in June. In the southern waters of Lake Michigan, salmon are feeding. Along the Eastern seaboard, alewives return to spawn, and the shad are running.

Daybook

1985: First small-flowered buttercup found in the grass. Early meadow rue foliage is six inches high, will blossom in a week and a half. Poison hemlock is two feet high in places, wild petunia three inches. Tulips and grape hyacinth full bloom throughout town. At South Glen, toothwort barely open, buckeye leaves have unraveled all the way, violet cress full bloom, first violet seen. Winter cress has sent up flower stalks, but the heads are tight still. Parsnips ready to dig, Dutchman's britches still open.

1986: First red bleeding heart. Peach trees begin to flower. Buckeyes, box elders, honeysuckles leafing, buds on sedum, sweet rockets begin to grow stalks, frogs chanting – ghostly chanting, shrill in the swamp – ragwort has some buds. Cowslips have yellow buds, should bloom next week. Some May apples a foot tall. Some bloodroot already gone. Mounds of lush water cress. Spikes of garlic mustard with buds. Hobblebush leafing. Skunk cabbage leaves a foot long, leaves starting on forsythia and pussy willows. First toothwort open, spring beauties beginning, red quince in bloom. Lil's maple flowering, and throughout the area, trees are greening in a radical, rapid transformation.

1988: First violet opens in the yard. Most buckeyes open. Two-thirds of the pussy willow catkins have fallen.

1990: Pussy willow catkins old and full of pollen, hanging on because of the cold.

1991: Pears opened today, afternoon in the 70s. Garden lilies up four inches, more tulips open, second patch of daffodils, box elder flowering, windflowers, scilla, glory of the snow holding. Grape hyacinth full. Pussy willows heavy with pollen.

1992: I haven't been to the woods in weeks. The cold has held since March 11th, all the progress of late February burned back by frost. Finally today, the second beginning of spring. The first cabbage butterfly seen, bees in the squills and star of Holland and windflowers. Front croci still bloom strong.

1995: Hard freeze this morning, maybe 15 degrees in the yard. The daffodils were frozen solid; I'll see what else was damaged tomorrow.

1999: The chorus begins between 4:30 and 5:00 a.m., standard time. Peak purple deadnettle now, full daffodils, squills, puschkinias, hyacinths, grape hyacinths. All the crocus gone. Early full dandelions in some areas. Early Spring beauty. Fringed loosestrife well underway, two to four inches of growth.

2000: To Cincinnati: Apples, pears, redbuds, daffodils all still at their peak like last Wednesday; except now the leaves are pushing out more. At the rest stop half way, the apple buds that were so tight a week ago were cracking open, just a bit ahead of Yellow Springs. And the tree line greening, Middle Spring coming on strong.

2007: Lil's maple has been blooming for several days. Many box elders leafing, their flowers coming down in the cold wind and covering the lawn. The pussy willow lost all its catkins at the beginning of the month, is now leafing.

2008: At the Moye Center along the river in Kentucky near Cincinnati, hyacinths and daffodils were open. Some lily-of-the-valley were up half a foot and budded. Daylily foliage had come six to twelve inches, depending on location. Spears were visible on older, established hostas. A few weigela leaves had come out. Chickweed, bittercress, blue eyes, periwinkles, spring beauties were all full bloom. Dandelions gathering momentum. Bellwort sprouts up three inches throughout the hillsides. Touch-me-not sprouts had two fat leaves. Dutchman's britches foliage common, but only one plant in bloom. Toothwort was budded, only a few buds open. Buckeyes unfolding, some red leaf clusters completely unfolded. Toad trillium up but not flowering. May apple umbrellas three inches, a few unraveling. Tea roses barely leafing. Trout lily foliage common, but only two flowers found. A few bloodroot in bloom. One blue butterfly seen.

2009: A soft, windy day before the cold front arrives with rain and snow tonight. Around the yard, many Asiatic and Oriental lilies have come up, are unfolding and about two inches tall. Buds have formed on the lilacs and viburnum, bleeding hearts and peonies are getting bushy, the lungwort has put out its pink flowers, the box elders are blooming, and the early orange and the yellow tulips are so wide open, their petals make flat disks to the sun; the later tulips are fully budded. The bamboo has shed about half its leaves. The primroses are all showing color. Ground ivy has joined the violets and the wild deadnettle. The wild onions are lanky and contribute to the shaggy appearance of the lawn and gardens. First cabbage butterflies seen, first blue.

2011: After the storms of yesterday, north winds and clearing sky, tousled and torn cumulus or stratus clouds. Grackles still feed heavily from about 6:20 in the morning. No crows today, less cardinal and robin song. In Dayton this afternoon, numerous star magnolias were in full bloom, and I saw a pear tree ready to open. Walking at sundown with Bella, I heard robins, doves, grackles and cardinals singing.

2012: Cool and cloudy, the mild weather moving east, cold winds through the next few days to accompany full moon. A cardinal sang once at 5:41 this morning, then twenty minutes later. Report of pawpaw trees blooming a month early. Lily of the valley foliage at Greg's house is up a good six to eight inches, starting to unravel. Apple blossoms hold. Bamboo up to two feet in some places in front of the south wall. Along the roads to Springfield and Fairborn, forsythia fully leafed, golden flowers falling, dandelions still in full bloom, but the first large patch of them seeding seen, the tree line completely flushed with green, the pastures brilliant in the afternoon sun.

2013: Santee, South Carolina to Yellow Springs: From dogwoods and redbuds in the Carolinas to several inches of snow on the ground for miles through the West Virginia mountains. Then down into southeastern Ohio, sun and 65 degrees, clumps of daffodils along the way.

2014: Light wind, cloudy, 36 degrees. First robin whinny at 5:36 a.m., then one cardinal at 5:37, then robins gradually into singsong, full by 5:42, then cardinals throughout the neighborhood at 5:45. The lateness of the birds, compared to other years, perhaps due to the wind, the amount of rain, the cold? At noon, John Blakelock reported hearing a toad sing in his pond. To the North Glen in the afternoon with Bella: The first Dutchman's britches had buds, and toothwort foliage had emerged, some plants budded also. I saw two spears of bloodroot, still not open, the stalk tightly wrapped with its leaves.

Along the river (so high from the past few days of rain), hepatica seemed in early full bloom, and at the swamp, skunk cabbage was sending out leaves about the size of tulip foliage. Near the path, speckled trout lily leaves were about three inches long. In wetter ground, I found touch-me-not sprouts, small and new. Chickweed was finally growing up around the autumn mulch. Leafcup foliage was bushy, maybe four inches long. Multiflora rose bushes just barely pushing out. At home, the nettles were visible, and I dug them out. Then I noticed that the thistles had emerged, leaves an inch to two inches. In the garden, spiderwort and catnip transplanted to their own beds. The catkins of the pussy willow by the front sidewalk are all puffed out and loaded with pollen.

2015: Clear, calm, chilly: Sleeping late this morning, I walked Bella half an hour after sunrise, the morning chorus of birds having been augmented by the addition of raucous blue jays and grackles, a chattering wren, the call of a pileated, the rattling of downy woodpeckers, calls of the red-bellied woodpecker, the robins and song sparrows and doves and cardinals continuing to sing.

Along the front walk, pussy willows were full of pollen, and the first forsythia flower from the old, tattered bushes had opened, its branch prostrate in last year's leaves. Throughout the day, the midseason crocus have held on well. Honeysuckle branches continue to green as buds break. Small, inch-long leaves on the last rhubarb brought here from Judy's in the early 1980s. Maybe I'll get one more pie. More finches to the feeder; they've reappeared just this past week.

2016: Frost and clear. The first robin whinny at 5:27 this morning; five minutes later the full chorus was underway, Sun throughout the day, but highs only in the 40s. Driving in the countryside I saw that the honeysuckle bushes were rapidly filling in. From Goshen, Indiana, my sister Judy reports watching, from her condo window, groundhogs cavorting, chasing each other and tumbling together. Ducks there are pairing up, she noted. And geese have been flying over Yellow Springs in pairs this past week.

2017: April 5, 2017: Yesterday at Eirexe, today at San Xulian. Yesterday and today climbing towards Santiago, the roadside vegetation becoming much less lush. Some butterflies. Blackberry vines and stinging nettles the constants throughout. As I walked west, the gray green leaves of eucalyptus trees became more prominent, the trees of Galicia invasive according to the pension proprietress. The newest markers of season: violet sweet rockets and brilliant gold poppies in a settlement past Palas del Rei.

2017: Spain: Yesterday at Eirexe, today at San Xulian. Yesterday and today climbing towards Santiago, the roadside vegetation becoming much less lush. Some butterflies. Blackberry vines and stinging nettles the constants throughout. As I walked west, the gray green leaves of eucalyptus trees became more prominent, the trees of Galicia invasive according to the pension proprietress. The newest markers of season: violet sweet rockets and brilliant gold poppies in a settlement past Palas del Rei.

The very beginning is perhaps the best part of a garden. Now the breeze feels as soft and sweet as it used to be on the first spring day that I could go barefoot. The whistle of a cardinal comes from far off through the hazy air. The sun, riding higher in the sky, arouses not only the buds and seeds but also the dormant hopes of the gardener. The memory of past mistakes and failure has been washed out by winter rain. This year the garden will be the best ever.

Harlan Hubbard

April 6th
The 96th Day of the Year

There grew pied Wind-flowers and Violets,
Daisies, those pearl'd Arcturi of the earth,
The constellated flowers that never set;
Faint Oxlips; tender Blue-bells, at whose birth
The sod scarce heaved....

Percy Bysshe Shelley

Sunrise/set: 7:12/8:04
Day's Length: 12 hours 52 minutes
Average High/Low: 58/38
Average Temperature: 48
Record High: 83 - 1929
Record Low:15 - 1982

Weather
Today begins a slight decrease in the average amount of daily cloud cover. From now on, there is at least a 40 percent chance for sun, and most days bring a 60 to 80 percent chance. Cool temperatures, however, are not uncommon on this date: due to the arrival of the second major high-pressure system of the month, there is a five percent chance for a high just in the 20s (the last day this spring in which 20s are likely), a 15 percent chance for 30s, twenty-five percent for 40s, twenty-five percent for 50s. Milder 60s occur ten percent of the years, and warm 70s come 20 percent. Snow falls two years in a decade, and rain comes twice as often.

Natural Calendar
When the days are mild, toads hop through the grass in search of ponds. The rare grouse is drumming. Downy woodpeckers are mating. Young groundhogs come out of their dens. In backyard ponds, the koi and frogs end their hibernation. Water rushes and purple loosestrife, water lilies and pickerel plants suddenly produce foliage. Gall mites work in the ash trees; pine

57

weevils and moths are eating evergreens. Birch leaf miners and elm bark beetles attack the birches and elms. Water striders court now in the still backwaters and pools. Along the Atlantic seaboard, azaleas reach full bloom from Norfolk south.

Daybook

1981: Apple tree leafing in the back yard.

1982: Worst April cold and blizzard in history for the East and northern Midwest, 30 inches of snow in New Hampshire.

1983: Covered Bridge: Blooming: violet cress, bluebells, twinleaf, bloodroot, toothwort, Dutchman's britches, violets, spring beauties. Downtown: Bradford pears flowering, cherries, quince.

1984: The cold spring continues: one dandelion budding at Wilberforce. Two bluebirds seen along Wilberforce-Clifton.

1985: Star magnolias blooming in Enon.

1986: Lil's maple flowering.

1988: First cowslip is open in the swamp across from the Covered Bridge. First periwinkle, apple tree leafing, box elder full bloom. Redbud flushed, ready to open (placing them parallel to the last redbud seen March 29th this year, 30 miles north of the Tennessee line... at that point, we were exactly nine days south of today).

1991: Apple tree just staring to leaf, first violets bloom, hops six inches, orange tulips full bloom, most big hyacinths open today, fleabane obvious now with three inch leaves, all the grass planted in February is up and thick.

1993: More daffodils budding in the yard, but only one is half open. The forsythia still has not bloomed, and none seen in the county, the latest it's ever been since I've come to Yellow Springs. Scilla full bloom in front of the house on Limestone Street.

1994: First yellow tulips open in the south garden.

1995: Magnolias in town badly hurt by the 17-degree freeze, but my trees at school were only partially killed, the heat of Wesley Hall holding enough through the night. Cabbages and new ranunculus badly hurt, but they seem to be still alive.

2000: Red middle-season tulips open in the garden this morning. The east hosta are up five inches, the north hosta just barely out of the ground. Grass getting too long to cut easily. Riding north along the path this afternoon, I saw chickweed, shepherd's purse, bittercress all full bloom, the peak season of the white *cruciferae* underway. Winter cress budding, pacing the money plant. Some garlic mustard sending up stalks. Full bloom of the dandelions, full dead nettles. Purple deadnettle turns the weedy pastures purple. Creeping phlox and spring beauties seen fully open throughout town. Then later this afternoon, I finally found toad eggs in the pond. They could have been spread as early as the end of March, maybe April 1st, when the toads were singing the strongest.

2001: First robins at 5:15 a.m., first cardinal at 6:07 a.m.

2006: Casey reports the first American toads singing this evening.

2007: Walking in the village with Bella, I noticed Don's cherry tree had opened during the warm spell. Half a block south of home, the young ginkgo is leafing. In Dayton, most of the pears have leafed out. Mrs. Lawson's red quince is opening in the snow.

2008: Ohio River: More walking at the Moye Center: Two question-mark butterflies seen. The great hillside of snowdrops was now deep green with foliage, all the flowers long gone. Throughout my walk, I heard nuthatches and flickers (or pileated woodpeckers). One pink magnolia was blooming. Leaving the river valley, I left the first week of Middle Spring to return to late March in Yellow Springs. At home, the forsythia had started to come out while I was gone, and a few pink hyacinths were flowering. The first violet, first grape hyacinth and the first primrose were in bloom.

2011: After a long absence, the finches have returned to the feeder, the males all gold, and even a red house finch. Pussy willow catkins continue to hang on. More hosta spears and oriental lily sprouts appearing. New England aster foliage one to two inches, peonies have started to bush out, up to a foot tall. Violets have started to bloom under the redbud tree. The lone white hepatica near the lungwort (full bloom) opened yesterday or this morning. Through the day, the song sparrow sings high in the maple between Moya's yard and ours.

2012: Our bluebells full bloom, the hepatica by the lungwort fading. Don's cherry tree almost completely gone. On the evening walks with Bella, birdsong seems diminished from a week or so ago. Robins calling with steady peeping but not the earlier singsong.

2013: Home from South Carolina: This morning, the robins sang at 5:25, full singsong chant at 5:30, cardinal at 5:40, and the song sparrow at 5:45. The new aconites have remained in bloom, and the small jonquils have come in, along with the grape hyacinths, many squills, more daffodils, more primroses, and the first two lungwort flowers. Ramp foliage has broadened out, waterleaf has started to spread, and at the old schoolhouse, some peony stalks are six inches high and leafing out little, way ahead of the peonies at home – which are only two inches high. In the east garden dooryard, most of the snowdrop inflorescence is withering, and only a few late crocus plants are blossoming. Around the yard, the lower honeysuckle branches are leafing; on the front fence, Japanese honeysuckle vines are greening. At Jacoby, the touch-me-nots have started to sprout, and skunk cabbage is getting its first leaves. Buckeye trees are not leafing, though, their buds red but small. Swamp iris foliage is thin and only three to six inches tall. Garlic mustard sprouts are everywhere, leafcup bushy in about four-inch clumps. A red, thin, cup-shaped fungus found. Jeni says tulips are in full bloom in Portland, Oregon and the tulip festival there just started this week.

2014: Today's inventory in the yard is almost exactly the same as last year's, but I did see that monarda leaves were up near the rose bushes. In the North Glen upper trail, I found violet cress budded.

2015: When I went outside at 5:13 this morning, the first robins were already starting to chirp. Around the yard, more daffodils, one allium bud, peonies coming on quickly, now some to three inches. Multiflora rose leaves half an inch. Grackles fed heavily throughout the day. I checked the pond thermometer in the afternoon, and it read above 50 degrees for the first time.

2016: Scilla and grape hyacinths graying a little, the white of pears shaded with green foliage starting to come on. Fields of henbit hold through the countryside. The orange early tulips hold by the pond, many of the red, purple, white ones maybe half full. Don's serviceberries still in bloom.

2017: Spain: sun and cool to Melide: huge primroses, tall stalked violet feathery flowers with onion like fat stalks, more afternoon butterflies one clump of small bright yellow cup-like flowers, some heal-all.

> *Mid April already, and the wild plums*
> *bloom at the roadside, a lacy white*
> *against the exuberant, jubilant green*
> *of new grass and the dusty, fading black*
> *of burned-out ditches. No leaves, not yet,*
> *only the delicate, star-petaled*
> *blossoms, sweet with their timeless perfume.*

Ted Kooser, "Mother"

Bill Felker

April 7th
The 97th Day of the Year

Violets dim, yet sweeter than the lids of Juno's eyes
or Cytherea's breath....

William Shakespeare

Sunrise/set: 7:10/8:05
Day's Length: 12 hours, 55 minutes
Average High/Low: 59/38
Average Temperature: 48
Record High: 83 - 1883
Record Low: 10 - 1982

Weather
Today is typically mild, dry, and mostly sunny. Twenty percent of the afternoons reach 70 degrees, 30 percent make it into the 60s, and another 30 percent into the 50s. Cold 40s occur 15 percent of the time, and 30s the remaining five percent. Skies are clear to partly cloudy 70 percent of the time. Likelihood of rain: 30 percent, snow ten percent. Frost comes one morning in three.

Natural Calendar
In average years, new beggarticks, touch-me-nots, and great ragweed have four leaves. Knotweed is eight inches tall, about as high as the nettles. May apples have emerged, announcing morel mushroom time. Buckeyes have unraveled. Columbine is three to four inches. Skunk cabbage is more than half size, ten inches long, eight across. June's chicory is six to nine inches. Ragwort and garlic mustard are forming clumps, seed heads visible, still tightly bunched. Dock is almost fully grown. Water cress has filled the shallow brooks. Half the ginger in the woods has emerged. Cabbage butterflies are out laying eggs on the new cabbage, kale, collards and Brussels sprouts.

Daybook

1980: First tulip blooms.

1983: Blue flag iris foliage up six inches. Lawn ready to be mowed.

1984: Leaves starting on the raspberries.

1985: Easter with snow and hail. In Washington D.C., cherry trees reported to be in full bloom.

1986: First cherry blossoms on our pie cherry tree. Nettles are now seven inches tall, still purple from frost. Small brown toad found in the field. First thrush sighted. Lawn ready to be mowed. Strawberries have their first blossoms. Locusts and ash leaf at Wilberforce. At South Glen, twinleaf, small-flowered buttercup and Dutchman's britches full bloom, but no toad trillium open yet. Some bloodroot gone. Wild ginger leaves almost full size now, in broad patches. Violets come into early bloom in the lawn and garden. Lizard's tail leaf spikes up two or three inches in the river mud. Zigzag goldenrod sprouts are fat, wild roses covered with leaves, the tree line starting to green. Some parsnip stalks a foot tall. Small flocks of bluebirds in the woods.

1987: Tiny flower buds noticed on the lilac as leaves emerge about an inch. Motherwort has grown about three inches in the past few days. Great ragweed has sprouted, unhurt by the frost. Lawns being mowed now.

1989: Motherwort is three inches.

1991: Blue flag foliage up six inches. Lawn ready to be mowed. Forsythia and Bradford pears full throughout town. First bumblebee in the grass. South yard bulbs are in full bloom: tulips, daffodils, hyacinth. Motherwort five inches. At the Cascades, first blue butterfly, first trillium grandiflorum and early meadow rue budding. Anemone flowering, first golden alexander and wild geranium leaves. Some bellwort up three or four inches. May apples up half a foot in places. In the apple tree, a dove was nesting in the branch by the back door. Two bats seen this evening.

1992: First asparagus is just coming up now. Comfrey is two to three inches, a little above the horseradish. First mint growing. Purple coneflower leaves have been up for a few days. Bleeding hearts holding at an inch or two high, Spring starting again after a long cold spell.

1993: The first steps into Middle Spring, a week late: first three daffodils at home fully open today, forsythia finally opens, periwinkle starting at Wilberforce. Covered Bridge: early violet cress, a few bloodroot, Dutchman's britches, first toothwort, bluebells budding, but buckeyes still not unraveling.

1995: Asiatic lilies found; they've been out of the ground for several days - and they survived the hard freeze of the 7th. Pears flowering throughout town. Dandelions are blooming in patches now, prelude to the Great Dandelion Bloom. Honeysuckle leaves are growing bigger, giving a green tint to the lower landscape, and the high canopy is turning orange from tree blossom (like southern Georgia in February). In the south garden, dark lychnis foliage is an inch high, the early orange tulips are in full bloom, also unhurt by the frost. Puschkinia and glory-of-the-snow are weakening in the east garden.

1998: Serviceberries are in full bloom, like the pears. Lil's maples and ours: peak blossoming. Red quince full, started a week ago. Hyacinth season is over, Early Spring closing.

2000: First redbuds seen halfway open on the way to south Dayton. Some red crabapples too, a little behind them. Full Middle Spring beginning. As in 1998, hyacinths are ending. One bluebell in the yard completely open, probably ten days behind the patches at the Covered Bridge.

2002: First robin twittering at 5:01 a.m.

2003: Knotweed up six inches.

2004: Dayton to Knoxville, Tennessee: The undergrowth was pale green going south toward the Ohio River. Pears were in bloom throughout Cincinnati, and the first redbud was flowering just above Lexington, Kentucky, and redbuds increased in frequency from that point south. Crabapples and dogwoods were blossoming in southern Kentucky, and coloration grew as we drove: golds, reds, oranges, violets. By the Tennessee border, dandelions were everywhere, winter cress was lanky, and there was a full green tint to the hillsides. In Knoxville: azaleas, dogwoods, creeping phlox in bloom. Pears, box elders, birch and apples leafing, dandelions going to seed.

2005: Inventory: Japanese honeysuckles and virgin's bower leafing, first ginger leaves in the woods. Wild rose well leafed. Toad trillium up. Violets, spring beauty, bloodroot at South Glen. Star magnolias full. Full daffodils grape hyacinth, scilla, hyacinths. Late crocus still open. The orange tulips opened today. Catmint bushy, stonecrop bushy at four inches. Allium twelve inches, cressleaf groundsel six inches. First pussy willows fall in the wind. Pink quince leafing. Stella d'oro lilies ten inches. Lungwort and forsythia full bloom. Peonies and daylily foliage are more than a foot high.

2007: Thin yellow tulips with pointed petals noticed open in Don's yard today, probably bloomed just before cold spell of the 4th.

2008: Inventory around the yard: Rhubarb shows red stalks now, leaves starting to climb. The box elder is flowering. Astilbe visible. Mock orange leafing. Pussy willows still without pollen. In the South Glen, the only wildflowers visible are the buds of purple cress and toothwort. Debris has been pushed above the path by the March floods, which obviously filled all the bottomlands. Bluebells in the North Glen seen at the same stages as those in our yard. Two robins in a field in a hard chase at full speed. In the alley, the pink magnolia buds are small but swelling; the willow tree has small leaves. This afternoon, Jeanie and I planted pansies and primroses in the front garden. In the house, small ants have started to appear; we haven't seen them at all throughout the fall and winter.

2011: Blue eyes and bittercress still blooming, yellow finches continuing to visit. Raspberry leaves have sprouted, some multiflora rose bushes all green with new leaves. Lace vine leaves well developed, came out in March's cold. Four yellow tulips along the south wall. Box elder flowers continue to bush out. The first bluebell under the mock orange opened overnight, and the pachysandra has started to blossom.

2012: At 5:30 this morning, the full moon was setting far into the southwest. Walk in the alley at 9:30: grackles, doves, cardinals loud. All around is green and bright. Most daffodils gone, tulips aging. On the way to Beavercreek, the first large areas of dandelions to seed, and many crab apples losing their petals, and redbuds losing their color. A red admiral butterfly came by while I was working on the pond. This evening, cardinals strong at 7:00, and robins continually peeping. Large seeds on the shag-bark maples along High Street. Pink quince flowers reaching full bloom.

2013: Large camel cricket in the tub when I got up. Soft but windy morning, thin crescent moon rising due east, robins beginning at 5:18, crescendo until cardinals at 5:35, song sparrow at 5:40, house sparrow chirping at 5:45. No grackles seen in the twilight, but they fed in the yard during the day. Doves and blue jays and the red-bellied woodpecker heard later in the morning. The first bright summer-yellow finch came to the side feeder, and carpenter bees were visiting the late aconites. Working in the garden this afternoon, I found spiderwort foliage –about three inches, the very first red knotweed, the first Asiatic lilies – three inches, blue flag foliage three to five inches, stonecrop three inches and bushy, motherwort two inches, new leaves of spring violets, Shasta daisy leaves an inch long, celandine and catmint clumps, nettles two inches, waterleaf foliage spreading now, first snow-on-the-mountain leaves, the very last snowdrop flower, ramps six inches and fat, lush, all the Lenten roses in bloom. At Don's house, and near Lawson Place, standard hyacinths are open, blue, white and pink. At the Kennedy Arboretum near Ellis Pond, the buds on so many trees are swelling and getting ready to leaf.

2014: Walking down Limestone Street, I noticed the first clump of tulips (red) in bloom and a scraggly forsythia bush in flower – both the tulips and forsythia the first of the delayed spring here. This afternoon, thunder! When I took Bella out between showers before supper, I came across henbit starting to flower.

2015: Bella woke me up about 4:00 this morning, thunderstorm coming in, the second of the spring. Walking the soggy yard this morning, I saw that catchweed had started to spread and that violet leaves were finally taking shape. Some great ragweed had sprouted. Waterleaf is now starting to spread and cover the ground along the west edge of the property. On the east border, the pussy willow catkins were heavy with pollen, but they had not started to come down yet. Across the street, the star magnolia is showing white buds. All around the north garden, the weeds are suddenly taking over: chickweed, crabgrass, bittercress, At the University of Dayton along the river, red maples were full of red blossoms, and some of the honeysuckles showed green shading. At a sundown with heavy altostratus: robins and cardinals.

2016: Rain and wind, mild in the 40s, deep cold wave on the way: first cardinal at 5:19 this morning.

2017: Spain: Walking toward Santiago from Melide to Arzua: Once again perfect weather, not a cloud in the sky, temperature quite warm in the sun, mild in the shade. The ginestra-like yellow pea-flower shrub has mostly disappeared. The eucalyptus forests protect and perfume the paths. Tall mallow plants bloom, as do ubiquitous ten-petaled white flowers that have thin, pointed, opposite leaves. Lamium has given way to heal-all. Approaching Arzua: the scent of cut hay, and the first field cut to my left. Many other fields lush and long, deep green, !ready to harvest. Most of the gardens have well-developed collard or Brussels sprouts plots, some plants only recently set out. Peas are just sprouting, grape arbors putting out first leaves. Bridal wreath seen here and there, pink magnolia blossoms down in many locations, camellias still in bloom.

April... the month of the swelling buds, the springing grass, the first nests, the first plantings, the first flowers.... The door of the seasons first stands ajar this month, and gives us a peep beyond. The month in which to begin the world, in which to begin your house, in which to begin your courtship, in which to enter upon any new enterprise.

John Burroughs

Bill Felker

April 8th
The 98th Day of the Year

My dream world today was a sunlit April woods at sunset time, beyond which were immense misty valleys.

Charles Burchfield

Sunrise/set: 7:09/8:06
Day's Length: 12 hours 57 minutes
Average High/Low: 59/38
Average Temperature: 48
Record High: 85 - 1883
Record Low: 15 - 1972

Weather
Today is typically mild, dry, and mostly sunny. Twenty percent of the afternoons reach 70 degrees, 30 percent make it into the 60s, and another 30 percent into the 50s. Cold 40s occur 15 percent of the time, and 30s the remaining five percent. Skies are clear to partly cloudy 70 percent of the time. Likelihood of rain: 30 percent, snow ten percent. Frost comes 30 percent of the time.

The Week Ahead
Rain is the rule for April's second quarter. After the third major high-pressure system passes through, however, a brief mid-April dry spell typically occurs on the 11th and 12th, chances for precipitation falling to 25 percent. The 11th is also the brightest day in the first half of April, bringing an 80 percent chance for sun, the best chances since the 7th of March. As for temperatures, chances for highs below 50 degrees fall to less than ten percent on the 11th where they remain until they drop to five percent on April 22nd. Milder highs above 60s occur better than half the time on all the days of this quarter except on the 10th, when cooler conditions typically prevail. Frost strikes an average of 30 percent of the nights.

Natural Calendar

The grass is ready to mow most years in the second week of Middle Spring. The shaggy grass reveals that parsnips are coming into bloom and that white tailed deer are growing their new antlers. Long grass says that all the garden weeds are coming in and that it's time to face them. Tulips bloom this week of the natural year. Even commuters see them as they drive through town.

And when the great annual dandelion flowering begins in lawns and freeway rest areas, then snakehead and morel mushrooms appear deep in the woods, the earliest spring wildflowers are at their best, May apples are shiny and tall, and giant leaves reach out from the wetland skunk cabbage.

Patches of wild geranium leaves glow with an orange tint in the sun. Forest sedum is budding. Stalks are forming on the sweet rockets. Cowslip is just opening in the wetlands. Peach trees are in bloom, along with forsythia, pears, quince, magnolias, crab apples, cherries, and the last of the *cornus mas*. Daffodils and grape hyacinth hold from March. Buds on the grape vines are flushed and swollen. Privets are filling out. Branches of the multiflora roses are almost completely covered with foliage. Pale spikes of lizard's tail are as long as dragonflies. Asparagus is big enough for supper. American toads are chanting, and tadpoles already swim the backwaters. Young hummingbird moths and bumblebees come out to sip the annual mass flowering of dandelions. Gnats become bothersome.

One thing always leads to another. Sheltered in a narrow habitat of work or obligation or limited mobility, we can still imagine further. For every world there is a parallel world to be touched or dreamed.

The Stars

Before the sun comes up, Hercules has moved to near the center of the sky. The Summer Triangle, which includes bright Vega, Altair, and Deneb, are just a little behind Hercules to his east. The Milky Way passes through the triangle, separating it from autumn's Pegasus rising on the eastern horizon. The Corona Borealis has shifted into the western half of the heavens, and the pointers of the Big Dipper point almost exactly east-west.

Daybook

1986: First asparagus pushes up in the garden. First ginkgo is leafing, first tree of heaven, ash, locust, and mulberry.

1988: Peony stems become green as they lengthen. Bleeding hearts are bushy, reach the tops of my boots. Young hummingbird moths were working the dandelions in the yard this afternoon. Purple deadnettle has turned Middle Prairie purple. Patches of white field penny cress through the fields. In the yard, all pussy willow catkins gone, daffodils a few days past their prime. Early tulips full bloom, late tulips ready. In the old leaf mulch, box elder sprouts have four leaves; in the greenhouse, one of the box elder sprouts has six leaves.

1989: Pussy willow catkins, pollen old, have dropped in the rain.

1993: Spring continues to break: forsythia now early bloom, some pussy willow pollen, the first two tulips blossom - the rest are forming buds, windflowers full bloom, the last of the large-flowered crocus gone, full bloom squills, full bloom glory-of-the-snow, rhubarb bushy and four inches, delphinium now six inches, summer lilies have come up an inch or two, Japanese knotweed spears are out, like red asparagus stalks, showing about the same time as the first May apples, but slower. Moths common on our evening walk. First sedum budding.

1994: Male gold finches have most of their summer color now. Sparrows have taken over the chickadee nest in the dead poplar tree.

1998: Foxglove six inches. Resurrection lilies have reached their peak, begin to become shabby. Asiatic lilies four inches, lagging behind the knotweed, which is a foot some places, other places two feet. Mid-season tulips have started along the north garden. Peas push up in the garden, the spinach has almost all sprouted. Bleeding hearts have their first red hearts. Almost all the hosta three inches (two or three plants still not up). Very first ferns show green. Woolly bear caterpillar crossed the road in front of my car this noon. The first American toads sang by the pond last night near nine o'clock, the green toad followed an hour later, his first call of the year.

1999: By the 3rd, the star magnolias had started; now they are at their peak. Within the last five days full Middle Spring arrived. Yesterday, the pears and the fritillaria broke out overnight, and various hosta leaves emerged. Forsythia at its peak. Some apple trees opening, full bloom of the smaller cherries and plums. Leafing of quince and lilacs, full leafing of the mock orange and honeysuckle. Yesterday in the Glen, the May apples were up. Dutchman's britches, violet cress, hepatica, anemone, early rue, first toothwort, mid-season bloodroot losing petals, the first trillium grandiflorum. Fish and frogs active in the pond the last two days, weather warm, highs in the 70s. First bat seen tonight at 7:06 p.m.

2001: Yellow and orange early tulips full bloom. Bradford pears ready to push out. Small plum bushes full bloom on Xenia Avenue. Apple trees leafing. White star magnolia flowers have come out through the day. Pink magnolia just starting to emerge in Dayton. A family of snakes has taken over our pond, swimming back and forth, searching the rocky edges; I don't expect any toads to sing here this year.

2002: Korean lilac has tight, purple beds. Mock orange bush has more leaves out than the white standard lilac. Foliage of the Dutch iris is five inches high. Asiatic lilies now two inches. New poppy leaves five inches.

2003: The robin chorus began just a couple of minutes before 5:00 a.m. this morning, even with the temperature at 37 degrees. Lilac budding at the corner of High and Dayton Streets.

2004: Asheville, North Carolina: Biltmore Estate: Although Asheville was at the blooming stage of southern Kentucky rather than at that of Knoxville, there were many shrubs and flowers open: helibores, early redbuds, early dogwoods, yellow-flowered hollies (Oregon Grape Holly – *mahonia aquifolium* and Leatherleaf Mahonia), periwinkles, wrinkle-leafed sow thistle,

Burkwood viburnum, yodogawa azalea, small-flowered white spirea, Japanese pieris with its white dredlocks, pink quince. Spicebush was budding, and oakleaf hydrangea leaves were still pale, maybe an inch long. Forsythia was common and spectacular. Some pussy willows still had their pollen. Some May apples had just emerged. Hosta leaves were over a foot long (they had just been emerging in Yellow Springs). Bellwort was unraveling, about six-inches long. Ragwort, bluebells, white bleeding hearts, trout lilies were in full bloom. Garlic mustard was just starting to flower. Chickweed was yellowing, and Early Spring bittercress was tall and lanky. A yellow tiger swallowtail passed us as we walked.

2005: First yellow tulips.

2008: Mid-season crocuses are just about done today. Some forsythia seen in full bloom. Service berry buds are swelling, may well open this week. The star magnolias are opening near my old building in Wilberforce; star and pink magnolias are blooming in Wilmington. Daffodils, grape hyacinths and squills are full everywhere, pansies set out in yards. Robinsong at dusk.

2009: It seems that like love, spring does not rise complete or whole from space or ether, is never a priori, in spite of the feeling that it may strike suddenly and spontaneously. Instead, like love, spring is precariously dependent upon a fabric of song and odor and tactile sensation and visual angle and color and chemical surges that build one upon the other day after day until it is much too late to return to winter dormancy and expectation and solitude.

2011: The first bamboo shoots are up about an inch. Downtown, the pears and serviceberries are almost ready to open. First orange tulip opens along the south wall. At the Covered Bridge, full bloom of twinleaf, henbit, cowslip, bloodroot, hepatica, spring beauties, violet cress, and a whole hillside of Dutchman's britches. Some toothwort in flower. Some toad trillium up but not blooming. Jacob's ladder and small-flower buttercup budded. All the skunk cabbage leafing, leaves maybe to a foot or so long. Seven blue butterflies seen along the path.

2012: A bright and cool and windy Easter. Middle Spring continues to deepen into Late Spring, some maples almost completely leafed, redbuds becoming tawny, the tips of rose bushes orange with new growth, full bloom still of the violets and deadnettle and ground ivy, fading of the wild deadnettle, bittercress to seed, ferns up to my thigh now, some of Greg's lily-of-the-valley with buds tucked way down. I work outside, and the grackles whine and cackle. From Madison, Wisconsin, my sister Maggie says that crab apples and lilacs were still in full bloom, that she had found Jack-in-the-pulpits fully formed.

2013: The first forsythia bloomed at home and in the rest of the village today, at least a week behind most past years. The upper catkins of the pussy willow developed pollen, bees visiting. Apple trees, peach trees, lilacs, privets, roses, box elders just starting to leaf. Buds of the serviceberries are straining to open, and Don's violet windlfowers are open. Salvia up two inches in the north garden, daffodils, puschkinias, squills, grape hyacinths reaching full bloom. Allium and resurrection lily foliage is tall and fat.

2014: Bluebells blossoming in front of Alice's house, and grape hyacinths at the corner of High and Dayton Streets. Henbit full early bloom at Tim's. First mint, New England asters and white Boneset seen just an inch high in the north garden.

2015: Red maple shedding onto the sidewalk along Dayton Street. All the privets leafing, crab apples leafing, violet windflower at Don's, daffodils and scilla and lungwort and puschkinias and grape hyacinths completely full, phlox now pacing the peony stalks, the ground suddenly surging from the recent rain and mild weather. Mid-season crocus gone, ending the phases of Early Spring. Perennial salvia has come up in the north garden, comfrey in the Antioch garden, chickweed flowering, white and pink magnolias coming out, pussy willows blowing down in the wind. And Casey called about 4:00 this afternoon: "I've got peepers!" he exclaimed. They had began a little yesterday, but today they were "going great guns!"

2016: The heliopsis has emerged (the earliest I've noticed it), the cherry tree has opened its first three blossoms, the viburnum seems ready to flower, and the weigela is leafing, despite the several days of very cool weather. Along Dayton Street, Don's service berry trees have started to lose their petals, a little ahead of the pears. From Spoleto, Italy, Neysa reports that her yard is full of violet cyclamens; they began to flower a week ago.

2017: Spain: On the Camino de Santiago between Arzua and Brea, sun and warm once again, through eucalyptus forest land: blackberry vines, lamium and violets continue faithfully along the paths, buttercups, cowslip, strawberry blossoms, Endless Summer hydrangea with growth almost a foot, a few large periwinkles and white clovers, dandelions throughout but one field of them half to seed, wisteria full, an orchard in full bloom, after a few miles, the ten-petaled white flowers with narrow opposite leaves reappears, first duckweed seen in the slower streams, a little watercress, unraveling ferns, a tall violet flowered cress with feathery alternate leaf branches wide apart, many large white-flowers prayer plants, large basal great mullein leaf clusters. From Yellow Springs, Jill sends photos: redbuds red, a few tulips out, spiderwort in bloom, circle garden with daffodils with hyacinths not dominant or adding color.

All our living is regulated by the revolving seasons. They determine what we do, what we think and talk about, what we eat, the pattern of each day.

Harlan Hubbard

Bill Felker

April 9th
The 99th Day of the Year

The grass of spring covers the prairies,
The bean bursts noiselessly through the mould in the garden,
The delicate spear of the onion pierces upward,
The apple-buds cluster together on the apple-branches....
The resurrection of the wheat appears with pale visage
out of its graves.

Walt Whitman

Sunrise/set: 7:07/8:07
Day's Length: 13 hours
Average High/Low: 60/39
Average Temperature: 49
Record High: 86 - 1883
Record Low: 20 - 1957

Weather

Today's temperature distribution: five percent chance for highs in the 70s, thirty-five percent for 60s, twenty-five percent for 50s, fifteen percent for 40s. And this is the last day of the season on which there is a full 15 percent chance for highs just in the 30s. There is 65 percent chance for precipitation, and snow falls more often today and on the 15th than on any other April days. A low in the 20s is still possible 50 years in a century, but frost stays away on this date two mornings out of three.

Natural Calendar

The second week of Middle Spring opens Strawberry Flowering Season and brings the peak of Daffodil Season, Squill Season, and Grape Hyacinth Season all along the 40th Parallel. Throughout the Ohio Valley, it's Creeping Phlox Season and Wind Flower Season. It's almost always Pear Flowering Season along the streets and Wisteria Season on the trellises. Middle Spring Wildflower Season keeps most of its early flowers and adds many more. It is full Spring Beauty Season in the lawns. In the woods, it is Toad Trillium (the small red-flowered trillium) Season. It is the peak of Virginia Bluebell Season, those flowers filling the hillsides. It is Cowslip Season in the wetlands, Trout Lily Season and Jacob's Ladder Season beneath the budding canopy. It is Redbud Blushing Season along the roadsides into Appalachia as redbuds get ready to open. In town, Tulip Season and Fritillary Season gain momentum.

Daybook

1984: First daffodils seen on Elm Street near St. Paul's in this very late arrival of Middle Spring.

1987: Raspberry bushes have small leaves now.

1988: Crow building a nest in Lil's pine tree. Silver olives leafing. Green ash buds just barely opening, first red quince flower seen, Lil's maple early bloom, and the first crab apple flower noticed beyond Polecat Road.

1989: First crab apple flower again noticed beyond Polecat Road. At the Covered Bridge, violet cress full bloom, bluebells and toothwort early full, first toad trillium open, rose bushes leafing, mint and wild geranium with two-inch leaves, May apples emerging, buckeyes just open, twinleaf, tall with buds, one bloodroot. Sedum thickens and spreads. Garlic mustard spikes have grown more than half a foot in places, with bud clusters at their tips. Honeysuckle leaves an inch long. Tulips in town are in full bloom..

1990: Isaac Walton: "Some have been so curious as to say the tenth of April is a fatal day for Carps." Not so today in South Glen.

1991: Pussy willow leafing begins. Color comes to the lower and middle tree line. Wisteria opening, and the first redbuds, Xenia, eight miles south, a day or so ahead of Yellow Springs. Winter cress comes into bloom at Wilberforce. Long box elder flowers waving in the wind, roadside water dock long and fat, peak bloom of cowslip, ash by my window leafing. A flock of buzzards seen engaged in mating rituals in the middle of a bright green field of winter wheat. Apples budding, showing pink.

1993: John calls from New York Mills, Minnesota: first butterfly of the year, a mourning cloak, seen April 4, the earliest he's ever recorded a butterfly sighting. Here in Yellow Springs, cool and rainy, not even a cabbage butterfly so far. Snow trillium found full bloom along the river. The first finches have turned, though; there were two with bodies almost completely yellow today.

1994: Spring still so late. Hepaticas and Dutchman's britches are almost all the way open in the woods, and toad trillium, bloodroot, toothwort, violet cress, bluebells are up and budding. But it's still the end of March or the 1st of April in the woods. Here at home in the north garden, comfrey leaves are just an inch long, phlox foliage has only begun. Bleeding hearts are an inch or two high, stems and all leaves still red. Astilbe has started, purple coneflowers have just come up, stonecrop getting new leaves. Flickers have been calling in the back trees for a week now. Grackles are in the yard. In the south garden, all crocus and snowdrops have gone. First wood hyacinths are blooming, grape hyacinths too. Blue anemones hold. Daffodils are in early full bloom now. Pansies, mallow, feverfew transplanted.

1995: Most pussy willow catkins are falling. Glory of the snow is gone. Squills are fading, and many of the early daffodils, putting an end to the second bulb season.

1998: Strange frog or toad call at 6:30 this morning, like an American toad, but lower and shorter. Wild phlox open at the mill. Cedar waxwings - a flock of them - outside my window at 1:15 p.m. Box elder flowers falling, branches leafing. Lower shrub line a third to half filled in now.

2002: Peak of daffodil bloom just as the first phase of the major dandelion bloom starts.

2003: Cowslip in bloom across from the Covered Bridge.

2004: Seen from the hotel window, the hills south of Asheville are gray, but they glow slightly gold in the sunrise. There is the palest tint of green to the far undergrowth, and the trees are still bare. The half moon lies in the southern sky. House finches fly back and forth around my window, must have a nest nearby.

2008: Willows are pale green against the horizon. Walking with Jeff beyond Cedarville, I saw several Dutchman's britches budded and one toothwort budded. One towhee, a pair of wood thrushes and a pair of large wrens seen. Jeff said Kit had told him about hearing a catbird. Some swamp buttercup foliage, but no flowers. Around town, some patches of glory of the snow are in full flower. Our red-leafed crab apple tree is leafing, and Japanese honeysuckle leaves pace the wild rose leaves, turning the front fence green. Pussy willows suddenly filled with pollen over night. The star magnolia across the street is coming into bloom. Astilbes and bleeding hearts are leafing, and candy lily clusters are an inch high. Red Japanese knotweed has emerged. On the bike path near Cedarville, small newborn snakes seem to have been drowned on the pavement in the recent rains. Five fingerlings counted in the pond. Don's pink and violet hyacinths are completely unfolded. Grackles cluck in the back trees and finches feed, but the loud cardinal songs during the day seemed to have stopped.

2009: Bamboo shoots seen this morning, some about three inches high. On Dayton Street, Don's serviceberry trees are starting to flower, and some blue windflowers are open. Some crab apple buds are cracking and showing color. A squirrel chattered in the alley this morning, the first time I've heard that in a while. More dandelions coming along the roads throughout the county. This evening as I walked Bella, grackles were clucking throughout the neighborhood.

2011: To Sharonville, 60 miles south of Yellow Springs: into a completely different season, one of full-blooming apple and pear trees and pink magnolias. In Dayton, pears are just starting in the rich center of daffodil bloom. This evening as I walked Bella, cardinals, doves, robins were singing. Pussy willow catkins almost all down in this afternoon's rain.

2012: Large comfrey leaves maybe nine inches long in Liz's garden, geranium stems tall and budded, and the first white wood hyacinths opening.

2013: First white cabbage butterfly seen today. The pileated woodpecker continues to call from the back trees, and the red-bellied is vocal, too. Several piles of algae removed from the pond. I had been waiting for the toads to lay their eggs in it, but the growth seems to be out of hand – and growth is out of hand also everywhere around the yard, Middle Spring surging. First periwinkle seen along High Street. At Ellis Pond, south wind warm and hard, blue-eyes, bittercress, and henbit in full bloom, hemlock a foot tall now. The buds of so many of the trees are swelling, pushing: white ash, redbud, Chinese maple, hornbeam, Chanticleer pear, plum, sassafras. Crab apple trees are leafing here and at home. The Red Sunset red maple is in bloom, and a star magnolia has opened downtown.

2014: Robins singing at 5:05 this morning, cardinal heard at 5:30. Chris sent a photo of a trout lily she found in bloom. In the garden, a little green showing on some ferns, the tips of a few hosta just pushing out, and the first of the delicate Asiatics and oriental lilies emerging. Walking Bella, I found one red tulip open, and a large patch of violets in bloom (and so their average blossoming date this cold year was only delayed three days). The buds on Don's serviceberry trees are straining to open. The pussy willows are holding their pollen.

2015: Last night, Bella woke me up; then came a great thunderstorm, and I lay on the floor with her so she wouldn't be so frightened. Hard rain, the yard flooded this morning. Crows heard at 6:00, grackles to the feeder at 6:30. The first of the mass dandelion bloom noticed on the way to Beavercreek this afternoon. The lone bloodroot by the lungwort opened over night, small, perfect, white.

2016: To Cincinnati in light snow and wind: pears definitely darkening with new foliage and petal loss, forsythia gold darkening, as well. Spring is on hold for the moment, however, high only in the 30s this afternoon. At the monastery of St. Clare: patches of the mid-April dandelion flowering, and the redbud in their garden outside the chapel windows is in early bloom. Their *cornus mas* is leafing, was bright with blossoms when I visited on March 13.

2017: Spain: a short four-mile walk from Brea to Arca, Full pink magnolia, apple, rhododendron, leafing pear. Weeping willows fully leafed, birches leafing and blooming, white oak leafing and blooming, box elder leafing, orchard grass and brome fully developed.

Reflections on the awareness of time and space as my body traverses the landscape of spring in Galicia, the linear nature of my pilgrimage, its intent fused into my motion,, the linear road ahead which I not only follow but also imitate and create, parallel entities each perhaps aware of the other, the changes in the landscape patterning or following or forcing changes in thought or physical energy. I am aware that my intent adapts, as well, to the motion of wind or the sound of birds, the stretching out of the plants, the leafing of the trees, following my daydreams as well as the dreams of my sleep, the intent always traversing the porousness of my mind and body, cleansing, strengthening, giving purpose and meaning, given purpose and meaning with the tidal conversation of beings and motion, desire and acceptance,

Much time to reflect on the entire cultural scope of Christianity and European history, combined with the realism of the walk itself, the sense of immediacy that comes from combining physical exertion and discomfort with the prayerful intent and request and offering of the pilgrimage itself.

Since I cannot do anything but accept the outcome of my physical journey, the walking is like an opening into lectio, waiting for the waters to move and the voice to come. The demands of the walk create a new space that is difficult to experience in daily secular life - or I suspect - in daily monastic life. As to what will happen in the end...that is not, thankfully, up to me. Which, of course, is the whole point.

The names we give to plants are important; more important are the

spaces between them which have no names, which hold the possibilities for endless variation, for infinite spontaneous generation.

Randolf Reich

Bill Felker

April 10th
The 100th Day of the Year

The seasons, like greater tides, ebb and flow across the continents. Spring advances up the United States at the average rate of about fifteen miles a day. It ascends mountainsides at the rate of about a hundred feet a day. It sweeps ahead like a flood of water, racing down the long valleys, creeping up hillsides in a rising tide.

Edwin Way Teale

Sunrise/set: 7:05/8:08
Day's Length: 13 hours 3 minutes
Average High/Low: 60/39
Average Temperature: 49
Record High: 82 - 1905   Record Low: 18 - 1900

Weather

Highs reach into 70s five percent of April 10ths; they find 60 degrees 25 percent of the afternoons, and make it into the 50s fifty percent of the time. Cold 40s occur fifteen percent of the days, and 30s come once in a decade or two. The sky is often overcast on the 10th, with totally cloudy conditions occurring 40 percent of the time. Rain is also common on this date: 40 percent of the days bring a shower, and another five percent bring a flurry. But from now on the chance of snow decreases each day until it becomes only one in 100 by April 20th. Frost still occurs an average of three mornings in seven.

Natural Calendar

Past the year's one-hundredth day, the Lower Midwest is overwhelmed by Middle Spring. The effects of rising temperatures and the longer days are cumulative. Suddenly, the tree line is greening. Mulberry, locust, tree of heaven, viburnum and ginkgo send out their first leaves. Magnolias, redbuds, lilacs, dogwoods, cherries, peaches, apples, quinces, maples, and pears are almost always flowering by the 15th.

At the forest edge, knotweed and nettles are tall enough to

cut for supper. Flower heads are forming on the sweet rockets and the garlic mustard. May apples spread their shade across the talus slopes of North Glen. Deep in the woods, the momentum of time and weather opens the soft ginger and raises morels from their mulch. Low patches of wild geranium leaves glow orange in the sun. Buds on the grape vines are swelling. Hobblebush and the privet are filling out. Branches of multiflora roses are almost completely covered with foliage. Along the Little Miami, pale spikes of lizard's tail are dragonflies.

In the garden, weeds are getting stronger. August's great ragweed grows its third and fourth leaves, keeping pace with September's beggarticks. June's Dutch iris spears surpass them now, shoot up more twelve inches. Asiatic lilies are emerging. Peony stalks are turning from February red to April green. Daffodils, tulips, and grape hyacinths fill the dooryards.

All across town, honeybees indulge in the seasons of flowering peach trees, forsythia, pears, quince, magnolias, crab apples, cherries, and the last of the *cornus mas.* Young hummingbird moths and bumblebees come out to sip the annual mass flowering of dandelions.

As lawn mowing season enters its second week, wild turkeys are gobbling. Late and mid-season daffodils are at their peak, and earlier varieties are gone. Tulip time is here. The delicate fritillary blossoms. Crab apples start their season (last year's fruit finally falling to make way for the new).

Although some snow trillium and twinleaf are done flowering, it's budding time for meadow rue, large-flowered trillium, trout lily, Jacob's ladder, ragwort and sedum. Bellwort leaves unravel. Virginia bluebell, hepatica, periwinkle, toad trillium, cowslip, rue anemone, chickweed, purple deadnettle, spring beauty, small-flowered bittercress, shepherd's purse, henbit, violet, small-flowered buttercup, thyme-leafed speedwell are now all in bloom.

Daybook

1979: First tulips open today in the south garden.

1981: First violets seen today, first periwinkle.

1983: Pussy willow catkins gone. Peach tree starts to flower.

1984: Mill Habitat, upper and lower, 62 degrees: May apples just up, geese scouting for nests along the river, snow trillium full bloom, violet and white hepatica all over. Water striders animated for the first time this spring, seem to be mating. Rue anemone blooming, harbinger of spring. Buckeyes still not leafing. A frog screamed as I walked by and jumped into the river, first frog of the year. At home, pussy willows suddenly have pollen.

1985: Pussy willow catkins almost gone. A year ago, they were just starting to turn gold.

1986: Cardinal sings 5:25 a.m. Along Grinnell, cowslip full bloom across from the Covered Bridge.

1987: Cardinal sings 5:30 a.m. Into southwestern Ohio: coltsfoot blooming by the roadsides. All across the middle of the state, the tree line is flushed, barely greening. Road kills: groundhogs common. At Wilberforce, early full bloom of dandelions. First pears bloom, bleeding hearts six inches, grackles building nests.

1988: Bleeding hearts have buds. Freeway grass near full green. Dayton tree line pale green throughout, but the countryside is still orange, red, and green. Jeanie reports from Midland, Michigan, 300 miles to the north, that the crocus are just blooming there.

1989: Even in the cold, the dandelions have started early full bloom.

1993: Another yellow goldfinch today, but maybe more than half of them still have their winter colors. First spring beauties seen at the Mill. Buckeye leaves just breaking out, not quite open yet. At home, beggarticks have sprouted at the north wall.

1994: Pussy willow catkins fell in the rain today, all over the new pansy plants. Squills bright blue, full bloom, throughout town.

1995: Hail and wind last night. A tree at the Antioch School was destroyed by lightning. At Grinnell pond, twinleaf has started to bloom. Dutchman's britches fully open now. First violet seen along the path. May apples are up three or four inches, their leaves starting to unfold. Box elders have begun to leaf out. Red-flowered toad trilliums are open in places; one trillium grandiflorum has a bud. The buds of the bluebells hang down, emerged from their sheaths of blue green. Henbit blooming throughout (I saw it open as much as a week ago). At the park up the street from my house, the red maple flowers are decaying, coinciding with the end of the second season of Early Spring bulbs. First cowslip seen across from the covered bridge.

1998: Dandelions in early full bloom. Forsythia old and turning deeper, decaying gold. Squills being covered by the grass of Middle Spring. Ashes and ginkgoes start to flower. Yellow and red tulips all open today. Toad calls at 10:00 p.m.

1999: First fleabane. Pink magnolias full early bloom now as the white ones fade. First frog croaks at 3:50 p.m. Giant blue hosta just barely visible under the mulch.

2002: Along Limestone Street, privet is pale green, pacing the color of the weeping willow there.

2003: Grass ready to be mowed. First patch of dandelions seen in town. Some white magnolia petals are falling on High Street.

2004: Returning to Yellow Springs from Asheville: Approaching the Tennessee boarder, we drive into a sudden change of season, the tree line green, and redbuds increasing in numbers. In Knoxville, it is full May, with even violet iris in bloom. Japanese knotweed is at least a foot tall about halfway to the Kentucky border. Redbuds in bloom remain frequent now into Cincinnati, then disappear by Dayton. In Yellow Springs, pears, plums, and the Dayton-Street serviceberries are in full bloom. At our house, the peonies are a foot tall, the red quince, the peach tree and the early tulips are open. The cowslips at the Covered Bridge have come into full flower.

2005: Inventory: Fields around town are purple with purple deadnettle. In the yard, fritillary in bloom, some small jonquils ending, crocus fading, crab apples in full bloom, along with most daffodils and grape hyacinths. Cowslip open at the Covered Bridge. Some full dandelions, red tulips starting at the red crab apples. First young snake seen in the sun. Leaves emerging on the spirea. Astilbe seven inches, cressleaf groundsel six inches, bamboo starting to push up out of the ground, purple buds on the Korean lilac, downtown pears bursting into full bloom, robins singing by 4:30 a.m., cardinals by 5:30. Peach leaves an inch long, Queen Anne's lace eight inches high, coneflowers three inches, all the bleeding hearts up. Thistles seven inches, flags eight inches, waterleaf fully leafed, first hosta spears, redbuds showing, peonies eighteen inches, orange and yellow tulips full.

2006: Yellow and brown fritillary open in the east garden. Purple magnolia opening in the High-Stafford Street alley. Star magnolia beginning to drop petals. Early full pears downtown. Pussy willow full of pollen. Early full dandelions along the road to Dayton, the undergrowth pale green. South to the Ohio River: a few trees puffed pale green throughout the hillsides. Apples blooming in Aurora, Indiana, trees greening in Rising Sun, forsythia aging, olives leafing, bright fields of purple deadnettle, fields and roadsides of yellow winter cress. Small-flowered buttercup at Patriot Landing, box elders in bloom, violets, two leaves on the touch-me-not sprouts, dock and hemlock boot high. Some pears leafing in Patriot village. Daffodils old, some garlic mustard heading. Faint blush to the redbuds. Red quince blooming on Market Street in Vevay. While I was gone, Jeanie heard the green frog croaking in the pond for the first time this year. And she said that one of her kindergarteners came to school with a cup full of baby frogs.

2008: First yellow tulip opened in the south garden this morning. The first pink lungwort flowered under the mock orange. The red quince is budding. In Wilmington, the decorative pear trees have started to come in; there are even a few flowers in Xenia but not in Yellow Springs. The first cowslip is open at the Covered Bridge.

2009: A cool Good Friday, but I saw one bleeding heart in full bloom. Grackles continue to cackle and cluck throughout the neighborhood. Robins are becoming less common, pairing up, perhaps, or saving their energy for early-morning courtship. All over Yellow Springs, pear flowering is at its peak. This evening at the park, I found the first crab apple breaking out.

2010: To the Cox Arboretum in Dayton: Crab apples, lilacs, Judd viburnum, Korean spice viburnum, dandelions, pale yellow *alchemilla alpina*, and redbuds full bloom. At home, hearts have formed on the bleeding hearts, Don's pie cherry full bloom, his wind flowers holding, serviceberry flowers almost gone.

2011: Weeding in the first day of temperatures in the 80s. The first carpenter bees noticed, and the first box elder bug, the first red tulip in the north garden. Daffodils have started to fade. Spirea leaves are thin, well developed. In the heat, Peggy's pear tree bloomed, and Don's serviceberry trees.

2012: More leaves appearing on the redbuds as the azaleas gradually open in the cool afternoons. Tulips hold and the last daffodils. On the road south of town, almost all the crab apples have lost their petals. The Korean lilac is trying to open, and the first of the purple wood hyacinths has started to come undone. The wisteria on the trellis is almost gone. Honeysuckle leaves are full-size, Lil's maple and burning bush leaves almost full. When I cut the grass today, I noticed that most of the violets were done blooming. In the countryside, many dandelion patches hold, even as more apple petals fall. Our redbuds hold at half violet/half tawny. Older sweet Williams budding. All the dogwoods still completely intact.

2013: Katherine says she saw a pair of pileated woodpeckers in her yard yesterday. My pileated has been calling all week – and the red-bellied, too. In the alley at dawn, grackles and starlings in small clusters, cackling and squealing and whistling as they socialize. The lawn is almost getting ready to cut, many areas tall enough, others hardly greening. Next week will be the time. More star magnolias flowering throughout town.

Into North Glen: The broad range of Middle Spring wildflowers in bloom: spring beauties, lesser celandine (found for the first time at the Cascades, all the flowers with eight petals), lush white, violet hepatica, yellow trout lilies, bloodroot, violet cress, and Dutchman's britches. Toothwort budded, one May apple about two inches out of the ground, and a tiny *trillium grandiflorum* just emerged. No bluebells or twinleaf seen, but our bluebells are budded at home. Spicebushes are in full bloom throughout the undergrowth on the way to the Yellow Spring. Got back just before the first major thundershower of the year, with hail, too.

2014: One star magnolia bud is almost ready to open across the street. The pussy willows are starting to come down in the wind. A few small tips of hosta found in my garden walk. Daffodils are still in full bloom, grape hyacinths coming in. Driving to Dayton, I saw the first patches of dandelions (very late!) and willow trees greening up.

2015: Spent the day with Tat transplanting. The first cabbage white butterfly of the year visited the northeast garden. The first hostas are visible now, some about an inch high. The early yellow tulips by the south wall, the first tulips Jeanie and I planted three decades ago, opened over night. Other tulips in the yard have buds. In rain and wind, almost all of the remaining pale bamboo leaves have come down with the pussy willow catkins. Compensation: the new bamboo is coming up.

2016: From Campello, in the hills above Spoleto, Italy Neysa sent photos of a huge patch of purple cyclamens and a tall lilac bush all in bloom, along with a cluster of wild asparagus. If this year's April hadn't been so cold, we would be neck and neck with central Italy. At home, the ancient oakleaf hydrangea is starting to leaf; it will have one more year, it seems. The Indomitable Spirit hydrangea is alive and has small buds. In the south garden, the rudbeckia that I planted in August are returning, leaves about an inch long, hiding in the weeds. Peach leaves on the new trees are an inch or so long, and the parent tree has bloomed a little is getting foliage, too.

2017: Spain: from Brea to Xan Xurgo a few kilometers from Santiago. The hotel is a masterpiece of charm and decoration surrounded by fields and farms. Most of the walk was through eucalyptus woods even past the airport and into the Lavacolla suburbs. Several clumps of cowslips, some spiderwort, yarrow (budding), many butterflies and songbirds, vegetation not so lush as it has been. Maples seen in flower, white seed tufts from flowering trees drifting by as we had lunch by the side of the road. Eucalyptus bark lay all along the path and throughout the forests, skin shedding like sycamores in July, (When do these begin?)

And since to look at things in bloom
fifty springs are little room,
About the woodlands I will go
To see the cherry hung with snow.

A. E. Housman

April 11th
The 101st Day of the Year

These days, the world
Is most beautiful of all:
Every seed is sprouting,
Buds are swelling.

Joannes Secundus
(bf)

Sunrise/set: 7:04/8:09
Day's Length: 13 hours 5 minutes
Average High/Low: 60/39
Average Temperature: 49
Record High: 88 - 1930
Record Low: 24 - 1892

Weather

On average, this is the sunniest and driest day since the 21st of March, the sky being clear to partly cloudy 85 percent of the years, rain occurring only 25 percent of the years. Highs reach into the 80s five percent of the time, into the 70s fifteen percent, into the 60s thirty-five percent, into the 50s twenty percent, and the 40s twenty-five percent. After today, an afternoon high in the 30s becomes a rarity. Frost, however, still occurs an average of one night in three on this date.

Natural Calendar

In the herb garden, wood mint is about eight inches tall, and sweet for tea. Chives are ready for salads. Pastures fill with golden winter cress, purple henbit and dandelions. Blossoms could be out on a few strawberry plants, and hearts are forming on the bleeding heart. Pussy willow catkins have fallen. Asparagus is coming up in the sun. The earliest grasshoppers and tadpoles swarm from their eggs. The first goslings are born. Tent caterpillars appear in the wild cherry trees. Along Nebraska's Platte River, sandhill cranes departfor breeding grounds in the North. In the lower Midwest, aphids become active, and ladybugs come looking for them.

Daybook

1983: Box elders leafing.

1984: First grape hyacinth bloomed behind the garden wall today. Full pollen on the pussy willows.

1985: Some of the maples are turning green. First strawberry bloomed today, first asparagus came up, first buttercups bloomed. Sweet rockets bushy like pineapples. At the Covered Bridge: toothwort, violets, purple cress, bluebells, bloodroot, Dutchman's-britches, toad trillium. May apples are three to six inches, one or two even a foot tall. First bumblebees at Middle Prairie. Twinleaf season over for the year. Some skunk cabbage fully leafed out like in June.

1986: 5:12 a.m., first loud birdsong. This morning, bees work the cherry blossoms in 45 degree temperatures, sun. Hops up six to twelve inches. Some red nubs on the grape fines, bleeding hearts early full bloom, pecan buds barely opening.

1987: Burr Oak State Park, southeastern Ohio: Spring beauties, coltsfoot, hepatica, harbinger of spring, toothwort. Buds on Jacob's ladder and large-flowered trillium. First grass heading.

1991: Hawthorns leaf out on Dayton Street. First cherry blossoms. End of scilla, glory of the snow and most wind flowers. Grape hyacinth, large hyacinth hold on. Violets have replaced all the Early Spring bulbs in the round garden.

1992: Full perennial sprouting time now. Bleeding hearts up to four inches. Small red leaves of the purple coneflowers are up, daisies three inches, lilies big and fat, three to four inches, blue flags coming back at six inches, first violets blooming, comfrey four to six inches, ahead of the horseradish. Ranunculus taking over. First tulip blooming. Pears full bloom downtown, squills holding, star of Holland old, some older hyacinths, knotweed up three to six inches, some mint emerging, phlox strong at three inches, clusters of lupine lush, cherry buds swelling, waterleaf spreading and turning the woods floor green.

1993: Grape hyacinth noticed booming by the garden wall yesterday. Pussy willows full pollen.

1998: Frog calls 5:00 a.m. Wild phlox full bloom, and creeping phlox in town. First apple blossom opens. Lilacs are open.

1999: A frog croaked at 6:34 a.m. Zelda, the huge orange koi, leapt into the air at 4:30 p.m., rare spring frisking.

2000: Cool weather keeps most of the apple trees from opening, although there are a few dark pink ones partially blooming. The pears are leafing, and some petal fall is occurring. Along Dayton Street, the serviceberries have lost most of their flowers now. In front of the house, the brown fritillaria has come into bloom. Money plant is budding, will probably open in the warm temperatures forecast for this weekend. In the backyard, the wild crocus leaves are turning brown. Still no hearts on the bleeding heart, but the lungwort is full of blue flowers. At 5:00 a.m. robins twittering in the distance.

2001: First cabbage butterfly seen. Strawberries start to bloom. Grass should be mowed.

2002: Now the roadside grass is really green, the transformation radical in the past two weeks. One azalea opened at school in Columbus.

2003: The sun is rising now from the north end of Lil's house at about 7:25. The peach tree is opening in the north garden.

2006: Peach tree opened completely today in the north garden.

2008: Jeanie said that worms were all over the bike path this morning, caught in last night's heavy rain. The peach tree's buds are pink, but won't open until after the cold forecast for the 12th through the 14th. Our daffodils are in full bloom, the peonies are a foot tall and unraveling, and the pussy willow catkins have begun to fall. The first cabbage butterfly of the year appeared in the north garden this morning.

2009: Walk at Clifton Gorge with Jeanie: Sun, wind, high in the 50s. We walked through early Middle Spring among full bluebells and Dutchman's britches, new miterwort, tall purple cress, hepaticas, spring beauties, early yellow bellworts, shy red ginger and large patches of large-flowered trilliums. A few toothworts were open. Some touch-me-not sprouts had a second pair of leaves. May apple umbrella foliage has just recently pushed up, leaves fresh and shiny, maybe six to nine inches tall.

2010: To Clifton Gorge with Jeanie: Sun, high 60s: The first tier of wildflowers was gone: only one hepatica, one bloodroot, fading purple cress, fading toothworts, a few tattered Dutchman's britches. The second tier was in full bloom: miterwort, large-flowered trilliums, late toad trilliums, bluebells, bellworts, meadow rue, Solomon's plume (budded), May apples well developed and budded, skunk cabbage leaves almost a foot long, ragwort budded, a few wild phlox open. Redbuds in full bloom throughout John Bryan Park, and in town, crab apples are coming in. At home, red and yellow tulips full, new deadnettle maybe half in bloom, a few hosta well leafed, red phlox foliage a foot tall, flags a foot. Trumpet vine has new leaves, buds on peonies (fully leafed). Tonight the toad called from the pond – after several cool nights of silence.

Judy writes from Goshen, 200 miles northwest of Yellow Springs: "Here's the list of wildflowers we saw Sunday (the 11th): coltsfoot, rue anemone, false rue anemone, bulbous buttercup, Spring Beauty, squirrel corn (the relative of Dutchman's Breeches), toad trillium, yellow trillium, white trillium, goldthred, May apples were budding. Today (April 15th) some crabapple blossoms are out; magnolias are starting to fall here and there; star magnolias and forsythia will be gone if we get rain with a wind tonight. I can't believe that some apple trees are starting to bloom--they're at least three weeks early, from what I recall of other years."

2011: A cardinal woke me up with loud, constant calls from 5:30 until 7:00 this morning. Last night, all the pears, the serviceberries, the pink magnolias, the red quinces, and the pink cherries came into bloom.

2012: Petal fall beginning on the pink quince.

2013: I went outside at 4:55 this morning, heard faint, rhythmic frog calls. The robins were just starting to talk, and by 5:00, they were chattering throughout the neighborhood. At 5:01 there was one very laud cardinal call, then no more cardinals for a while. At 5:05, the song sparrow came in, and the crescendo of robins and song sparrows filled the dark and then the twilight until cardinals came in steadily at 5:35 and doves at 5:45, then the house sparrows by 6:00. The green frog was sitting by the pond at 9:30 – the first time I've seen him this year. No grackles or starlings around this morning. In the west garden, the pachysandra opened overnight. The pussy willow now is bright with pollen along the sidewalk, and the first tulip, a red one, has come out. In the south garden, some peonies are a foot high, unraveling. Close to the house in the east garden, the very first hosta spear is protruding about an inch. At Ellis Pond, small field peppergrass all about, has been blooming for quite a while, seed pods numerous. Willow hornbeam catkins. Red maples flowering, ashes, oaks, sugar maples still holding back. The star magnolia on High Street is in full bloom, a pink magnolia and a plum tree also open down Stafford Street. Rob reports his wife saw a mourning cloak butterfly and a blue, and he saw a polygonia this week.

2014: To Gethsemani near Louisville, Kentucky: I left Dayton still a little before forsythia bloom, finding quickly the undergrowth filling green near Cincinnati, and rows of daffodils up to and then across the river down into the knob country. Very little color, nevertheless until we entered the area around the monastery. And there, I found that the eastern Kentucky spring was about two weeks ahead of southwestern Ohio spring, but still only at the level of what a Yellow Springs season would be at this time of year (if the weather had been typical), and so instead of driving down into the first week of Yellow Springs May, we found the middle of

Yellow Springs April at Gethsemani: red quince, forsythia, cherries, daffodils, anemone, violets, small-flowered buttercups, pink magnolias, periwinkles, white trout lilies, ground ivy, spring beauties, dandelions, decorative pears (a few even leafing), toothwort, spicebush, blue fields of henbit in full bloom. Redbuds blushing. A seven-petal white flower (just three of them) with rue-like leaves, probably a rue. May apple umbrellas rising, some open and a foot tall, most of them still only a couple of inches.

Dogwood blossoms still small but starting to unravel, the tree line greening, so many buds starting, here and there, some patches of red maples flowering. Toad trillium full size by the creek but not open. Cabbage whites and small blue butterflies. Grackles (the most prominent) and robins and cardinals and mockingbirds calling throughout, chickadees and red-bellied woodpeckers and nuthatches at the feeders. Steady push of a south wind throughout the day, sometimes gusting, gibbous moon in the east at dusk, shining so bright through Vigils the next morning, ceding to the tresses of cirrus clouds. At home this evening, John Blakelock left a message: "The toads have begun to sing."

2015: More transplanting of lilies today. By the shed, the bluebells are budded, the bloodroot holds. Daffodil and squills still at full bloom. Box elder tree flowering. Peonies: some gangly to almost a foot. Evening primrose sprouts about an inch tall, started from seed last summer. Gloldenrod sprouts – also seeded last summer – have leaves an inch long. Now the large ferns show green knuckles, and some of Jeanie's ferns by the redbud tree have curled through the mulch. In the southwest garden, the established astilbes are up about six inches. But in the dooryard east garden, no sign of the new plants set in last fall. The first red-winged blackbird sang and fed in the yard through the afternoon, the first red-wing here for years.

2016: Mild in the 50s, light rain: First cardinal called at 5:03 a.m.

2017: Spain: to San Marcos near Santiago: Only red clover among the thinning suburban vegetation. At one rest area, sycamore leaves quite well developed, maybe to two or three inches, Space slipping by more easily the more we walk and our bodies become used to movement, The correlation between landscape and mind melds. The world is no longer separated from us by machine or walls. We are simple figments of the surrounding roads and woods. In reality, we and they are porous, almost interchangeable.

In a flash, I realized that the world was not formed by random accidents, chance, and fate but that behind the dizzying diversity is a seamless stream of predictable patterns.

Adrian Bejan

Bill Felker

April 12th
The 102nd Day of the Year

All Nature seems at work. Slugs leave their lair –
The bees are stirring – birds are on the wing –
And Winter slumbering in the open air,
Wears on his smiling face a dream of Spring!

Samuel Taylor Coleridge

Sunrise/set: 7:02/8:10
Day's Length: 13 hours 8 minutes
Average High/Low: 61/40
Average Temperature: 50
Record High: 87 - 1930
Record Low: 19 - 1940

Weather

Thirty percent of the afternoons reach 70 degrees on this date, 20 percent make 60, forty percent 50, and just ten percent remain in the 40s. Skies are clear to mostly sunny 65 percent of the time, and rain falls just one day in four. Frost occurs one morning in three. Today marks the beginning of a dramatic increase in the possibility of warm weather. Afternoons above 70 degrees occur three times more often between the 12th and the 30th than between the 1st and the 11th.

Natural Calendar

Summer's jumpseed and zigzag goldenrod sport four to six leaves apiece. Comfrey and lily-of-the-valley are seven-inches high. Wood mint is at least eight inches tall, and sweet for tea. Chives are ready for salads. Raccoons are born. Woodcocks spiral into their mating rituals. Eagles and goslings hatch. Tent caterpillars appear in the wild cherry trees.

Daybook

1983: Covered Bridge: purple cress, bluebells, twinleaf, chickweed, violets, Dutchman's britches, toothwort, spring beauty, purple deadnettle, henbit full bloom. Sedum budding.

1984: Grinnell Swamp: Toad trillium open, Dutchman's britches and hepatica full bloom, trout lily foliage six inches. A few leaves out on the umbrella-like May apple spears. At home, the first tulip blossomed.

1985: Yellow trout lilies and swamp buttercups blossoming along Yellow Springs Creek. Twinleaf and snow trillium gone, same as in 1983. Miterwort six inches. Large-flowered trilliums look like they've been up for several days. Bellwort leaves unraveling from their stalks. Meadow rue budding. First of August's jumpseeds have emerged. Leaves start on apples, cherries, peaches, and pussy willows.

1986: First strawberries bloom in the garden, one day later than last year. Grape vines beginning to grow. Grackles still building nests in the back yard.

1992: Finches courting in the apple tree.

1993: Maple seeds sprout in the garden and in the hard dirt at Wilberforce. First substantial numbers of dandelions are opening now. Daffodils full bloom: every plant is open in the south garden. First magnolia flowers push out next to my door at school. Large-flowered trilliums have just emerged at the frog pond on Grinnell, touch-me-not leaves have gotten fat and wide, cover the stream banks like newly hatched, sleek, green butterflies. First swamp buttercup blooming at the swinging bridge.

1996: Everything seems to be happening at once now that the cold winter and Early Spring have given way to real spring. Yesterday the first bicolor tulip, yellow and orange, opened in the south garden, today, three more. Blue eyes are blooming beside the wilting crocus. Pink hyacinths started yesterday, are filling out today. This afternoon, the first bumblebee and the first two cabbage butterflies of the year in the daffodils – which are reaching full bloom all at once. Aconite leaves are big, flowers long gone. Puschkinia full and holding. Rhubarb leaves up to three inches, horseradish an inch or two, the honeysuckle leaves suddenly pushing out, pussy willows have full pollen, the magnolia on the east side of my building at Wilberforce opened all the way today. Scilla still full bloom. I saw the first crab apple flower opening on Monday, and now many of the fruit tree leaves are coming out. Raspberry leaves half an inch, too.

1998: Budding white mulberry in the back yard. Toad sings in the pond at 1:00 p.m. Full petal fall for pears. Toad eggs seen by Neysa.

2000: First money plants flower in the yard. First backyard apple opens. Redbuds and other apples coming in around the village. Very first garlic mustard along the path, large pink five-petaled honeysuckle open there. Daffodils in the yard are almost gone, tulips full bloom. Late maples in flower, box elders leafing. Most magnolias, white and pink, are decaying.

2001: First meal with asparagus, sweet and fresh, from the garden.

2002: Casey called: Toads began to sing on April 8th, about a week late.

2003: At North Glen: Bloodroot almost gone, Virginia bluebells and spring beauties in early full bloom. Toothwort, violet cress, hepatica, Dutchman's britches, yellow trout lilies full. Hepatica has new leaves. Serviceberries, red quince, pink magnolias, and the downtown pears are still their best.

2005: Willows very green. Lilacs budded. Grass and pastures bright April green, just barely long enough to ripple in the hard wind today. Red quince fully opened. Pears, dandelions and daffodils full. Redbuds and beach show more color. At South Glen, bloodroot common and full flower of spring beauties, purple cress, toothwort. Toad trillium cracking. Grandiflorums and May apples – a few are up. Ginger leaves are well developed. Midseason tulips are coming in around the yard. The small, low red tulips are gone. Ginkgo leafing in front of Rachel's house, stubby leaf clusters. White birch flowering at the same time as box elder. The woods clearly greening and filling in. Buckeye leaves about three inches long.

2008: To Dayton: Plum trees in full bloom along Memorial Drive. Full–pollen pussy willows seen here and there. Bluebells at home show blue and pink buds. More yellow tulips are budding.

2009: A chilly, sunny Easter, light frost but no damage to the magnolias or the bleeding hearts. The serviceberries are in full bloom now on Dayton Street, and the pears are lush along Xenia Avenue. Daffodils, squills and grape hyacinths continue at the peak of their flower, the cool weather keeping the trees and the bulbs from burning out.

2011: The sweet cherry tree is leafing now, and the first leaves are coming out on the blueberry bushes and the river birch in the back yard. Serviceberries, pink magnolias, decorative pears, star magnolias (losing petals in the wind) and weeping cherry trees all full bloom. One bud is almost open on the peach tree. Honeysuckle leaves are offering a modicum of privacy from the neighbors. A red velvet mite seen in the dirt as I was weeding this afternoon.

2012: Peggy's geraniums are in bloom this morning. Our vibunum is in early full flower in spite of two nights of light frost.

2013: Wind and mist in the dark. The song sparrow was the early singer this morning: When I went out about 4:45, he sang once. Then I walked into robin song half a block later, maybe 4:50, then more robin song. Then the song sparrow again at a little before 6:00.

Drive to Gethsemani, Kentucky, two-hundred miles southwest of Yellow Springs: When I was packing the car for the drive, I noticed that many pussy willow catkins – full of soggy pollen – had been blown down in last night's rain. The honeysuckle undergrowth was very light in south Dayton, thickened quickly on the way to Cincinnati, white flowering pears and plums coming in as I approached the Ohio River. (I had left Yellow Springs at the very cusp of pear flower emergence, the day that the pears were sure to blossom.) In northern Kentucky, the grass was so rich and bright, more pear trees in bloom, the high canopy flushed, and many taller trees presenting mounds of April green, redbuds and fields of dandelions and winter cress all along the freeway west, box elder flowers prominent from time to time, pink magnolias in the countryside. At the monastery, plums, red quince, redbuds and forsythia in bloom, the Kentucky forsythia still light yellow, as though it were as new as the Yellow Springs forsythia. In the old graveyard, cherry petals were blown down in the wind, rolling across the stones and along the driveway. In the cloister walk, I found a medium-sized (maybe one inch) pale yellow flower with six petals on a thin stem, like a wild onion stem. Here the field peppergrass and the bittercress have gone to seed, lush chickweed in bloom, violets common. Outside the monastery chapel, 7:45 p.m., robin vespers ongoing.

2015: Pachysandra suddenly open full. Lilies-of-the-valley uncovered in the north garden, two to three inches. A few red nubs on the domestic roses. Some ferns up six inches. Squills, daffodils, grape hyacinths, forsythia all hold at their peak. Bluebells, hepatica and bloodroot open in the wildflower corner. The pale orange tulips joined the yellows (both planted in the 1980s) by the southwest corner of the south wall. Doves and sparrows mating, grackles courting, red-winged blackbirds singing through the day.

2016: First cardinal sang at 5:06 this morning. Pachysandra, east garden late, golden crocus and the west-garden scilla almost all gone, very first stubs of bamboo felt as I walked to the pond, forsythia and pear trees turning to leaves, serviceberry flowers gray, crab apples open in various places, the orange and yellow tulips fading, some snowball viburnum open along Dayton Street. A crow came to the back yard, first time I've seen one land here in a while. At the Cascades: trillium grandiflorum, miterwort, meadow rue, and bellwort in full flower, many spring beauties and hepatica hold on, and even Dutchman's britches from Early Spring, one very old purple cress, a few toothworts.

2017: Spain: Walking from San Marcos into the old portion of Santiago: once again, a clear day, warming in the afternoon, Throughout the walk through town, through traffic and noise and construction - an urban spring: full azalea, rhododendrons, sweeping plantings of cherry trees, their pink blossoms strong against the harsh city cement and stone, The ancient area near the cathedral had a few small plantings with tulips and even pansies. At the hotel, late flowering apples, thousands of the minuscule daisies that have been with us from Madrid.

The flowering pears are holding up the sky
Like a mother whale bearing her baby up for its first breath.
This one stands like flowing horse curried by the wind
Singing to star-slathered canyons and coral-draped islands
In the turquoise eye of Spring
This one's a pyramid of small-leafed acrobats balancing darkness.
A shaving brush shadow of Van Gogh's cypresses
Dusted with powdered sugar, dipped in half-lit green salsa.
It's clear some inner geometry directs the buds.
That flowers can watch the petals of the sun unfold.
That a raindrop disappears into ground, then pokes its head out
Like a white rabbit from crabapple bloom.
That Venus holds up a candle as monkish moths
Illuminate the book of night.
That a tree, embossed with globular rosettes,
Spilling perfume like a broken decanter,
Is both particle and wave.
The breeze weaves sun/moon breath in the branches.

Robert Paschell

April 13th
The 103rd Day of the Year

Loveliest of trees, the cherry now
Is hung with bloom along the bough,
And stands about the woodland ride
Wearing white for Eastertide.

A.E. Housman

Sunrise/set: 7:01/8:11
Day's Length: 13 hours 10 minutes
Average High/Low: 61/41
Average Temperature: 50
Record High: 85 - 1887
Record Low: 19 - 1950

Weather
Chances for a high in the 70s are 20 percent today, and 60s come 40 percent of the time. Look for cooler 50s on 25 percent of the afternoons, and for chilly 40s fifteen percent of the time. The 13th is often cloudy, with totally overcast conditions four days in ten. Rain falls one day out of three, but frost usually stays away, burning sprouts only one morning in five.

Natural Calendar
Japanese knotweed catches up with the rhubarb (just about big enough for a small pie). Water rushes and purple loosestrife, water lilies and pickerel plants have suddenly produced foliage. Snakehead mushrooms, which have a tall, light-colored stalk and a small, dark cap, begin to appear now in the Middle Atlantic region, and their season typically lasts through the end of the month. Black and gray morel mushrooms generally come up at this time of the month, too.

Daybook
1981: Bleeding hearts have pink buds.

1982: Honeybees are out gathering pollen from the pussy willows. Leaves starting on the fruit trees.

1983: Forsythia is leafing now.

1984: Bees in the pussy willows again. First dandelion. Magnolias just start to emerge.

1985: First cherry blossoms. First forget-me-nots in the garden.

1986: Late magnolias hold on in a few places. Bees were all over the cherry tree today. Several cabbage butterflies seen. First apple blossom in the yard. Red quince is full. Forsythia fading. Most trees seem to be leafing.

1988: First cabbage butterflies seen today. First cherry petals show at the top of the tree. Middle Prairie is purple with purple deadnettle. Violets are early full bloom, daffodils are fading quickly. Apple leaves an inch long, redbuds beginning. Some magnolias gone at Wilberforce, some full bloom. Winter cress is budding. The tree line has soft green patches where box elders are strongest.

1991: Bleeding hearts well into bloom, but still tightly clustered and low.

1993: Daffodils and hyacinths peak of bloom.

1996: Off to the Luddite Conference in Barnesville, Ohio. Standing on the street before at 5:10 a.m. after packing the car, I heard the high-pitched chant of American toads. East on the freeway, the roadside grass was greening. Daffodils were in full bloom in wayside pockets near Columbus. Seven migrating cedar waxwings seen at rest stop near Cambridge, all eating the centers out of last year's crab apples.

At the Quaker meeting house in Barnesville, spring beauties and dandelions were in full bloom in the lawn. Down the hill near a little stream, coltsfoot was flowering in the sun. I found a bloodroot open, two skunk cabbage plants, one just blooming, another with a six-inch leaf.

1998: Early apple blossom time begins. End of pear flowers and forsythia and mid season daffodils. Serviceberry flowers disappeared about April 9. Full bloom forget-me-nots at King's Yard downtown.

1999: Frog croaks off and on around 9:30 a.m. Now full bloom spring beauties. Scillas fade, daffodils too, and grape hyacinths so quickly.

2000: First winter cress plant open along the bike path. Blackbirds singing constantly on either side as I ride along, and cardinals flying back and forth in front of me. At home: scilla becoming overgrown in the east garden.

2001: At South Glen with Mike and the puppies: call of the field sparrow identified, high-pitched, frequency increasing at the end of its song "like the way a ping pong ball speeds up as it comes to the end of its bounce," Mike said.

2002: First carpenter bee of the year came out of the woodwork today.

2003: First strawberry flower in the garden. Bleeding hearts are budding. Very last pussy willow catkin falls.

2004: Last year's crabapples falling to the sidewalk along Dayton Street, pushed from their branches by the emerging leaves.

2006: Stopped at Jacoby to let out a rat I'd caught last night in the laundry room. Walked down into the wetlands, the sun emerging over the hill, found cowslip in full bloom, a few bluebells, skunk cabbage big and fat, buckeyes with young red leaves and well budded, an early wild phlox, touch-me-nots with four large leaves. A pair of nuthatches seen, flickers calling throughout. Two deer crossed Grinnell Road in front of me as I drove home, then a wild turkey. On Dayton Street, the serviceberry trees have come out all the way, and it's full bloom time for them and village pears.

Carpenter bees have been out for several days scouting the eaves. Bleeding hearts have hearts, pussy willow catkins hanging on. Early tulips full, and the first midseason varieties seen in town.

2007: Inventory at the end of the early April cold spell. I went looking for damage from almost a week of nights in the 20s. New leaves burned on box elder, maple, crab apple, redbuds, ginkgo, viburnum, spirea, climbing hydrangea, mock orange, hobblebush, serviceberry, privet, purple lilac, forsythia, tree of heaven, peach, tea roses. Korean lilac unhurt, and Dutch iris, asters, penstemon, most tulips and daffodils, monarda, sweet rocket, poppies, sweet Williams, oregano, dead nettle, wood and other hyacinths, helibores, ramps, bluebells, waterleaves, thistles, mallow, mint, achillea, stonecrop, azalea, hostas. Daylilies and purple coneflower foliage burned but seems all right. Covered Asiatic lilies were ok, uncovered ones frozen back. Astilbes and bleeding hearts melted in the frost. Very little prospect for any apple blossoms or redbud bloom this year.

2009: Pear flowers are starting to cede to leaves in downtown Wilmington.

2010: The circle garden is full and lush now with solid banks of purple violets and deadnettle. There are buds on the large allium stalks. Very first leaves push out on the trumpet vine stalks. Hops vines are at least four feet long. A small bright green bee noticed near the porch, possibly an *augochlorella* or a sweat bee.

2011: The pussy willow, with a few catkins left, has started to leaf. Dandelions are gaining momentum at Peggy's and about town.

2012: Yellow Springs to Gethsemani Abbey in west-central Kentucky. When I left home, almost all the apple trees in the park had lost their petals, all the snowball viburnums were full, the tulips and daffodils in their last days, the maples were full of fat seeds, and lawns were full of maple or box-elder seeds turning into trees. Redbud trees at least half gone. The first honeysuckles were starting to come in downtown next to Sam and Eddie's store. In the countryside, the fields are mostly plowed and disked, ready to be seeded or already planted. Many lilacs were almost gone. Silver olives and wintercress common along Dayton-Yellow Springs Road, and many high oaks coming in.

By the time I reached Cincinnati, fifty miles from home, I saw locusts and honeysuckles in full bloom, and by Lexington the high canopy was definitely filling in with luminous leaves, globes of pale-green light sometimes emerging from less advanced woodlots. From Lexington west, wild cherry trees, locusts and honeysuckles in bloom dominated the roadsides, the flowers creamy white in the April green. Red and white clover along the highway. Thistles were tall and budded near Bardstown, and turning down toward the monastery, I saw iris and roses and yellow poplars in bloom, and then I heard the constant call of the abbey mockingbirds.

I walked the fields after I got settled into my room. The inventory: late hawthorn flowers, full locusts, dogwoods and tulip trees, redbuds - interestingly enough - still holding on like in Yellow Springs, blue-tailed dragonflies and black dragon flies at the pond, golden iris in the swampy shoreline of the pond, full ranunculus, cress, very late chickweed all tawny and gone to seed, pink fleabane every where, yellowing deadnettle (and in the middle of the field I noted, as I had more than once this spring, how I must define time and season by where I am and what is happening rather than by relationship to a calendar), star of Bethlehem, shamrock flowers, scraggly bellwort, wild strawberry, blue speedwell, poison ivy leaves recently remerged, the plants covering the ground and about three-inches high, the monastery chestnuts all burned from a recent frost, thin-leafed bluets were the most common deep woods wildflower, a few spring beauties found in bloom, white-flowering sedum by one of the statues, blue violet and white violets, a few Jack-in-the-pulpit plants in bloom, May apples full bloom, poke weed up to four feet, cow parsnip also tall, ground ivy full, small toads about an inch long hopping along the swamp floor, blackberry bushes starting to blossom, one black swallowtail, many blues and sulphurs seen, and many smaller orange and brown butterflies, boneset with five-inch leaves, hemlock very bush and three feet tall, rust on raspberry bushes, yarrow budded. Grasses were fully developed, and I gathered a few.

2013: Gethsemani: Robin singsong begins outside my monastery window at 4:35 a.m. South of the graveyard, the foliage of three large sweet gum trees is about a fourth of its mature size. An apple tree and a cherry there are in full bloom. Willow catkins are aging, willow leaves about an inch long. Fleabane with a heavy stem like Robin's fleabane just coming into bloom. A miniature grape hyacinth flower is growing about the enclosed garden, does not seem domesticated. In a small tree on the way to the monastery entrance, a dove sitting on her nest.

2014: Gethsemani: In the gusting wind this morning, I lay down at 4:45, no birds singing. I woke up at 5:00 to full robinsong. Some blooming redbuds, several crab apples, and more full pears seen in the countryside. A dove is sitting in the same nest as last year on this date. In the courtyard, maples are seeding, green and red. Walking around the monastery west and south walls, I found one fleabane variety and several types of cress in bloom.

2015: On the way downtown, I passed the first pear tree with blossoms. Full bloom dandelions throughout the area.

2016: The last pachysandra dissolved overnight. Lily-of-the-valley about three inches high, ready to be transplanted. The dooryard garden is in transition to its hosta phase, simply looks like weeds at the moment. Walking at John Bryant State Park: Full bloom of trillium grandiflorum, bluebells, toothwort, meadow rue, a few white violets, late scattered hepatica, late but prominent Dutchman's britches, the "honeysuckle high" spring filling in the undergrowth, box elders leafing.

> *The hawthorn whitens, and the juicy groves*
> *Put forth their buds unfolding by degrees,*
> *Till the whole leafy forest stands displayed*
> *In full luxuriance, to the sighing gales,*
> *Where the deer rustle through the twining brake,*
> *And the birds sing concealed.*

James Thomson

April 14th
The 104th Day of the Year

April to perfection, such a sentiment of spring everywhere. The sky is partly overcast, the air moist, just enough so to bring out the odors, a sweet perfume of bursting, growing things. One could almost eat the turf like a horse.... The soil calls for the plow...the garden calls for the spade, the vineyard calls for the hoe. From all about the farm voices call, Come and do this, or do that. At night, how the 'peepers' pile up the sound!

John Burroughs

Sunrise/set: 5:59/7:12
Day's Length: 13 hours 13 minutes
Average High/Low: 62/40
Average Temperature: 51
Record High: 84 - 1887
Record Low: 22 - 1950

Weather

Rain occurs seven years in a decade on this date, making it the wettest day in my April weather history. Highs reach above 70 degrees 30 percent of the time, make it into the 60s on 40 percent of the afternoons, into the 50s ten percent, and the cold 40s the remaining 20 percent. Frost strikes just 15 percent of the mornings.

Natural Calendar

The Great Dandelion Bloom is the most common and the most radical marker for the third week of Middle Spring Of course a few dandelions started blooming in February and March – and often they bloom year around. Now, however, comes the *Great Dandelion Flowering* that begins in the Deep South - where Middle Spring comes much earlier than it does in the North - and it spreads up through the Border States like robins, reaching the 40th Parallel, the lateral midline of the United States in April, and then creeps up to the northern states in May.

Whenever it occurs, the Great Dandelion Flowering turns lawns and waysides golden with their blossoms and announces the greening of the high trees: the maples, oaks, mulberries, locusts, and ginkgoes sending out their first leaves. It trumpets tulip season and the budding of peonies in the garden. The Great Dandelion Bloom in the alleys and along the freeways lets you know that - if you had time to take to the woods - you could find hepatica, periwinkle, toad trillium, cowslip, rue anemone, and buttercups in flower. In the vegetable garden, you might find fresh asparagus, new herbs for seasoning, maybe lettuce leaves long enough for salad.

And above golden fields of dandelions flowers the more exotic, yet no less powerful, marker of the third week of Middle Spring: all the fruit trees coming in: first the cherries and plums and the pears put out their white blossoms, then the pink peaches and then the roseate and white and red crab apples. Like the seas of dandelions, the cherries and plums pears and peaches and apples reveal the season from New Orleans to Maine and Minneapolis, telling time far better and more beautifully than any paper or digital calendar.

Daybook

1982: Dutchman's britches past its prime, woods full of flowers that have butterfly-shaped foliage and chalice-like white flowers, eight petals: twinleaf. Ginger emerging with its small, soft, arrowhead leaf. Buckeyes leaves unraveling. Maple hulls fall to the street.

1985: Covered Bridge: First cowslip, first Greek valerian, first ragwort. Violets, phlox, toothwort, and bluebells perfect full bloom. Dutchman's britches about a week past its prime. Violet cress fading. Garlic mustard and sweet rocket stalks shooting up. Toads chanting at the Covered Bridge. Some touch-me-nots have four leaves, some six. First cherry and quince blossoms appear, first forget-me-not blooms in the yard. Mulberry buds greening.

1987: First cowslip, first strawberry flowers, first ragwort. Red-winged blackbirds nesting in the goldenrod fields. Grackles have been mating for a week now, bobbing up and down, spreading their wings, building nests. Grass long enough to cut. Comfrey leaves eight to nine inches. Apple leaves a half inch to an inch long. Box elders, maples flowering everywhere. Peonies are a foot tall now, leaves unfolding, bleeding hearts not far behind.

1989: Cascades: the cold has kept bloodroot from fading, angel wing leaves pierced by the chalice of white petals. September's zigzag goldenrod is three inches high, with three to six leaves. The American colombo has six-inch leaves. Wood betony, two inches, tightly clustered together, heading. First thick, three-fingered golden alexander is up. Delicate, early white rue anemone in bloom. Bellwort three inches. Trillium grandiflorum: first one bloomed today. Spring beauties early bloom. Red foliage of spicebush paces the honeysuckles. Violets full at Antioch. Dutchman's britches declining. Bradford pears downtown leafing before they blossom. First cabbage butterfly seen today.

1991: First daddy longlegs, maybe a fourth grown, seen in the pile of poplar wood. At the nursery, barberry was in full bloom, yellow flowers, serviceberry full, white, plums and sand cherries full, some viburnum too.

1993: First cowslip blooming by the Covered Bridge. Willows greening, soft color to the lower woods as honeysuckle leaves get bigger. Upper tree line reddening with buds, box elders and maples in full bloom, bleeding hearts shoot up in the warm afternoon. Pussy willow catkins, puffed out with pollen, fall and scatter in the wind. In the east garden, the last of the snow crocus disappear. Beside them, purple coneflower leaves are up an inch or two, thin astilbe stems unravel, veronica thickens.

1994: High 75. First cabbage butterfly seen today. At the Cascades, hepatica and violet cress in full bloom, toothwort beginning, Solomon's plume or seal are up several inches, early meadow rue is up to a foot too, pacing the growth of the columbine, flower clusters forming. Along Grinnell Road, box elders, buckeyes, roses, black raspberries, and honeysuckles are turning the undergrowth pale green, fleshing out the winter branches. At home, bluebells have grown up quickly, but still not budding. More early tulips open (first the yellow, then the orange). Comfrey a couple inches high now. Asiatic lily clusters are up.

Violets bloom here and at Antioch. Apple trees have been leafing for several days. John called yesterday from northern Minnesota; he found the first wood tick, his rhubarb was just beginning to show its stems, and frogs were croaking.

1996: Coming back from Barnesville across central Ohio: a red and gold tint to the mountains from the flowering trees.

1998: Weeds out of control now, I should have started pulling them ten days ago. First garlic mustard seen open along Grinnell. Full apples and red buds and dogwoods now, and all lilacs and tulips. Center of late Middle Spring. Tulip tree paces ginkgoes and willows.

2000: First ichneumans seen at home and at work. Almost all the hosta varieties have emerged, some leafing at about six inches. Asiatic lilies are up about four inches. Carpenter bees starting to look for nests along the west roof line, more of them lying dead too at the back porch. The pond toad finally sings briefly after maybe two weeks of silence.

2002: Snow-on-the-mountain has emerged in the east garden. Buds on the sweet rockets, clematis, bleeding hearts, and azaleas. Peonies and some hosta unraveling in the west garden. Astilbe leafing out, eight inches tall under the apple tree. Asiatic lilies up to six inches in the north garden. Honeysuckle getting enough leaves to form a barrier against the street. Black raspberry fully leafed. Grass past ready to cut. Cabbage butterflies seen all week. Bats in the evenings now, and toad song coming from the river. Snakes have taken over the pond.

2005: Knotweed knee high. Some fresh bamboo stalks are four inches tall. Periwinkle continues full. Purple fields of purple deadnettle, yellow fields of dandelions. Crab apples emerging. Lil's maple full bloom. Hydrangeas and viburnums have been leafing for a week now, their leaves at least an inch. Silver olives coming out. Full bloom of the serviceberry trees across from Don and Miri's house on Dayton street (those trees parallel the cycle of the pears). Foxtail grass full bloom in Dayton. Blackberries leafing, wild roses and honeysuckles half leafed. Some pink magnolia petals falling in the wind. Peonies past knee high and budding.

2006: At South Glen, a flock of wood ducks sitting in a tree. Spring beauties blooming below them, a few wild phlox and bloodroot. American toads or tree frogs loud upstream. Geese screaming out their warning to the dogs all along the river path. In the yard, the grackles have been clucking throughout the morning. The grass is getting long. At the north fence, the red quince is flowering, and some of the forsythia is leafing. Apples are just starting to open at the park. Along High Street, coral berries have all withered, and most of them have been pushed off their branches by new leaves. Above them, the bittersweet berries are also almost gone. Rachel's ginkgo buds are starting to turn to leaves. The sweet gum near Lawson place has developed huge buds.

2008: Walking at South Glen with Mike: Bloodroot, purple cress, and spring beauties in bloom. Toothwort and toad trillium budded. Wild ginger leaves are unraveling from the soil, and buckeye leaves have opened, some revealing bud clusters. Sweet rockets very tall and bushy, garlic mustard starting to rise. Geese patrolling their nesting areas. Towhee calling. At home, more lilies coming up, bleeding hearts with small heart buds. Pussy willow catkins falling, almost all gone. Greg's lily-of-the-valley has just emerged.

2009: The late-planted crocus are finally winding down, and the daffodils and grape hyacinths are starting to fade – but are still full flower. I noticed that all the berries are gone from the coral berry bushes along High Street and that the privet berries are fast disappearing. Oak leaf hydrangeas are just starting to leaf. Some ferns are up three inches. Hobble bush is leafing. One burdock along the front walk has six-inch leaves. The bittercress that bloomed so vigorously last month is now seeding. Lily stalks are up four to six inches now. The mid-season tulips are opening now, and the early orange and yellow tulips are holding in the cool weather.

2010: Covered Bridge habitat: Soft carpet of chickweed across the open areas, skunk cabbage leaves full size, the last toothworts, early phlox, budded ragwort and May apples, one blooming Jacob's ladder, full bluebells (but the undergrowth is rising, hiding the ones on the upper slopes), full dandelions and violets. A huge patch of twinleaf foliage near the flat rock landing, a patch to watch next year. In town, full dogwoods, apples, pears. In the yard, the peach flowers are fading. Oak-leaf hydrangea leaves are between two and four inches. Bittercress seeding. First buds on Greg's lily-of-the valley.

2011: First creeping phlox seen in the plantings in front of the store. On Stafford Street, maples forming seed pods, box elders leafing. Redbuds blushing throughout town. Birdsong not so prominent this evening, robins and an occasional grackle. Rachel's ginkgo buds leafing. Peach tree almost full bloom. Puschkinia season suddenly over.

2013: Gethsemani: I was up early, my third-floor room window open, waiting for the birds to start singing. Suddenly at 4:26 the robins burst into song, the sound magnified by the architectural valley over which my room is located – the church on the north side, the guest house wall on the west, the monastery garden wall on the east, the cobblestone walkway in the middle. So I heard the birds nine minutes earlier today than yesterday; is that because the temperature was milder, because the wind had shifted or because I wasn't paying attention yesterday?

Reading back over the daybook notes, I can see how the cold March has put the Gethsemani spring back to what a Yellow Springs spring is usually like in the middle of April. Brother Paul said that this area had been seven degrees below normal in March (versus five degrees below normal in Yellow Springs).

To the woods: Two tiger swallowtails, one mourning cloak, two azures, a polygonia, numerous cabbage whites and several medium-sized black butterflies. One bright green tiger beetle and one dragonfly. Two small webs full of webworms. Small-flowered buttercup, bluets, spring beauties, late toothwort, periwinkles, early Jacob's ladder, holly, cherry in bloom. May apples range from just emerged to budded. Blackberry leaves an inch long. Throughout the woods, very little canopy coverage, very little foliage in the undergrowth.

2014: Home from Gethsemani: While I was gone, lots of changes: mid to late-season daffodils following the fading early ones; forsythia blooming; early tulips starting at the south wall and around town; pear trees and serviceberry trees starting to flower; pink and star magnolias in full flower; grass getting long enough to cut; Asiatic and Oriental lilies are up a few inches; heliopsis foliage found; peaches are leafing, some budding; late crocus still prominent; all the pussy willow catkins knocked down in the weekend's gusty wind; no sign of ferns yet; first leaves on the Anna Bell hydrangea; creeping phlox in many yards. The most obvious differences between Gethsemani and Yellow Springs today are the leafing of the pears and the blooming of the redbuds there, compared to pears just starting to flower, and the redbuds not even blushing here. Among my messages: John Blakelock reports toads in full song.

2015: Listening for birds: Early robins at 4:35, song sparrow heard at 5:12, cardinals finally coming in at 5:13, woodpecker tapping, doves, blue jay, titmice waiting until 5:54, grackles and crows at 6:00. In Dayton, I saw a large planting of tulips starting to open. The woods along the river was greening. The decorative red maples was full bloom, seeds dangling. At home, more pears in flower, and all the serviceberry trees,, white as I walked at dusk. In the back yard, the sweet cherry is opening – with more buds than it's ever had. At Ellis Pond: yellow buckeye and horse chestnut are leafing.

2016: Sun and 60s: As I was walking the north garden, a red admiral butterfly passed me to explore the new sprouts. Along Dayton Street, the fragrant snowball viburnum shrub has put out all its flowers.

2017: Spain: Throughout Santiago de Compostela, fruit trees, azaleas, other flowering shrubs in bloom, daffodils well past prime at the Alameda park, some pear trees fully leafed and a sense of middle and Late Spring throughout the park.

The first in time and the first in importance of the influences upon the mind is that of nature. Every day, the sun; and, after sunset, Night and her stars. Ever the winds blow; ever the grass grows.

Ralph Waldo Emerson

April 15th
The 105th Day of the Year

I had no inclination to read or to write, but only to spend the hours looking upon the earth's April beauty, so lavishly spread before me here, listening to the field sparrow's song, and smelling the fragrances of the leaves, the musk of the turned soil, the delicate perfume of the pasqueflowers, spending the hours in the sure knowledge that none would ever come again.

August Derleth

Sunrise/set: 5:58/7:13
Day's Length: 13 hours 15 minutes
Average High/Low: 62/41
Average Temperature: 51
Record High: 80 - 1976
Record Low: 23 - 1907

Weather

Highs in the 70s occur 20 percent of the time; 60s come 30 percent, 50s are recorded 30 percent, and 40s fifteen percent, 30s or 20s five percent. The sky is often overcast, with two April 15ths out of three showing no sun at all. Even though precipitation falls six days in a decade on this date, making the period of April 14th-15th the wettest days of the month, today also marks the close of the rainiest part of April in an average year.

The Weather in the Week Ahead

The chances for a high above 50 degrees are 85 percent on almost every day during April's third quarter, and temperatures above 60 come at least half the time. Cold 20s are rare (just a five percent chance on the 17th and 18th), but frost still strikes an average of one night in four. Beginning on the 20th, the chances for an afternoon high in the 70s or 80s jumps from an average of 25 percent way up to 45 percent.

Rain or snow falls an average of 35 percent of the time this week of the year, the today, 15th, being the wettest day of all – carrying a 45 percent chance for rain and an additional 20 percent chance for snow. Beginning on the 16th of the month, a major increase in the average daily amount of sunlight takes place: a rise from early April's 50/50 chance for sun or clouds up to a brighter 70 percent chance for clear to partly cloudy conditions.

Natural Calendar

In cooler years, this is usually apple blossom week along the 40th Parallel, and redbud week, and dogwood week. By this time of the season, honeysuckles and spice bushes have developed enough to turn the undergrowth pale green, and color rises throughout the tall tree line. Pheasants nest, and bird migrations peak with the arrival of whip-poor-wills, red-headed woodpeckers, catbirds, cedar waxwings, yellow-throated vireos, meadow larks, indigo buntings, scarlet tanagers, Baltimore orioles, cowbirds, kingbirds, and more than a dozen varieties of warblers.

Daybook

1981: First pie cherry blossom in the side yard this morning.

1983: First winter cress just past Clifton Road. Field peppergrass, too. Village tulips full bloom. All the uncut grass in the lawn is heading.

1984: To Cincinnati: Magnolia, dogwood, forsythia all blooming together, willows green. At home, box elders and maples flower, lilac leaves coming out. At the Mill, snow trillium fading as tulip tree buds expand. First violet in the woods. Water cress opening.

1985: Poplars leafing.

1988: The first cherry opens, at the same time the ginkgo, poplar, and sweet gum buds get read to leaf, and the redbuds brighten. Frog or toad eggs reported from Mrs. Bletzinger's pond (about five miles west of town).

1989: First yellow flowers on the holly bushes in King's Yard. First leaves on the hobblebush at Grinnell swamp. Some garlic mustard heading up. Early cherries open in town. Peonies budding. Comfrey leaves nine inches long, hops a foot to a foot and a half. *Cornus mas* done blooming, and leafing forsythia drops its flowers.

1990: First cherry blossom this Easter morning. First blue speedwells open under the pussy willows. Red tulips past their prime, but the yellow and pink are full. Last yellow crocus gone. Only a few daffodils left. Anemone and squills, white and blue hyacinths are still strong. Two redbuds seen blooming. Forget-me-nots open in the south garden

1992: First carpenter bee.

1993: The year continues to pace 1984 almost exactly.

1996: While I was in Barnesville over the weekend, the crocus season abruptly ended here in Yellow Springs. The cherry tree garden is empty now. But daffodils are in full bloom, and squills still offer blue. On the way to school, I saw that the swamp cowslip in South Glen had opened. In Fairborn, the first pears were starting to flower. At home, box elders were starting to bloom. All around the town, a major leafing has begun: honeysuckles, lilacs, mock orange, Japanese honeysuckles. The garlic is high now, equal to the daffodil foliage. Japanese knotweed is about three to six inches.

1998: The pond toad loves the rain today, sings and sings. Azalea buds red and ready to open. Blue speedwell full bloom for about four days. Peak of dead nettle bloom. Early locusts bud. The best of money plant flowering starts now.

1999: Petal-fall for pears and pink magnolias begins. White magnolias mostly down in the rain. Red quince full now. Frog calls through the gray morning.

2000: A few tadpoles have left their eggs. Money plant full bloom. Snakes hunt the pond. Now more apples are blooming, more redbuds. Most of the daffodils flowering are the white, later varieties. The tree line is still predominantly gray-brown, but there are prominent patches of pale green, and the undergrowth has filled in. Clear bell calls of the blue jays off and on through the days. This is the high tide of Middle Spring, the fulcrum on which the next season turns. In the next six weeks, all the leaves push out and the world becomes solid with foliage, the ground covered with crops.

2003: Pushed by this warm April, lilacs came in today, both the white and the purple. A few purple azalea bushes seen in town, but ours in the east garden are still just budding. Forsythia is still bright, but green leaves are filling in around the flowers. Tulips are full, daffodils beginning to deteriorate. In the south garden, coneflower leaves are an inch to two inches long. At the Covered Bridge, violet cress and toothwort have withered, but wild phlox, Jacob's ladder, violets, and ragwort have taken their place. Between here and Washington Court House, 35 miles away, dandelions are everywhere.

2004: The first cabbage butterflies seen today. Weeding in the garden, I found the lilies-of-the-valley up about four inches.

2006: Cardinals first sang near 5:30. No screech owls heard for a while now. Drove to Dayton to look for porch stones, saw pears leafing, purple magnolias shedding, star magnolias gone, apples coming in, redbuds showing a lot of color – but not blooming yet, dandelions at their peak flowering everywhere. Pansies and primroses bought for the east garden. The pussy willow catkins have all fallen to the front sidewalk along High Street. Bleeding hearts are prominent now, rhubarb is ready for pie, all the hydrangeas are pushing out, the bi-colored leaf hosta have well-developed leaves, fall stonecrop is bushy and four inches tall, the honeysuckle hedge around the yard is filling in, the *pieris* is in full bloom, the earlier daffodils fading, and mid-season tulips opening all at once. Against the north wall, the bamboo is coming up. This is a clear pivot time when early Middle Spring cedes quickly to the center of the season and the rate of change accelerates, the passage of time bursting from its February and March lethargy, rushing towards May and summer.

2008: Pears, star magnolias, pink magnolias are in full bloom in Wilmington. One plum completely open along High Street in Yellow Springs. More and more trees getting ready to flower, buds swelling. In the evening about 8:30, robins and doves singing steadily.

2010: First azalea and the red–flowered crabapple open at home. Sidewalks downtown white with pear petals. Tulip tree has two-inch leaves. Black walnuts half inch and flowering, red oak flowering. Cherry done blooming. Honeysuckles and garden raspberries budded, strawberries starting to flower. High-Street maples a third to half leafed. Alley dogwood in bloom. First ladybugs found in the garden. Toad still sings, but no sign of eggs. John reports no signs of peonies yet in Lanesboro, southern Minnesota, daylilies four inches.

2011: The new cherry tree has a few blossoms this morning. A few buds are cracking on one crab apple in the park, and a few of our azalea buds are showing some color. Rhubarb has six-inch stalks, but it's not ready for pie yet. Some garlic mustard heading up, and one sweet rocket plant with buds. I mowed the lawn today, cutting mostly to even out the wild onions. Robins continue to sing at dusk, but the grackles have pulled back in the past few days, and the song sparrow has stopped singing.

2012: Gethsemani to Yellow Springs, pushed by a strong south wind, temperatures in the 80s throughout the drive: Little change observed in Kentucky from the drive down on the 13th, but I noticed that the locust bloom had crept north about thirty miles beyond Cincinnati over the weekend and was moving quickly toward Dayton, accompanied by a parallel intensification of honeysuckle bloom. One patch of lush wisteria along the freeway near Centerville, garlic mustard full throughout the Miami Valley (but not noticed at all around the monastery grounds). At home: reports of tulips in Chicago and Portland, Oregon.

2013: Gethsemani: The robins are even earlier this morning than yesterday morning: 4:17 ! Home in Yellow Springs, the pears are in early bloom, and it is hard to distinguish the difference now between Kentucky and Ohio.

2015: More tulips coming in around the yard, Middle Spring deepening. Portions of the back honeysuckles gradually obscure the houses beyond. All the maples on High Street in bloom, and violets are coming in all around the yard. The first azure butterfly glimpsed in the yard. Monk the cat killed a dove fledgling this afternoon. In the cool evening, I transplanted New England asters and white boneset, dug the first rows of the annual bed.

2016: Yellow Springs to Gethsemani, Kentucky: Sun, no frost, the lawn ready to be mowed a second time, crab apples coming on Limestone Street: Along the highways south, the honeysuckle and silver olive hedges have gained in density these past days but still define the height of the foliage. Even though the trees are bare, though, the landscape is heavy with spring. Then approaching Louisville: it seems that the mood of the woods changes suddenly, the bright leaves rising above the honeysuckle. Into the country roads, the dramatic shift in season is obvious: sprawling patches of dandelions gone to seed, several Robin's fleabane – one with violet petals, golden fields of tall ragwort and winter cress, dogwoods in full bloom, redbuds in late bloom, tiger swallowtails, black swallowtails, webworms in their webs, simple, clear signs of passage from middle to Late Spring.

2017: Spain: Jill sends photos of tulips and creeping phlox, full Middle Spring. Similar here, but it seems that the fruit tree blossoms are not as abundant.

You may hold it as matter true and undoubted,
That he who lives the more hidden
And the more removed from the multitude
Lives better.

Jacopo Sannazaro

April 16th
The 106th Day of the Year

I will love you in the thyme-leafed speedwell,
I will love you at the Ragweed Moon.

Hepatica Sun

Sunrise/set: 5:56/7:14
Day's Length: 13 hours 18 minutes
Average High/Low: 62/41
Average Temperature: 51
Record High: 87 - 1896
Record Low: 23 - 1962

Weather

Highs reach into the 80s five percent of the time, into the 70s twenty-five percent, into the 60s fifteen percent, into the 50s forty percent, and into the 40s fifteen percent. Beginning today, a major increase in the average daily amount of sunlight starts to take place: a rise from early April's 50/50 chance for sun or clouds up to a brighter and more spring-like 70 percent chance for clear to partly cloudy conditions. Snow rarely falls on April 16th, but rain comes 35 percent of the days. Frost strikes one morning out of every three on this date.

Natural Calendar

In the Northwest, Kestrel hawks are nesting, and aspens flower. Wood ticks follow the receding snow, and grizzly bears come out of hibernation. Sand hill cranes migrate through the western wetlands. In Vermont, trout fishing time begins. Croci are blooming in Minneapolis. Rhododendrons are open in St. Louis. Dogwoods are at their best throughout the South. Along the north Atlantic coast, mackerel move toward inshore waters.

Daybook

1981: First strawberry blossoms seen.

1982: Dandelions prominent now. Lawn needs mowing.

1983: Comfrey leaves eight inches long. Full dandelions.

1984: Comfrey leaves only two inches long, measuring the cold spring.

1985: Asparagus up in the garden. Comfrey leaves six inches long. Ginkgoes begin to leaf, spring beauties in full bloom in lawns throughout the village. Dandelions full bloom.

1986: Cardinal wakes me up 5:12 a.m. Maple flowers forming wishbone shaped seeds half an inch long, and viburnums at Wilberforce have big new green leaves. Thyme-leafed speedwell identified, first blossoms in the north lawn.

1988: Small butterflies, the blues, are out. Dandelions everywhere.

1989: At the mill, down river, the first leaf is out on the lizard's tail. The first wild phlox has bloomed, the first ragwort, the first wild geranium, the first grandiflorum. I saw the first bumble bee. The first cabbage butterflies are spiraling, mating. Pussy willows and forsythia are leafing. One strawberry plant has buds, quince is budding, winter cress is budding, first flower open on the cactus cress, bees working the peach flowers.

1991: Jacoby: clear, 70 degrees, intense sun. Out to take photographs. First garlic mustard flowers, first phlox. Toothwort and spring beauties dominate in patches, skunk cabbage leaves in their prime, some a couple of feet tall. Cowslip full boom, wild iris up and budding. Ferns unraveling, buckeye flowers budding, violets everywhere, purple, yellow, white. Four to six leaves on the touch-me-nots. Purple cress gone, no hepatica, twinleaf, bloodroot. Some parts of the woods floor covered with chickweed, others with dense garlic mustard. Some tree lines show bubbles of green, but most are still brown.

At Wilberforce, the star magnolias are gone, a few last petals holding. Doves nesting in the ginkgo outside my window. Cherry full bloom at home, sweet gum and tree of heaven starting to leaf.

Celandine suddenly blooming. Hosta pacing the lily-of-the-valley at about three inches, similar spear of green. Ferns show color at the north wall. Some grape hyacinth are gone, others full. New growth on the pines is well underway.

1993: Purple deadnettle full bloom in the pastures now, patches of deep purple. Very first buds on the bleeding hearts, wisteria buds swelling.

1994: Bleeding hearts have gotten hearts in the past few days, and the clematis has leafed out. More tulips are opening, ten in all so far. Lupines strong, maybe five inches high. First ferns just barely starting to open in the west garden. Daffodils full bloom everywhere, and scilla, glory-of-the-snow, hyacinths.

1995: Yesterday the first strawberry flower was open. Red quince is in full bloom all over town. Fruit trees, star magnolias leafing. Cabbage butterflies spin through the north garden, carpenter bees are mating by the side of the house: lumbering, lurching unions.

1998: First celandine opens. First tadpole today. John reports from New York Mills, Minnesota: rhubarb is an inch high, the same as in early May other years. They are having an Early Spring like we are. Hostas leafing now here, ferns six inches to just emerging.

1999: Major petalfall of pink magnolias in the April 16-18 cold front.

2000: In Dayton, violet lilacs completely open. At the Covered Bridge, buckeyes budding with their leaves only half developed. Purple and white violets, chickweed, white wood hyacinths, spring beauties, cowslip, bluebells, an occasional swamp buttercup, Jacob's ladder full. Early wild phlox. Late toothwort. Sweet rocket stalks extending a third of their way. Skunk cabbage leaves fully developed. No violet cress seen or other Early Spring flowers. In the yard, first daisy bud, peonies budding, early fleabane. I think there's enough rhubarb for pie. This afternoon, I saw two female ichneumans laying eggs in two different locations, one in the garden, one in the damp soil near the woodpile.

2002: Sudden dramatic collapse of pear flowers: the trees move from full bloom into full leafing after two days in the 80s, seasons all around me exploding, beginning, ending overnight. Creeping phlox are open everywhere. Cottonwoods, silver olives flowering, red quince flowering. In Columbus, full tulips, crabs, redbuds, snowball viburnum. Tree line alive, box elders getting leaves and flowers, white mulberry budding. In Yellow Springs, purple magnolias transition the landscape to red buds. At Grinnell Pond: toothwort, spring beauty and violets. Peak dandelions along the freeway east. Now the road grass is full summer color. Toads strong at night.

2003: Ticks reported in the Glen. Crab apples open in town, and the ancient apple in the back yard. Purple loosestrife stalks are a foot high. Peonies have small buds. Thin lily-of-the-valley foliage is at least six inches high. The first white bleeding heart has a half-inch heart, and water lily leaves have reached the surface of the pond.

2004: At South Glen, buckeye trees are well leafed and budding. The wildflowers have been preserved by the cool first two weeks of the month. Bloodroot and violet cress are still open. Some bluebells are only budding. Geese on the river were calling loudly, their heads moving back and forth.

2005: The very first robin chorus started at 5:00 a.m. this morning. Doves finally joined in at 5:17, and the cardinals sang consistently beginning at 5:25. Jeanie found the first tick at school near this date.

2007: First really bright yellow goldfinch eating at the feeder this afternoon, only a few signs of the molt left. Lilac buds and Korean lilac buds are limp, and most will not bloom this year. Clematis leaves noticed withered from the frost also. Jeanie saw a bright green beetle fly away along the Gorge path this afternoon, probably a six-spotted tiger beetle.

2008: More pink magnolias and plums blooming in town. All of the early yellow and orange tulips in the south garden are open. All of the daffodils are in full flower, only a few past their prime. Now the Asiatic and Oriental lilies are pushing up everywhere in the north garden, and the primroses have all unfolded – red, violet and yellow – under Janet's redbud (which is well budded). On a ride to New Carlisle, I noticed a few large patches of dandelions. Seems like Middle Spring is finally coming in hard.

2009: Pink magnolia petals falling in Wilmington and Yellow Springs.

2010: Porch wisteria leafing, hyacinths budding. First wild geranium seen at Peggy's.

2011: In the rain, to Miamisburg, 30 miles southwest of Yellow Springs: The season has deepened there, redbuds starting to bloom, some pears losing petals, developing leaves. Russian olive shrubs seen in bloom. Back in Yellow Springs, serviceberries are losing petals, zelcova leaves an inch long, buds formed. Tat says that a few daffodils have opened in Madison, but snow is in the forecast.

2012: While I was gone this past weekend, star of Bethlehem bloomed in the garden, and garlic mustard reached full flower. Now the ferns are tall and nearly all unfurled. The first few hyacinths, white and violet, are opening. The Korean lilac and the small blueberry bushes are in full bloom, and the red azalea in the dooryard has opened up completely, the honeysuckles are coming in more, and the red-leafed crab apple has lost its petals, the pink quince dropping its flowers through the day. Numerous small daddy longlegs found as I worked on the pond's stonework; sometimes when I lifted up a rock, I would reveal five or six of the fledglings clinging to the irregularities in the stone.

2013: Inventory upon return to Yellow Springs after four days in Kentucky: So much has happened. Downtown, all the pears and serviceberry bushes have blossomed. The tulips that grow next to the south wall have opened. The lace vine, the Anna-Belle and the hobblebush hydrangeas and the pink quince have one-inch leaves. Bamboo is up an inch. Box elders and the red quince and the pink spirea bushes are flowering. Poppies and celandine are bushy and big. Lilacs are budded, a few with shades of purple. The leaves on some of the peonies, sixteen inches high, are open and developed. Early daffodils and squills and grape hyacinths are fading quickly. Mateo's weigela is leafing. Waterleaf and lungwort are lush, hide the ground beneath their leaves. Redbuds and many crab apples are straining, their flower buds almost open. Jeanie's river birch and blueberry bushes have tiny new leaves. Astilbe is up and leafing. Pachysandra is in late full bloom. Ramps are fat and long and floppy. Oakleaf hydrangeas are starting. Many Asiatic lilies about three inches, daylily spears one to two feet. Ferns are showing, but not up yet. Achillea and perennial salvia strong, maybe nine inches long. Knotweed and hops vines at least in length. First few leaves found on the butterfly bush. The peach tree is blooming. Evening primrose, white boneset, and New England aster foliage is one to two inches. Raspberries and roses leafing well. Rhubarb up to eighteen inches long, bushy. Violets full bloom, tulips gathering momentum. Nettles nine inches, catmint clumps six to twelve inches. Catchweed budded. The Lawsons' black walnut tree has fat, dark red bud clusters. Maples in the neighborhood are setting seeds. Privets are packing the honeysuckles, slowly bringing privacy to our hedges. John Blakelock reported the first toad sang in his pond at 5:00 p.m. today.

2015: Lawn mowed for the first time.

2016: At Gethsemani: Cardinals singing at 4:55 this morning. From Goshen, Judy writes her northern Indiana update, her wildflowers just a little behind what is happening in and around Yellow Springs: "Bill and I went wildflower hunting at Benton this afternoon. The below-freezing temps of the last of March and first weeks of April resulted in some teeeny-tiiiny plants, I think. The violets and yellow nodding trilliums looked stunted. Everything else was pretty sturdy: henbit (of course, nothing kills that, unfortunately); spring beauty, pink & white; bloodroot; early meadow rue; false rue anemone (carpets and carpets of the latter two), toad trillium and emerging may apples and giant trillium. We saw a garter snake and a turtle sunning themselves and heard some small frogs ribbeting--nothing like the impressive bullfrogs that inhabit the ponds at DeFries Gardens out near New Paris. I guess they respond to the sound of the cars on the speedway there."

Tomorrow may you love
if you have never loved before.
Tomorrow may the lover love again.
For spring is a new song.
Spring is the earth reborn.

From the *Pervigilium Veneris*

Bill Felker

April 17th
The 107th Day of the Year

Spring hangs her infant blossoms on the trees,
Rocked in the cradle of the western breeze.

William Cowper

Sunrise/set: 5:55/7:15
Day's Length: 13 hours 20 minutes
Average High/Low: 63/42
Average Temperature: 52
Record High: 88 - 1896
Record Low: 22 - 1904

Weather

Today's high temperature distribution: 15 percent chance for 70s, thirty-five percent each for 60s and 50s, ten percent for 40s, five percent for 30s. Rain falls one day out of three; snow occurs 15 percent of the years, as does frost. Sixty-five percent of the days bring fair to partly cloudy skies.

Natural Calendar

Now winter wheat, the pastures, and the lawns are the brightest of the year. Winter cress and violets turn some fields gold and purple. Bluebells nod on the hillsides. Bellwort, meadow rue, ragwort, columbine, white violet, winter cress, small-flowered buttercup, large-flowered trillium, wood betony, miterwort, and Jack-in-the-pulpit are out. Forsythia flowers turn a darker gold and magnolia petals fall as locusts, mulberries, ash, tree of heaven, ginkgoes, Japanese honeysuckles, wild roses and virgin's bower leaf out. Grub worms come to the surface of the lawn, and grasshoppers are born in the fields. Weevils appear in the alfalfa.

Daybook

1981: Bleeding heart blossoming today.

1983: Lily-of-the-valley shoots are six inches high. At South Glen, snake sunning in the leaves at ten in the morning, temperature at 35 degrees.

1984: First patch of violets at Antioch library, first star magnolia blossoms start to unfold at Wilberforce.

1985: Crab apples open in the village. Pheasant seen along Wilberforce-Clifton road. At the Cascades, toothwort still full bloom. Bellwort advanced stems and leaves, but only one seen flowering. Leafcup knee high. Meadow rue blossoming. Buds on columbine. First large-flowered trillium, Jack-in-the-pulpit open, hepatica still strong, still a few Dutchman's britches, full bloom rue anemone. Hobblebush leaves an inch long. The fields on the way to Clifton starting to burst with yellow winter cress.

1986: Cardinal sings at 5:10 a.m. Geese fly over at 6:48 a.m. At the Covered Bridge, bluebells late full bloom, twinleaf and bloodroot gone. Only a few toothwort and violet cress left. White and yellow violets full. First phlox flower seen, toad trillium full bloom, some sedum with white buds, May apple with a bud. At Wilberforce, white magnolias have fallen.

1987: Cherry trees starting to bloom. Bees out strong, their low buzzing monotone fills the yard.

1988: In the hills between the Covered Bridge and the Swinging Bridge, grasshoppers, only a few days old, swarmed across the path, clicking on the dry leaves. Phlox and ragwort, purple and gold, throughout the woods. One May apple budding. Great wide patches of chickweed now. A few hidden ginger plants are blooming, some meadow rue, the first bellwort, the first Jack-in-the pulpit, first thyme-leafed speedwell. First peonies budding. Forsythia half yellow, half green.

1989: Apple and quince bloom today.

1990: Most of the pear flowers have fallen.

1991: Reading Thoreau's journals the first time, I wanted him to tell more about himself. I thought all his notes on the thickness of ice at Walden Pond or about the dates the asters bloomed were frivolous. I wanted him to talk, just once, about his most secret passions. I wanted him to stop hiding behind nature. Then I started keeping my own notebook and found this history of the Yellow Springs year was more important to me than the other kinds of history I'd encountered. Starting from an old assumption that the course of the seasons can be a metaphor for the span of human life, I saw that the closer observation of that metaphor revealed parallels I hadn't thought about before. Each entry in the notebook, the times of cardinal song, the measurements of leaves, the dates of blossom and petal fall, not only contributed to a grand design, but gave me insights into all the minor, isolated actions, which I used to feel were meaningless in the cycle of my life. The more closely I looked at what was happening around me, the more detailed and myopic the notes became, the more I understood the extent of the metaphor, and the better I started to understand myself, my own passions, and Thoreau's.

1992: Dandelions full bloom at Wilberforce. Parsnips two-feet tall, woods floor covered with waterleaf. The Early Spring garden is gone on the south side of the house. Wind flowers hold in the east garden.

1993: Star magnolias full bloom at Wilberforce.

1995: Box elders are flowering and leafing all over town now. The first blossoms are coming out on the cherry tree. Dandelions, violets, periwinkles are peaking together. The Antioch green along Corry Street is suddenly full of spring beauties. The seeds on the silver and red maples grow quickly, and now Lil's maple and our maple are blooming.

1996: First violet seen in the yard today. First lupine foliage noticed; it's maybe an inch across now. First lily-of-the-valley seen pushing out of the ground. Pussy willow catkins, laden with pollen, fell in the wind yesterday morning. Many still hang on today.

1998: Last of the peach flowers. First tadpole emerges in the pond.

Buckeyes head up to flower. Full bloom of shepherd's purse in the fields. Winter cress full by the roadsides. Honeysuckles budding, leaves half size. Phlox: a foot high, knotweed: four feet, motherwort and Asiatic lily: two feet.

2002: Dandelions, creeping phlox, violets, and spring beauties all at their best together. My maple and Lil's are in full bloom.

2004: The bamboo has started to push out of the ground along the south wall, new stalks several inches high.

2005: Ferns up from three to eight inches. Pears are leafing. White and pink magnolias coming down. Red quince full. Crab apples reaching full. Dandelions totally full. The first lilacs seen in Xenia.

2006: Spring picks up more speed. The peonies have budded. The new euonymus leaves are almost as big as the old ones. The serviceberry trees have dropped their petals after only two days of bloom. Redbuds have suddenly opened. Yellow bellwort-like flowers blossoming at the corner of Dayton and High. Dogwoods, which had just cracked enough to reveal their flower buds, are opening here and there throughout town. Bamboo is shooting up, some stalks eight inches.

2007: The landscape trying to recover after the long cold spell. Tulips and dandelions are in full bloom all around Yellow Springs. The white birch near the apartments is leafing, and its catkins have emerged. The redbuds, burned all the way back, have fresh buds. At the Gorge, bluebells were unhurt, and the large-flowered trilliums have survived pretty well. Small-flowered buttercups are in full bloom, and bluets were open along the upper trail. Meadow rue, flowering at the end of March, had survived and was still in bloom. A few Dutchman's britches and hepatica were holding on. I saw the first wild phlox open, and several ragwort plants were coming undone. In the woods, almost no trees appeared damaged, whereas in town, so many of the maples, trees of heaven, and the fruit trees suffered major setbacks.

2008: Don's pink magnolia is just starting to open; a few petals are falling from the star magnolia across the street. Service berry buds are so fat. The box elder in the back yard is lush with the tassels of its bloom. Sweetgum has huge, fat buds. An orange question mark butterfly visited the circle garden this afternoon. Pears suddenly full bloom downtown, peach tree starting at home. Dandelions coming into bloom along the highway south. In Wilmington, leaves are joining the flowers on the pear trees, and the first redbud has blossoms. One Xenia redbud almost in bloom. At 8:40 this evening, robins were still chattering, and I saw bats for the first time this year.

2010: Mrs. Lawson's pointed yellow tulips full in Don's yard. First viburnum flower on the north side of our house. Bamboo shoots have grown several feet tall.

2011: Inventory in the yard: Bamboo shoots nine to twelve inches, early tulips dropping petals, mid-season tulips full bloom now, algae growing thick in the pond, peonies with small buds, violets, ground ivy and deadnettle full, redbuds starting, squills gone, early daffodils and grape hyacinths withering, forsythia and serviceberry flowers falling, garlic mustard and allium budding, penstemon a foot tall, "white bells" have been in bloom for several days, starting to fade, white bleeding heart with buds, ferns three to nine inches with the smaller ferns coming on quickly, variegated knotweed just starting, hobblebush with one-inch leaves, blue flags twelve to eighteen inches, phlox twelve inches, purple coneflowers three inches, red quince and primroses hold, some hosta leafing, Russian sage with half-inch leaves, some lilac buds show color, bluebells, hepatica and lungwort full.

2012: Some bamboo shoots are now over seven feet tall. In Beavercreek, fields and entire lawns full of dandelions go to seed. A few scattered apples in bloom, and the first rows of blue iris along Xenia Avenue. Yellow Springs locusts appear budded but not blooming yet.

2013: Ellis Pond Kennedy Arboretum: Toads calling in the distance. Trees leafing: Persian parrota, hybrid filbert, Lawson false cypress. Trees budded: White ash, yellow buckeye, red horse chestnut, sassafras, *cornus florida.* Weeping flowering cherry in early bloom, crab apples getting ready. At home, I cut the lawn for the first time, planted a few zinnias directly into the garden. In the yards of Yellow Springs, the Great Dandelion Bloom has begun just as lily-of-the valley reaches up three or four inches and the first hosta leaves unravel. Rachel's ginkgo has very small new leaves pushing out.

2014: To South Glen: Dutchman's britches and violet cress full bloom along the river, late full toothwort. Multiflora roses with leaf clusters like clover foliage. All but one bloodroot gone. Hemlock up to a foot and a half, parsnip half a foot. Budded ragwort and wild phlox (one phlox flower). One mint cluster, dusky and soft. Cowslip bright and dominant by the swamp across from the Covered Bridge. Two azure butterflies. In the yard, box elder flowering and leafing. Pears full in town, full magnolias and the more precocious hosta all burned by last night's frost. Early blue-eyes. Lily-of-the –valley up to six inches, bamboo has appeared, two inches up now.

2015: Yellow Springs to Gethsemani: A warm summer-like day throughout the trip. Redbuds opening, red quince full bloom, daffodils, serviceberry, pears holding, Peggy's peaches flowering, one crab apple with breaking buds. Full dandelions all the way to Cincinnati, then Lexington. The tree line greening , more and more as I went southwest. Full flower of crab apples, lilacs, redbuds (some shedding) and winter cress near Gethsemani, some pears leafing, and fields of dandelions gone to seed. Most trees blooming or leafing (sycamore leafing, but still holding last year's seed balls, quince here full as in Yellow Springs, anemone and Jacob's ladder in the woods, and two Jack-in-the-pulpits, May apples tall but not in bloom, water cress and ginger without flowers, peonies with buds almost an inch across, one tall ragwort plant full bloom, two yellow sulfurs. Several bright green beetles on the paths. The dove nest above the entrance to the monastery was empty this year.

2016: Gethsemani, Kentucky: Sun and 80s: a four-petal "blue eyes" (with stem and leaves like ground ivy, and a five-petal stitchwort-like plant, several fleabanes, two cut over daisies. Tulip tree leaves are about a third developed. Foliage is starting on the upper branches of cypress trees. One sulfur butterfly and several field moths seen on my walk. Scott climbed Vineyard Knob this afternoon, and at the top, he came upon a huge and dense confluence of butterflies, all colors (especially yellow and black, most likely tiger swallowtails), he said, a great hatch that flew around him "like angels." From Yellow Springs, Suzanne Patterson called to report that she had seen a red admiral butterfly near the Dharma Center gardens.

2017: Spain: Jill sends a photo of the north-side white viburnum and the deep pink apple blossoms all out, Here in Castelo among rolling hills and late Middle Spring, a definite change from before we reached Santiago de Compostelo,.After five days in the city, I see the canopy foliage has thickened considerably, oak, maple and tulip tree leaves at least half size and grape vines becoming bushy with new growth. Brome grass common and orchard grass blossoming, Black medic and strawberries in bloom. A hemlock-like plant is opening, The low, five-pearled white flowers (petals divided in two) have been replaced by smaller, similar white flowers (but undivided)with tiny opposite leaves have replaced them he bright blue borage continues in the roadsides, but most of the ubiquitous yellow, thorny, pea-flowered shrub - although still everywhere - have become brown, replaced by a tall plant with a similar flower but soft stems and feathery foliage. Ferns, low and just starting to unravel two weeks ago, have grown up to line the roadsides, Bushy fennel is up to my knees.Swamp buttercups in wet places and another low five-petaled blossom the same size and color in drier parts, some purple vetch. Campion still grows in the ditches. Several fat field thistles are about to open, Approaching Castelo, I saw dogwoods open for the first time and white jasmine in full flower, thickening the air with its fragrance, The small rusty petaled thyme-leafed speedwell noticed tucked into the grasses in one place.

There is a time when spring's new leaves are just opened, the grasses are growing to their first tallness, violets- yellow and blue, -- cowslips, crowfoots, woodruff, false Solomon's seal are in bloom, the woods are dense against the evening sky, but not yet as dark as in Late Spring, the time when the evening air echoes with the songs and cries of warblers, thrushes, pewees, and the frogs, with the trilling of toads ringing through the twilight, the time when the evening air in the lowlands is a perfume none other in the year ever equals – the intoxicating perfume of the opening leaves, the essence of leaf and blade, of petal and bud, of ground and water.

August Derleth

April 18th
The 108th Day of the Year

Then came the lovely spring,
With a rush of blossoms and music
Filling the earth with blossoms
And the air with melodies vernal

Henry Wadsworth Longfellow

Sunrise/set: 5:53/7:16
Day's Length: 13 hours 23 minutes
Average High/Low: 63/42
Average Temperature: 52
Record High: 88 - 1896
Record Low: 25 - 1983

Weather

Today, for the first time since October 14th, there is a ten to fifteen percent chance for a high in the 80s. Seventies come five percent of the time, 60s fifty percent of the time, 50s twenty percent, 40s five to ten percent, 30s five percent. The sun shines seven days in ten, rain comes four in ten, snow two in ten. Frost burns tender plants one morning out of three (the last time this spring that odds are so strong for freezing temperatures).

Natural Calendar

The third week of a typical Middle Spring brings Bumblebee Season and Carpenter Bee Season, Great Egret Migrating Season (through southwestern Ohio), Asparagus Cutting Season, Crab Apple, Cherry, Dogwood, and Redbud Season. It's Lawn Mowing Season, Buckeye Leafing Season, the Great Dandelion Bloom Season, Winter Cress in the Pasture Season, and the best of Late Middle Spring Flower Season with watercress and ragwort blooming in the wetlands, thyme-leafed speedwell in the lawn, early meadow rue, rue anemone, wild geranium, large-flowered trillium and columbine all filling the Glen. In the parks, Pink Magnolia Season replaces White Star Magnolia Season.

Buttercup Season and Money Plant Season complement Snowball
Viburnum Season and Bridal Wreath Spirea Season.

The Stars

This week, the Big Dipper comes deep into the sky
overhead; its pointers (the two outside stars of the dipper) are
positioned almost exactly north-south after dark, marking the
center of Middle Spring. Now Cepheus and Cassiopeia, which
were nearly directly above the Northern Hemisphere in early
winter, have moved to the far side of Polaris along the northern
horizon. Scorpio and Sagittarius share the southern sky when the
robins first sing in the morning.

Daybook

1982: Chinese crab apple blooming.

1985: Redbud, watercress, miterwort all blooming. Cattail leaves
are two feet tall. Cactus cress is a foot and a half, budding. Ash
leaves have started outside my window. Red and black ladybugs
seen at Wilberforce and Yellow Springs.

1986: Cardinal sings at 5:00 a.m. Cascades: First bellwort, last
Dutchman's britches. Meadow rue, large-flowered trillium,
miterwort, Jack-in-the-pulpit, and rue anemone are in full bloom.
First columbine, winter cress, wood betony. Small tadpoles in the
backwaters. Wild geranium and common fleabane budding,
hepatica fading. Squirrels chasing each other in the trees. Off year
for garlic mustard, very few plants this year; they seem to go in
cycles: the even years are the lean years, the odd are plentiful
ones. Forsythia flowers completely gone at home, lawn grass going
to seed in spots. Redbuds declining.

1987: Buds on daisies and bleeding hearts. Small-flowered
buttercups have been out for a week along the front walk. Pines
have put out new growth. Tulips early full bloom in town. Rhubarb
big enough for one pie. Box elders leafing, all the maples
flowering, hops moving into the honeysuckles. Forsythia and pussy
willow leaves are almost an inch long.

1989: Very first cherry blossoms in the yard.

1991: This is the week Yellow Springs gets out of hand. Through Early Spring, I could track the movement of time by measuring daffodil foliage and recording the progress of crocus, pussy willows, aconite, and snowdrops. There were only a few leaves to check, only a few wild flowers were in bloom. Now everything is happening at once. In the next thirty days, every kind of plant and tree, something like a thousand species, will sprout new leaves or flower. I want to join them, to be like them, to stand for them, to have them stand for me, to be part of them, have them be part of me. I want them to have meaning. I want to know that I have meaning.

1992: First cherry flowers in the yard. Hosta are one to two inches, first bleeding heart flowers, peonies are knee high.

1993: First strawberry blossoms. Astilbes and peonies are unraveling, stems thickening. Phlox now bushy and about four to five inches. Most of the tulips budding. Daylilies up to a foot tall, Asiatic lilies strong at half a foot. First asparagus comes through the straw. Three blue jays courting in the garden box elder, bobbing up and down, singing. Mountain maple blooms at Antioch School.

1994: The first bumblebee was out yesterday, the first wood tick picked up in South Glen today. (John reported them in northern Minnesota a week ago - along with frogs croaking.) The season accelerating: apple tree leafing, pears near full bloom in Xenia, starting to open here, the first daffodils fading, bleeding hearts have hearts, ferns are protruding in the Glen and in the yard, rhubarb is long enough to cut for pie, quince is leafing, maples flowering in front of the house and across the street, mid- season tulips starting, some roses with new shoots.

1998: Purple loosestrife in the pond is seven inches high. Monarda about the same height in the east garden. Great mullein has nine-inch leaves, the plant a foot tall. Virginia creeper leaves one half to fully developed, depending on the exposure. Roses well leafed, maybe a third of summer size.

1999: In Madison, Wisconsin, bloodroot time is almost past, says Maggie. Here in Yellow Springs, one purple lilac seen in bloom in the south side of town. Ragwort, phlox, creeping phlox opened last week. First bellwort today.

2000: Cool and rainy, gray this morning. I look out the back door: the apple tree is white and pink with all its flowers. In the pond, a few stalks of the loosestrife is at eight or nine inches, a little ahead of 1998; the rest of the stalks are a little behind. Small-flowered dogwood near the Mills Lawn park is open.

2001: For me, the lush blooming and leafing of the land in Middle Spring is accompanied by a sense of fulfillment and relief after the gray of winter. Little by little, I gather more confidence and dare to hope. The flowers become a kind of visible troth, a promise quieting my fear that winter will never leave.

But a sharp cold spell often strikes in mid to late April, burning back new growth, and the month can close without a flowering tree, with perennials black from frost. And so the warmest springs can also bring a feeling of suspense, a suspicion that the new season could be too good to be true.

I don't feel the same uneasiness at the approach of autumn. Instead of disquiet, I feel disbelief. It is not possible, my body tells me, that summer could disappear and that the leaves might come down. On the other hand, like the residue of a night's dreams that pushes against my consciousness, the uneasiness about an April or early May freeze may linger as vague anxiety, sometimes metastasizing, growing far out of proportion and blending with other unrelated anxieties and fears.

Then I get disgusted for letting myself feel like this. After all, weather is changeable. Why take seriously an abortion of April? Isn't there enough to worry about? Things balance out. They always do.

Still, the suspicion that everything will suddenly and unfairly fall apart can linger until the first heat wave finally convinces me that all is well. It takes tall rhubarb and sweet strawberries; I need raspberries and blackberries setting fruit, peonies, iris, lupines, poppies, and all the clovers in bloom to cure the neurosis and settle me into mindless denial: Summer will never end.

2002: In Columbus: dogwoods, snowball viburnum, azaleas, and even lilacs in bloom. Silver olive bushes along the highway three-fourths leafed.

2003: Apples close to full bloom now, and small-flowered dogwoods open throughout town. At Mrs. Lawson's, sudden bloom (after decades of being mowed back) of bright yellow tulips with six pointed petals, each flower the size of a trout lily.

2004: The new rose-red tulips in the east garden are in full bloom today, the deep red buds of the new crabapple above them are soft and ready to open. I cleaned off the elephant ear bulbs this evening, many of the them had sprouted quite a while ago. Steven's allergies suddenly started today.

2005: This is the first day redbuds and crabs are in full bloom in town, and the tree line flushed and filling in. Lil's maple and the Danielsons' maple are full of yellow green flowers. The ashes are all leafing, foliage maybe a fourth of full size. Tree of heaven leaves are starting. The first azaleas are open in Cedarville and in front of our house here. A cardinal sang today at 4:55, another at 5:10, before the full cardinal song started at 5:25.

2006: Lilacs fully budded in the alley and at home. In the east garden, the small pink azalea is opening, creating a palate of pastels with the violets and the purple dead nettle. The viburnum in the north garden is starting to bloom, forsythia leaves outnumber its flowers, and buds have formed on a few honeysuckles. Lil's maple and the Danielson's maple are in bloom. Celandine is flowering at the side of the house.

2007: At Bryan Park, spring beauties in full bloom throughout the wide expanses of grass. Bluebells, toad trillium, toothwort, anemones, meadow rue all flowering. Along High Street, a few periwinkles and grape hyacinths are still in bloom. Only the small white daffodils are open in our yard. In the alley, I noticed that all the willow leaves had been destroyed by the frost. Mateo's apple tree is flowering, and one red-flowered crab apple is opening along Dayton Street.

2008: An earthquake struck this morning at about 5:40. Very little damage except at the center in southern Illinois. The very first serviceberry flowers are opening along Dayton Street. One of our bluebells is starting – which means that probably all of the Glen's bluebells are blooming. More and more hostas and lilies are pushing up, viburnums and hydrangeas leafing out. Comfrey leaves, very late this year, are about four inches long. Purple coneflowers and monardas are bushy and strong, maybe two inches high. By nightfall, all the serviceberries were in full bloom. Petalfall increasing on the star magnolias. Grackles more prominent than robins at dusk.

2009: Tulips and bleeding hearts are in full bloom around the village, as are our tulips – but our bleeding hearts still do not have hearts. Purple coneflower foliage is about two to three inches high. The first lilac seen in bloom downtown. Redbuds are showing considerable color. Dandelions full bloom along Elm Street. Creeping phlox is open at Peggy's and in other yards, too. In the afternoon, Jeanie watched a pileated woodpecker land on our back birdfeeder and search all its openings for seeds, and later in the afternoon, we saw a flock of cedar waxwings come to the south edge of the property. A wisteria and two blueberry bushes planted this evening. And transplanted a clematis, which the wisteria replaced. Jeanie put in a row of mesclun in the raised bed. Bats seen in the evening.

2010: From Judy in Goshen, Indiana: "We don't have the variety of wildflowers that you are blessed with in Ohio. However, over the weekend (the 18th) we saw (in a venue different from last week): globeflower, white violets, moneywort, budding early meadow rue, marsh marigold, spring beauty, trilliums, and some kind of what looked like nightshade. Garlic mustard is abundant in the vacant lot at the end of our street.."

2011: Strong cardinals and song sparrows and house sparrows through the alley. A pair of starlings in Judy's lawn. Mrs. Lawson's yellow tulips are opening, only two left from years ago. The buds on Rachel's ginkgo tree have become minute fourth-inch leaves. Grackles and finches and sparrows at the feeders. First two cabbage butterflies mating in the yard this afternoon.

2012: The first iris are in bloom along the south side of the house at the corner of Limestone and Stafford. Our iris our budded, as are many others along the street. The Stafford Street buckeye has huge flower stalks with fat buds. Dogwoods hold throughout my walk. Bluebells almost gone in the south flower bed. In the garden, the rhubarb is definitely ready for pie, and the raspberries are budding. Many hostas are almost full-size. At 10:15 this morning: the first zebra swallowtail of the year! Then, a fritillary around noon. Walking at the Oakes Quarry Park, part of the Beavercreek Wetlands preserve, I made the following inventory: sulphurs, metalmaks, blues, cabbage whites, a black swallowtail and a white spotted skipper (and another skipper seen at home when I got back); honeysuckes, pink and white, and silver olives in full bloom; winter cress, dead nettle, dandelions, fleabane, white-flowered wild strawberry all in flower; other plants not blooming: sweet clover, large-leafed thistles, asters, multiflora roses, vetch, plantain, teasel, mint, hemlock, wing stem, dock, cattails, yarrow, great mullein; trees: sliver maple, sycamore, water willow, blackwalnut, and dozens of two-to-three-foot poplars filling the flats (What will they make this rocky landscape look like in twenty or thirty?), mulberry, Chinese elm, panicled dogwoods; minnows seen in one pool, lazy, fearless tadpoles in another; redwings, killdeer, field sparrows, and a red-bellied woodpecker calling, nesting ducks and geese; dragon flies mating, spitbugs on a few stems. Temperature about 65 degrees, sky hazy. A soft wind was blowing throughout my walk, and the air was sweet with honeysuckle. The quarry was surrounded by higher ground, filled with high trees just starting to leaf out.

2013: High in the 80s today, strong southwest wind, and I went to the Mill, walked along the river with Bella: Grasses so green, river high, muddy, flowing hard: Red-bellied woodpecker, cardinals, pileated woodpecker calling, buzzards swooping, American toads screaming their mating calls in the backwater, chickweed carpet blooming across all the woods floor, honeysuckle leaves an inch long, forming their dense summer wall, winter cress budded, bloodroot gone, new wild ginger foliage, toothwort and spring beauties and late Dutchman's britches and wild phlox and meadow rue and ragwort (most ragwort tall and budded) and violets (white and purple) and bluebells and violet cress and toad trillium and small-flowered buttercup and swamp buttercup, one trillium grandiflorum, and box elder trees in bloom, winter cress and Jack-in-the-pulpit budded. At home the first wild strawberry flowered, first star of Bethlehem bud found. The garden is starting to fill with quack grass, henbit, catchweed, too many violets.

2014: North Glen: Dutchman's britches and many toothworts throughout, bellwort six inches, rue anemone and meadow rue in bloom. The skunk cabbage has huge, fat leaves, maybe a foot high, at least half that wide. In the yard at home, ten astilbe planted, several lilies transplanted, the ground still soft. Peonies unraveled, knee high. Ramps lanky just like in the Glen.

2015: Gethsemani: Waiting for birds from 4:00 a.m. Mostly clear above me, fog all round the hills, cool in the 50s, no wind, Scorpio in the south. At first only roosters across the countryside. One robin whinny at 4:38, and the first cardinal at 4:41, much later than in some years past.

2016: Gethsemani: Curious that I heard a robin whinny at exactly 4:38 this morning before I left for Yellow Springs.
2017: Spain: I climbed from Castelo about a thousand feet to the San Jose albergue in Negreira, Middle Spring continues to retreat, Late Spring approaching, one mock orange flower emerging, most of the canopy and shrubbery well leafed, snowball bushes full of white clusters, one purple loosestrife, bridal wreath rusting, wisteria starting to break down, yellow thorn bushes less frequent and browning, many yellow daisies, and the tall pea flowered yellow bushes almost tree size (ginestra-like). Some constants: borage, buttercups, red and white clovers. One section of a roadside had dozens of Japanese iris, buds golden, ready to bloom.

All our cells are affected by the sun and moon; every time the sun goes down they change, and again at dawn. By daylight the cells assert themselves, at night they are more receptive to external forces.

Taisen Deshimaru

Bill Felker

April 19th
The 109th Day of the Year

For you the roving spirit of the wind
Blows Spring abroad; for you the teeming clouds
Descend in gladsome plenty o'er the world;
And the sun sheds his kindest rays for you,
Ye flower of human race!

James Thomson

Sunrise/set: 5:52/7:17
Day's Length: 13 hours 25 minutes
Average High/Low: 64/42
Average Temperature: 53
Record High: 84 - 1985
Record Low: 22 - 1983

Weather

Today is yet another pivot point for spring: from now on a high temperature below 40 degrees is extremely unlikely until October. Chances for highs in the 80s are five percent, for 70s thirty percent, for 60s thirty percent, for 50s twenty-five percent, for 40s ten percent. And from this point forward, the number of frosts in any given seven days declines by nearly two percent per 24 hours. The sun shines 65 percent of the time on April 19th, and rain falls one day out of every three.

Natural Calendar

The third week of Middle Spring punctuates the end of tobacco bed seeding (and half the beds show leaves) in the Border States. Farmers seed spring wheat in New England, sugar beets all across the Midwest. Field corn planting is in full swing throughout the South, cotton planting along the Gulf.

The boxwood psyllid starts to attack the boxwoods as Middle Spring deepens. Dogwood borers are at work on the dogwoods. The great spring dandelion bloom fades between now and the first week of Late Spring. In Japan, cherry blossoms have reached their best. Wisteria and azaleas will bloom in early May there, rhododendrons from mid May to mid June – not unlike the blooming patterns in the Lower Midwest of the United States during cooler years.

Daybook

1982: Mill Habitat: Watercress has white flowers in the small pond behind the dam.

1984: Upper Grinnell path at North Glen: Trillium grandiflorum have been up a few days, spring beauty budding.

1985: Redbuds and crab apple trees open overnight. Viburnum is coming in along Limestone Street. Winged ants (maybe termites migrating) are falling from the trees along the river. Grapes have been leafing for three or four days.

1987: First small bleeding hearts formed today.

1988: Some pokeweed three feet, the same height as at Jekyll island on the Georgia coast in mid-March. Bleeding hearts with one-inch hearts.

1990: Fishing at Caesar Creek: no bites all day, but the land full of sound, frogs chanting, flickers mating, nesting.

1991: To Wisconsin, from Yellow Springs and full Middle Spring, with the maples and cottonwood starting to leaf, forsythia and daffodils fading, apple and cherry trees in full bloom, tulips mid season, grass long and green. Past Dayton, lilacs seen, silver olive leafing, poplars pale green. The landscape stays almost unchanged until I get above Urbana, Illinois.

At El Paso, Illinois, above Bloomington, the apples are no longer flowering. A few miles north, near Peru, redbuds become paler. At Rockford, the tree line is suddenly bare. Only the willows, yellow green, stand out in the suburbs. Near Madison, only a few patches of flowering trees (this is Yellow Springs a month ago; I have traveled 600 miles and 30 days back into winter at the rate of one day for every 20 miles). Just willows and honeysuckles leafing. Early tulips, daffodils, magnolia just opening, peonies and rhubarb only six to nine inches.

1992: Ginkgoes leaf. Maple full flower, exotic, waving in the wind, watercress full bloom, magnolia and ash leafing.

1993: Into Xenia today, some weeping cherry trees with pale violet blossoms, full bloom. In the evening, the first ichneuman flies around the light in my office. The first bumblebee of the year working in the purple deadnettle after supper, temperature only in the 50s.

1995: At South Glen woods, phlox and early meadow rue have headed up. In town, crab apples start to open. Outside my classroom in Wilberforce, one apple, deep red-purple, is almost in full bloom. From my office window, I notice the ginkgo leafing for the first time. Across the lawn, the sugar gum is coming out too.

1999: Spring beauties hold full, daffodils declining, mid-season tulips full, quinces full, many pears full, many leafing. No toads heard yet this year.

2000: To Cincinnati and the zoo: viburnums all in bloom here, the bridal wreath too, red and violet azaleas, large white dogwoods, lilacs, and wisteria. Late tulips still quite strong, but only the latest varieties of daffodils, the white and the miniature yellow jonquils. Blue wood hyacinths and tall, six-petaled, pale blue star hyacinths were also in the middle of their season. Columbines at their peak here and forget-me-nots, candytuft, yellow comfrey, exotic snow wreath shrub (*neviusia*). The first honeysuckles were starting to open, and Jacob's ladder had just ended.

2001: Visited my ginkgo at Wilberforce: leafing out on schedule.

2002: First cressleaf groundsel, first garlic mustard, first white wood hyacinths, first fleabane, first water lily leaves (brown from winter). Poison ivy leaves are between a half inch and an inch long. Some Virginia creeper leaves up to two inches. Full bloom white bleeding heart, money plant, and winter cress. Buds on the peonies. Hemlock foliage knee high, purple loosestrife ten inches, black-eyed Susan three inches, large blue hosta and mallow eight inches, Asiatic lilies and motherwort 12 inches, knotweed two to four feet, Dutch iris 18 inches. Pussy willows, honeysuckles and forsythia at least half leafed.

2003: The north garden ferns have grown from nothing (six days ago) to about a foot tall. Garlic mustard, a few daisies, some fleabane budding, sweet rocket stalks rising. White bleeding heart – and the pink – have several large hearts. Pink lungwort flowers remain in bloom. Now the garden weeds take off just as the lilies reach three or four inches. Pears leafing, linden leaves the size of a quarter, Lil's maple filling in quickly. At South Glen this morning, delicate cobwebs, shining in the sun, were hanging in the dry corymbs of last year's ironweed. We passed one large web, too, woven between wingstem stalks.

2004: Crabapples are early flowering as pears and forsythia leaf out. Petal-fall is rapid on the pink magnolias (the white fell about a week ago) and on the Dayton Street serviceberries. Mid-season daffodils are almost done, pink hyacinths hold but are getting a little raggedy. Windflowers and early tulips continue to blossom. One purple azalea bush in Cedarville was in full bloom. In the wind, the winter wheat quivers, but it is not long enough to ripple.

2006: Strawberries and cressleaf groundsel have buds. Japanese knotweed has grown up to my waist. Lindens, red oaks and ash all have one-inch leaves. Many apples and redbuds in full bloom. Garlic mustard has started to open.

2007: A female starling started to attack the chimney for the first time this morning. I made a note of this on May 1 last year, but the activity had begun before that date.

2008: The redbuds blush in the back yard, and the western tree line is golden with box elder flowers. Japanese knotweed is about a foot high. Grackles, cardinals, doves, robins, starlings, song sparrows singing, a background like the sky. In Madison, Wisconsin, my sister Tat says that she has a couple of daffodils, one tulip blooming and that her peonies are about three inches, daylilies almost six. Hail fell this afternoon about 3:00 o'clock. The ginkgo at the corner of Limestone has finally started to leaf out. Red quince flowers at both ends of the block. Sweet gum buds are huge, straining to unfold. Crab apple trees have all their buds. Redbuds are fully budded now. Squills and grape hyacinths are fading in the yard.

2009: Don's pie cherry opened during the night, and the serviceberry flowers are looking old. I have never seen so many birds courting and flying back and forth: grackles, starlings, robins, cardinals, blue jays, sparrows. Garlic mustard heading but short in the alley.

2011: Thunderstorms to the south all night, and heavy rain flooded the backyard in places, filled the pond. The flowers on Don's serviceberry trees have turned to berry buds, and leaves have formed around them. Oakleaf hydrangeas are leafing, and one snowball viburnum seen opening in the village. In the park, one apple tree has come into full bloom, others well budded. The hawthorn has small buds. Some of Greg's lily-of-the valley is leafing. More rain in the afternoon, the entire back patio and side yard flooded, streets and stores and cars flooded in Kettering. Robins, doves and grackles still call in the evening.

2012: Peak of violet hyacinths, white hyacinths, Indian hyacinths, bridal wreath spirea, sweet Cicely, *lamium purpureum*, honeysuckles, late dogwoods. Bamboo is up to ten feet tall now, and knotweed in the Phillips Street alley is over my head. Redbuds are all to leaves, many Asiatic lilies budded. Many ferns are completely developed. Another red admiral butterfly came by the yard again today. All of the pink quince flowers have fallen now. The new bamboo, so tall, has started to shed its sheathes.

2013: The cherry tree Jeanie and I planted maybe four or five years ago, a tree with a gangly shape and few leaves, is finally in bloom, having come in with the storm and the cold front last night, looks like it might have a handful or two of sweet cherries for the grackles. North wind throughout the day, flurries, rain, stratus clouds coming across all the lush pear and cherry and plum and serviceberry flowers, the first redbuds, delaying the crab apples and the dogwoods. In all the chill today, I found the first watercress in bloom at Ellis Pond in one of the narrow backstreams.

2014: The river birch in the back yard is just starting to push out., the cherry not flowering yet. Mid-season daffodils hold and several tulips. No sign of life on the roses. At Ellis Pond arboretum, lots of budding: sawtooth oak, linden basswood, ginkgo, Norway maple, red horse chestnut. Yellow buckeye buds are bursting into two-inch palmate leaf clusters. Persian Parrota, Katsura tree and mountain ash have small leaves. Pears and serviceberries full throughout town, some star magnolias that survived the frost.. Some red quince opening on the north side of the yard and along High Street. Puschkinias all gone now, squills fading with the early daffodils. Foliage of snowdrops floppy, will soon be covered by the hosta (now one to three inches throughout the garden).

2015: Return from Gethsemani: A weekend of heat and rain has pulled Middle Spring down on top of everything. The changes a litany: the early yellow tulips gone, the mid-season tulips full, the yellow daffodils gone, the bicolor and white daffodils still strong. The fruit trees coming into full bloom. Peonies are tall and just beginning to bud; heliopsis three inches, monarda low and bushy, lily-of-the-valley to four or five inches, some hostas are leafing now, others just emerging, bluebells in the back yard and the alley all blue, day lilies full and up to two feet tall, Asiatic and oriental lilies to three inches, Jeanie's fern garden coming back with at least five varieties emerged, the other ferns tall as the peonies, a few lilac blossoms along the south garden, waterleaf covering the redbud garden and growing tall around the pond, more bamboo piercing the ground, some (like the alley knotweed) up to my waist, hops tangling around the tall decorative grasses, new astilbes starting up in the dooryard, garlic mustard budded, lamium deep pink, profusion of violets and dandelions in the grass, allium, Indian hyacinths and wood hyacinths budded in the circle garden – ready to replace the daffodils, weeds getting out of hand throughout the more neglected garden patches, a snowball viburnum seen along Limestone Street, bittersweet starting to leaf in the alley. I saw a fledgling dove by the stone wall, brother or sister to the one Monk caught a few days ago. Hopefully this one will stay alive. As always I am behind in getting the ground prepared for seeding annuals. Hard wind this evening, cold spell moving in quickly.

2016: Return from Gethsemani: All the grape hyacinths and scilla are gone. Blooming celandine and the red crabapple in the yard, the first lilacs at home and down Greene Street. Ferns up a foot or two, bamboo to eight inches, the early tulips gone, standard tulips full bloom, the daffodils considerably thinned but still beautiful, the first hyacinths at Jill's with first petals, mine with flower stalks rising, bluebells and lungwort very bright and strong, lily-of-the-valley about ready to bud, the earliest hostas well leafed but others just emerging or unfolding, garlic mustard budding, all the crab apples in town, including my red one, open, many dogwoods too. . Violets fill the lawns all about, matching the abundance and timing of the Great Dandelion Bloom. Rhubarb leaves are almost the size of my hand. Milkweed stalks are three inches high. The deep pink azalea in front of the house is cracking. Lizard's tail has put out a few short leaflets. Hops is rank, running through the honeysuckles. From Fontanelli in Italy, Neysa reports her cyclamens continue to flower, but they are being covered by their own foliage.

2017: Negreira to Vilaserio, Spain: Once again perfect weather for a climb into the mountains. A drier habitat, less rich variety of plants. Borage, lamium, violets, clovers, buttercups, ginestra, English plantain and tall-flowered plantain common. Some flax seen, some blue speedwell, a few hyacinths, several clumps of wild purple columbine. Blackberry brambles appear again in the fences. Like yesterday, relatively few eucalyptus trees. Crab apples with half their flowers down. The pathway cluttered with catkins from last week's bloom.
As Middle Spring loses its power, I continue to walk parallel to it, conscious of how I have moved beside it. So the season and my trek stay connected with motion, developing together without conscious purpose or intent.
I realize that I have left the height of April behind in Santiago and

Madrid. That flowering I associate with my own presence, that my presence was parallel to those events and was defined by them.

The stream of my travel deliberately holding to the unfolding of Galician April, disorienting me from my American experiences so tied to speed and at the same time to home, in which I separate myself from the long deliberate walk beside apparently at the same speed as the unfolding, erasing separation.

For us the winds do blow,
The earth doth rest, heaven move, and fountains flow:
Nothing we see but means our good,
As our delight, or as our treasure.

George Herbert

April 20th
The 110th Day of the Year

The wind blows sweet from the west
through Jupiter, locking away the winter,
thinning the gray clouds now
that the sun alights on Taurus.

Carmina Burana:
(bf)

Sunrise/set: 5:51/7:18
Day's Length: 13 hours 27 minutes
Average High/Low: 64/42
Average Temperature: 53
Record High: 85 - 1915
Record Low: 21 - 1897

Weather

Chances for a high in the 80s surge to a full 20 percent today, the first time all spring that they have been so good. Seventies come 15 percent of the time, 60s thirty-five percent, 50s twenty percent, 40s ten percent. The sun shines seven days out of ten; rain falls three in ten. After the 20th, the steady advance of the year's cold waves slows, and relatively long periods of stable, mild weather encourage the advent of full spring growth. High temperatures almost always reach 70 at least once or twice in a week. Spring rains often diminish, their frequency dropping at least ten percent from last week. From now on, a cold day in the 30s is virtually out of the question. Snow falls just once or twice in a century. Frost, however, can still be expected two or three mornings out of seven.

Natural Calendar

The sluggish nature of winter, its interminable cold and gray skies, its sameness that lasts from the beginning of December through the middle of February, reflects the slow movement of the sun between October's Cross Quarter Day (the 24th) and

February's Cross Quarter Day (the 18th).

For more than four months, the sun lies at its lowest position in the sky. For more than a hundred days, nothing seems to change. By the 20th of April, however, the increased acceleration of the year becomes apparent. A season is always the sum of its parts. The pieces of Early Spring are few and subtle, but Middle Spring, reaching its zenith this week, leaves little to the imagination. The meager inventories of change that characterized equinox quickly fill with new details each day. Trees leaf and flowers bloom, unmistakable, their numbers catching the eye of almost everyone.

All the habitats, from rich talus slopes to alleyways, reveal the prints of change. The first leaf is out on the lizard's tail. The first wild phlox has bloomed, the first ragwort, the first wild geranium, the first trillium grandiflorum. Honeybees find the peach and crab apple flowers. The cabbage butterflies are spiraling, mating. Pussy willows and forsythia are leafing. Strawberry plants have buds, quince is budding, winter cress is budding. The days finally grow warm.

The earth seems to spin faster now, time ceding to the eye of the spectator. The days suddenly stretch out to their summer length. The floral and faunal fragments multiply, literally filling in the space of Earth with tangible, visible clockwork, the months of waiting through winter and Early Spring repaid beyond counting.

The Sun

Cross-Quarter Day, the day on which the sun reaches halfway to solstice, occurs at the end of April's third week. The sun enters the sign of Taurus at the same time.

Daybook

1982: First strawberries flower, periwinkle full bloom.

1983: A few remnants of Early Spring are holding on: a handful of bloodroot and twinleaf. Violets are strong, along with spring beauty, toad trillium, toothwort, violet cress, periwinkle, henbit, purple deadnettle. Flowering trees are at their peak in town. Dandelions full bloom.

1985: An eight-day heat wave has turned the town green. Celandine is blooming, and garlic mustard. First fleabane bud, first peony bud found. Mulberry leafing. The first lilacs are out.

1986: Most cherry blossoms fell in the wind today - they usually last about ten days; the petals were also dropping from the pears downtown.

1987: Mrs. Bletzinger reports: "My pond is alive!" She tells me she can't sleep at night for all the carp jumping and the frogs croaking. Frog eggs all over in the water, she says. At Wilberforce, some maples almost solid green. Ginkgoes coming out too, and sweet gum pacing its development. Crab apples in the village come into full bloom as the pears downtown leaf out through their blossoms. Most of the garlic mustard is budding. Early meadow rue blooms. Asparagus about three inches in the garden, Japanese knotweed a foot and a half tall.

1988: Japanese knotweed killed back by heavy frost. Early bloom time for winter cress.

1989: Cross-quarter Day measurements of the sun: sunrise at a 75 degree azimuth from the front porch, about east northeast (it was 90 degrees on March 17th). Sunset is at 285 degrees, west northwest (it was 270 degrees March 17th).

1990: Grape hyacinths fading, with the daffodils and tulips. Some windflowers and scilla keep their color. First question mark butterfly seen today. Crab apples flower a little more at Wilberforce, but still hold back some. Viburnum flower clusters are two inches wide.

1993: Deep warm wind this morning, moaning in the pale green trees, birds silent. Then it lets up a little, and the cardinals sing. The first Bradford pears on Xenia Avenue opened this afternoon. The redbud at the west entry to the Glen is getting ready to bloom. Pink magnolias still full bloom throughout the county.

1995: Along Grinnell, down to the creek: Buckeyes are budding now, and garlic mustard has buds, too. Ginger is up. Violet cress flowers have withered. Swamp buttercups are blooming. First Jacob's ladder open, first yellow violet seen. The first trout lilies open shyly, protected by sepals, flowers bowing to the ground. Chickweed is getting lanky in its late prime. Bloodroot gone here. Several new shrubs are open, a snowball viburnum, and one with clusters of fine, white, five-petaled flowers, the bridal wreath. The small cream-colored dogwoods are open. The first purple lilacs have opened.

1998: The first batch of toads has hatched in the pond. The other string of eggs is not elongated yet.

1999: First toad of the year sings in the pond at 8:50 p.m.

2000: Cascades: Trillium grandiflorum, miterwort in full bloom. Early Jack-in-the-pulpit, early garlic mustard, and first columbines, wild geraniums and wood betony. A patch of yellow trout lilies. American colombo sending up first stalks about two feet. Toad trillium old. Ragwort early, wild phlox common. Early meadow rue and the small anemones, a few hepatica and cut-leafed toothwort still in bloom, a last few Dutchman's britches.

2003: Cardinal sang at 5:20 a.m. (like yesterday morning – and at about the same time as in the third week of August). At the Covered Bridge, buckeyes are in bloom. Bluebells, Jacob's ladder, violets, and phlox make pale purple the dominant forest floor color. Around them in a tangle lie all the flowers of the mouse-ear chickweed. Sedum is budding. A few white wild hyacinths (*camassia scilloides*) blooming at the far end of the woods; I saw some along Dayton Street yesterday. Dandelions cover the green on Corey Street.

2004: Mrs. Lawson's yellow tulips were open this morning when I went by her yard with Bella. In the pond, the leaves of the water lily have almost reached the surface. By afternoon, lilacs – both the violet and the white – were opening. In the north garden, the first cressleaf groundsel and garlic mustard were flowering. In the east garden, the first fritillary was blossoming. All over town, dogwoods are coming in as crabapples reach full bloom. Along the street, Japanese knotweed is almost chest high. Now the bamboo is sprouting out in the lawn.

2006: At North Glen along the high path, the bluebells and spring beauties are in full bloom, but most Dutchman's britches and toothwort have faded. Redbuds at the entrance to the park are completely open. The first lilacs open in unison throughout the village.

2007: Early dogwoods are open at Antioch and along Elm Street. Tulips and dandelions open throughout town. Casey told me that his white lilacs, like mine, seemed ready to bloom. Also, his red buckeye apparently did not get damaged by the freeze. The library weigela is in full bloom today, but Mateo's hasn't started yet. This afternoon, Jeanie and I drove down to Chillicothe and Portsmouth, then back through Ripley and then north again. Approaching Portsmouth, spring returned – the frost had not killed the flowering trees or the leaves. We saw a few redbuds, many dogwoods, purple lilacs and crab apples in bloom. There were fields of tall winter cress, and the wheat fields were bright April green, the brightest I've seen this spring. Creeping phlox was common. Dandelions were still in full bloom, but a few places along the river they had gone to seed. In the Glen, the high tree line is still brown; along the Ohio, the pale green is spreading through the hills.

2008: Dandelions are coming in now throughout town, an early phase to the peak. Some hosta leaves are unraveling. Monarda is about an inch tall, a few garlic mustard plants heading in the strawberry bed. Rhubarb almost a foot tall. Summer phlox bushy and six inches. Primroses under Janet's redbud reaching full bloom. Viburnum leaves an inch long, hobblebush leaves up to two. Red quince full flower, honeysuckles budded at the same time as crabapples. Sparrows and starlings with nesting materials. Robins singing at dusk.

2009: The serviceberry flowers turned brown last night. Bleeding heart hearts are forming in our front garden, and allium buds have appeared. The carrot seeds finally sprouted: the salad garden is taking place. Rhubarb is big enough for pie. No peach flowers this year, and many crab apples show no buds. Peonies, however, still red, have started to form their buds. Redbuds are increasingly pink in early bloom. The east dooryard garden is almost solid green now, the ground covered with lanky snowdrop and crocus foliage, hosta leaves filling in around them. Some of our ferns are over a foot tall. Many maples have large seeds now, some red like the maples that lined the highways in Louisiana two months ago. Tat says daffodils are blooming now in Madison. Robins were strong at 5:00 a.m., and a cardinal sang at 5:15. I heard a screech owl in back for the first time this year. Along the way to Wilmington, most pear trees have lost their petals; in Yellow Springs, petal fall has begun. This evening, sun and rain, wind and dark clouds. I cut a little wood in the back and worked at katas before the storm hit.

2010: Into North Glen with Jeff: Morning with sun and mild 50s: The woods was full of anemone, trillium grandiflorum, bellwort, garlic mustard, Solomon's plume and seal, meadow rue, Jack-in-the-pulpit, late miterwort, wild phlox, wild geranium, small flowered buttercup. One golden Alexander and a few wood betony open.

2011: Overnight in all the rain, Don's cherry tree came into bloom. In the circle garden and in Liz's, the Indian hyacinths are budding. Some white lilacs pushing out at Don's, a pink snowball hydrangea open on Stafford Street. Maple seeds coming down in the wind. The backyard redbuds are in early bloom now, and one apple tree along Dayton Street is beginning to open, more apples seen in Fairborn. Pears quickly losing their petals. The song sparrow, the red-bellied woodpecker and lots of grackles calling this morning. Black walnut buds huge and round, tree-of-heaven buds starting to push out, pubescent, some small leaves appearing on the rose of Sharon. One dogwood coming in. House sparrows mating high on the gutters along Limestone

2012: White moths at the porch light this morning - the first time I've noticed them this year. Earlier in the spring, flat, dappled moths came to the light. This afternoon, the first yellow tiger swallowtail seen, and a polygonia. I found a toad that had gotten into the new pond and died because it apparently couldn't get out. Zinnias seeded in the east garden. All but a handful of the small late daffodils, and just a couple of tulips still hold on.

2013: Cold throughout the morning, but finally sunny and moderate in the upper 40s by mid afternoon: Some weeding and transplanting in the north gardens, weeds moving in, some north ferns up a foot or so, leaf size expanding on all the hydrangeas so quickly. At the Covered Bridge, the river high and brown and fast, and the usual litany: bluebells, cowslip, very late toothwort, one lesser celandine, chickweed in bloom and catchweed (not blooming) rising across the forest floor, Jacob's ladder with very early flowers, toad trillium, spring beauties, wild phlox, crowfoot, swamp buttercups, budded ragwort, skunk cabbage with full-size leaves – fat and long, one bloodroot leaf still. Along Corey Street, a dogwood seen in bloom, and one apple is starting in the triangle park. Here on High Street, the maples in front of Lil's house, the Danielsons' and Mrs. Timberlake's houses are all setting seeds. Rachel's ginkgo has half-inch leaves now. Peggy's virgin's bower is coming on at about the same rate as the lace vine on my porch. In front of Moya's house, the first rose of Sharon leaves are starting to show. From the San Francisco area, Paul W. Rhea wrote: "Recently took a splendid seven-mile ramble in Henry Coe SP, where emerging oak leaves glowed lime green against a cobalt sky. At one point, we beheld a patch of blue *brodeia* with literally dozens of spangled butterflies dancing overhead. Truly magical and memorable."

2014: This Easter Sunday morning, Moya announced over her south fence that she had found a praying mantis ootheca (egg sack) in her spirea bush, the same place she had found one last year. That year, Rick found the mantises emerging on May 5, and Moya's ootheca gave birth on May 25.

2015: The zelcova by the post office fully green with thin and delicate adolescent leaves. Don's serviceberry trees: flowers going to berries; his pie cherry loaded with blossoms.

2016: Now hyacinth season creeps up to replace the daffodils in the circle garden. Jill says the lilacs in Delaware, Ohio, are in full bloom, just starting here. Blueberry bushes leafing ahead of the beginning river birch branches, wild strawberry yellow found in the lawn, the earliest star of Bethlehem, the first budding of the tall alliums, now bamboo surging up to almost two feet and fat. The pink quince tree is in full bloom, most likely came into flower while I was gone last week. At the Indian Mound near Cedarville, twinleaf found still in bloom, skunk cabbage giant leaves, cowslip, tall swamp buttercups – very prominent in one bog, ragwort and tall ragwort, bluebells, wild phlox, garlic mustard all in flower, one yellow tiger swallowtail seen. And Peter and Mary Sue sent pictures of three Great White Egrets in the sycamores near Ellis Pond – the appearance this week of April fitting with the migration dates in my references, but the sightings are quite rare in the area. Mary Sue wrote a few days later: "For at least 3 or 5 years, give or take a year or two, about this time we see one passing through. Never for more than a day or two. It is possible they've done this longer and we just hadn't noticed, but, we've been in this location about 16 years and I'm always glued to the scene across the street, but I only started a bird journal in 2012 so other sightings are possible, and who knows what we miss. My notes recorded this: In 2014 on April 24 one large white egret and one on August 15 same year. In 2015 on April 12 one large white egret. Then this year April 20, the sighting of three. Sometimes we see a few small white cattle egret but I haven't any notes on them."

2017: From Vilaserio to Casa Pepa in Santa Marina, Spain. Walking through major agricultural lands, many hay fields cut, harvest lined up row after row; large tractors and plows working deep rich brown soil; people out in their gardens planting. Along the roads, the canopy thins, the result perhaps of elevation - well above Santiago - and well north of Madrid. At the pension in Santa Marina, an assortment of the vegetation of previous days, dandelion seeded, some violets, much celandine, white and pink clover, the first rare tall red tropical clover (like in southern Georgia), dock, lamium, large periwinkle, tall mallow in flower, sow thistles, brome, plantain, tall flowered plantain, borage, lanky chickweed, bladderwort, hawkweed, catkins all about, many from what appear to be silver olive bushes, the plants I thought were

Angelica or cow parsnip are really, I believe, very tall poison hemlock, an idyllic stream filled with ferns and hemlock, water striders hunting the slowly spinning surface. As I walk, I reflect how in all of this I often confuse the timekeeper markers with time itself, spring with its pieces, the sum with its parts.

God Almighty first planted a garden; and, indeed it is the purest of human pleasures; it is the greatest refreshment to the spirits of man.

Francis Bacon

Bill Felker

April 21st
The 111th Day of the Year

You watch the afternoons of Spring across the river,
and you know that nothing only is or happens once,
and that our hearts spin like the Earth around the Sun.

bf

Sunrise/set: 5:50/7:21
Day's Length: 13 hours 31 minutes
Average High/Low: 64/43
Average Temperature: 53
Record High: 84 - 1985
Record Low: 26 - 1904

Weather

Highs in the 80s come 20 percent of the days, 70s another 20 percent, 60s another 20 percent. Fifties occur 30 percent of the time, and 40s the final ten. The sky is overcast 50 percent of the time, and rain falls 50 percent of the time, too. Frost: one morning in a dozen.

Natural Calendar

Cross-Quarter Day, the day on which the sun reaches halfway to solstice, occurs at the end of April's third week. This is the time the antlers of deer begin to grow. In average years along the 40th Parallel, the first parsnips bloom, and all major garden weeds are sprouting. Honeysuckles, the rose of Sharon and spice bushes have developed enough to turn the undergrowth pale green, and the high trees are blossoming and leafing: ginkgo, elm, tree of heaven, black walnut, pussy willow, box elder, sweet gum, ash and locust.

Redbuds and pie cherry trees blossom as pear petals come down. Hepatica sprouts new leaves as it comes to the end of its April cycle. Wood mint is at least eight inches tall, and sweet for tea. Wild ginger foliage has pushed up through the mulch. Toad trillium, Jacob's ladder and large flowered trillum are budded, some in bloom. Virginia bluebells and spring beauties still hold.

Daybook

1982: The red quince at the north corner of the yard opened today.

1983: Cascades habitat: May apples tall, some fully developed, toothwort, spring beauties, hepatica, rue anemone, Dutchman's britches still in bloom. Some early white spring cress. Trillium grandiflorum is almost opening.

1985: Cascades habitat, after ten days in the 70s and 80s: First wild geranium, wild ginger, sedum, wood betony, and golden alexander. Toad trillium, Jack-in-the pulpit, early meadow rue, ragwort full bloom. At home, the first thyme-leafed speedwell in the lawn.

1986: Cardinal sings at 5:05 a.m.

1987: Asparagus is up four inches. Redbud finally opens in the Glen. First garlic mustard blooms, first wild phlox, first white violets.

1988: Daisies budding now.

1989: The redbuds are open in Xenia, a few days ahead of Yellow Springs. First strawberry flowered today. More and more crabs are flowering. Mrs. Bletzinger talks about the great chanting of frogs and toads, their migration to the neighbor's pond, but not to hers this year. Purple violets early full, the first yellow violets open, tree line thickening with blossoms, magnolias leafing on the south side of Wesley Hall, flowers holding on the north. Tulips still full bloom, daffodils late but holding. Everything happening so quickly, the sub-seasons over in a week or two, blend into other segments of seasons.

1991: Wisconsin to Yellow Springs: First white clover seen near Indianapolis. Above Janesville, the land is orange and gold with buds in the middle patches of pale green. Huge stretches of dandelions 60 miles south of Madison – the furthest advance north of the Great Dandelion Bloom. Forsythia blooms 15 miles further.

1992: Cowslips still in full bloom across from the Covered Bridge. Bradford pears leafing. Redbud three days out. Patches of green in the high trees across Yellow Springs valley.

1993: First killdeer noticed on Wilberforce-Clifton. Ferns just starting to unravel in the yard.

1995: One hundred and twenty miles north of Yellow Springs in Norwalk, Ohio, one azalea in full bloom against the doctor's office wall. Northern Ohio daffodils are in full bloom, whereas ours in Yellow Springs are gone except for the late varieties.. The fritillaria against the east wall opened today. Tonight in the warmth, the first ichneuman of the year stumbled about the living room.

1999: The toad cried in the rain at 5:08 a.m. Earlier, the frog barked. White bleeding heart early full, red bleeding heart early, small tooth-leafed bleeding heart full, dead nettle full, earliest tulips gone, some of the mid-season tulips are wilting as well. The first ferns have green nubs, knotweed three-feet plus.

2000: Redbuds still early bloom, apples hold in the cool rain. Honeysuckle leaves are shutting off the back yard from the street, maybe two-thirds of the way so far. The north side ferns are just starting to unravel. Cowslips along Grinnell declining.

2001: Today in the rain, the April green is so exquisitely bright: the great pubescent green of the world, the transfiguration of the earth, its shining garments.

2004: In Dayton, the first patches of dandelions have gone to seed, moving the area into the final phase of Middle Spring. At home, the first small pink azaleas are starting to open, and the new crabapple tree has just begun to flower.

2005: Celandine and fleabane, dogwoods, too, are starting. Some one-inch creeper leaves. Oak leaves some one to two inches, the scarlet and red oaks and rose of Sharon just pushing out. Hosta to about a foot tall. Green frog seen in the garden pond. Many maples and box elders a third to a half fully leafed.

2008: First celandine seen in flower today by the stone wall. Redbuds reddening, dandelions reaching full bloom throughout town. Lil's maple and all the other maples on the block are leafing and flowering. Peaches and pears full. The south ash and the hackberries are also coming in. Nate's black walnut and Moya's both have distinctive, fat, dark bud clusters, but Don's tree shows no sign of blooming. Daffodils are starting to decline now, but in the South Glen, a new twinleaf had opened. Toad trillium had developed its red flowers. Violet cress and toothwort were still strong. Foliage of wild geranium and wild phlox was appearing, ragwort budding. Along the east border of the yard, the white bleeding hearts have finally come up, and an old pink bleeding heart emerged over night next to the new ones. A few ferns are a couple of inches tall, but most are still just slightly swelling and showing no green. Cowslips along Grinnell still full. The television news showed a full-blooming dogwood as a backdrop for a local political story.

2009: Two of Greg's lily-of-the-valley have unraveled to reveal green buds. In the garden, variegated knotweed is up, flushed red, some stalks six inches. Endless summer hydrangeas have started basal leaves. Early Judd-type viburnums are in full bloom in Wilmington.

2011: Bright sun after days of rain and clouds, titmice and song sparrows calling loud, grackles all over, white birch and mall river birches with catkins, red mulberry, white mulberry, sweet gum leafing, more lilacs blooming, just a hair ahead of the apples. Lil's maple in flower. From Goshen, Indiana, Judy writes: "Bill and I saw bloodroot, Dutchman's breeches, spring beauties, early rue, and toad trilliums beginning to bud. May apples aren't up very far. Violets aren't out yet except here and there in our back yard. The forsythia are blooming, and a few daffodils, but the large bunches are still in bud. The hellebore, however, is magnificent."

2012: Many roadsides covered with brown maple seeds.

2013: Another sunny but cold day. Still, the sidewalks along Dayton Street are lined with the fallen petals from the serviceberry trees, and the very first violet lilac opened above the pond. Don's pie cherry is in full bloom like our sweet cherry. Paulownia tree buds have become enlarged over the past few days, should be ready to leaf when the weather warms. A few allium in the circle garden have buds. More zinnias planted around the yard. Fed the fish, and they actually left their hideout to move around the pond, first time this year. The birch at Lawson Place has bright catkins now. At the Kennedy Arboretum and Ellis Pond, the yellow poplars have one-inch leaves, scarlet oak and sawtooth oak buds are just breaking out, the chestnut oak a little ahead of them. Red oaks are leafing, have small half-inch leaves. Shingle oaks have tiny catkins. Hackberry in full flower, garlic mustard heading up. The ashes are flowering, pecans beginning to leaf. Willows and sugar maples have one-inch leaves.

2014: Walking through the neighborhood, Bella and I found mid-season daffodils and tulips in full bloom, and one broad-leafed azalea starting to flower.

2015: Hard wind today, temperatures in the 50s. I dug more annual beds, transplanted the evening primrose and the Shasta daisies. Squills, yellow daffodils, grape hyacinths and pachysandra all ended their bloom season at about the same time a day or so ago.

2016: First annual beds dug. Late daffodils, windflowers and glory-of-the-snow and tulips still hold.

2017: Spain: To Olivieroa just thirty kilometers from Muxia and the ocean. More large landholdings throughout, much hay cut and to be cut, large tractors plowing. The vegetation thins with the altitude and the change in soil and the increase of agribusiness. Some stone outcroppings have appeared in the hills. As the landmarks recede with the differences in land and land use, so does the season become thinner and less clear.

Surely
there is a great Word being put together here.
I begin to hear it gather in the opening
of the flowers and the leafing-out of the trees,
in the growth of bird nests in the crotches
of the branches, in the settling of the dead
leaves into the ground, in the whittling
of beetle and grub, in my thoughts,
moving in the hill's flesh.

Wendell Berry

April 22nd
The 112th Day of the Year

In the flowers find a solace,
Fleeting cure for every sadness,
Fragrant physic for your longing,
Certain aid for loneliness.

Celtus
(bf)

Sunrise/set: 5:49/7:22
Day's Length: 13 hours 33 minutes
Average High/Low: 65/43
Average Temperature: 54
Record High: 86 - 1985
Record Low: 28 - 1907

Weather

Fifteen percent of the highs today exceed 80 degrees, 15 percent are in the 70s, thirty percent in the 60s, thirty percent in the 50s, just 10 percent in the 40s. There is only a 15 percent chance for frost this morning. The sky is completely overcast one day out of three, and rain falls one day in four. And this is the last date of the season when the chances for snow are even close to ten percent.

The Weather in the Week Ahead

Late Spring arrives this week, the warm weather creating unmistakable markers in the progress of spring. Among those landmarks:

The 26th and the 30th record freezing temperatures less than five percent of the time, the first time that has happened since late September.

After the 22nd, chances for snow drop below five percent.

Chances for a cold day in the 30s or 40s fall to only ten percent on the 22nd, then plummet another eight percent on the 26th.

Beginning on April 27th, highs in the 90s become possible, and the chances for a high in the 80s pass the 20 percent mark. The chances for a high above 70s degrees are now 50/50 or better for the first time this year.

April 29th and 30th are usually the mildest days this week, with the 30th bringing a 90 percent chance for highs above 60 degrees for the first time since late September.

The driest days this time of year are April 26 and 27, each with just a 20 percent chance for rain. The wettest days: April 29th and 30th - both carrying a 55 percent chance for precipitation.

Natural Calendar

Now new beggarticks, touch-me-nots, and great ragweed have four leaves. May apples are a foot tall and buckeye buds have unraveled. Skunk cabbage leaves are more than half size in the swamps. Ragwort and garlic mustard are forming clumps, seed heads visible, still tightly bunched. Watercress has filled the shallow brooks. Peony stems are a foot and a half tall, leaves developing and spreading out, turning from red to green. Cabbage butterflies are out laying eggs on the new cabbage, kale, collards, and Brussels sprouts. Mulberry, locust, tree of heaven, viburnum, and ginkgo send out their first leaves. break dormancy.

Red-bellied woodpeckers, towhees, catbirds and thrushes sing in the woods. Grackles settle in to feed and mate. Buzzards roost and turkeys gobble. Mallards pair up, and geese nest near parking lots and riverbanks. Bees, flies and mosquitoes emerge. Rhubarb climbs taller than your boots. Worms breed in the wet earth, and the first young grass snakes hatch and explore the undergrowth.

Early tulips continue to flower, but the seasons of grape hyacinths, daffodils and scilla are ending. Many of the earliest Middle Spring wild flowers - bloodroot, purple cress, twinleaf, toothwort, Dutchman's britches, and periwinkle – have completed their blossoming periods.

Redbuds complement the last of the crab apples as the land gets ready for May: wild phlox, wild geranium, wild ginger, celandine, spring cress, sedum, golden Alexander, thyme-leafed speedwell, garlic mustard, and common fleabane are budding and blooming. Sweet clover and wild lettuce are already a foot high.

Hosta and lily-of-the-valley foliage will be four to six inches, poison ivy vines two to four inches, dock and great mullein and comfrey leaves eight inches.

The Stars

The Milky Way fills the western horizon as Orion sets just behind the sun. Now the middle of the heavens are in their prime spring planting position, Castor and Pollux to the west, Leo with its bright Regulus directly overhead, and Arcturus dominating the east. At morning chore time, Vega is the brightest star above you. Arcturus is the brightest in the western sky. Deep along the northern horizon the brightest star is Capella.

Daybook

1984: Jacoby, 55 degrees: Buckeye leaves emerging, leafcup full and lush, four and six leaves on the fat touch-me-not sprouts. First mosquitoes, first cowslips. Hepatica getting new leaves, coming to the end of its cycle, ragwort tall with purple buds, Dutchman's britches and bloodroot still holding, yellow-flowered toad trillium found, winter cress budding.

1985: Late Spring measurably closer: At South Glen, sweet clover, parsnips, and wild lettuce are a foot high already, waterleaf and sweet rockets have buds, four leaves now on next year's garlic mustard, white spring cress opens, clumps of June's cinquefoil leaves are common, locust and grape vines well into leafing, sweet Cicely foliage like delicate lace. Garden chives blooming today, first tall grass heads up in the yard.

1986: First buds on the raspberries. Ragwort seen in full bloom by the roadside near Wilberforce. Ferns emerging.

1987: Day flower and first mid-season hosta foliage is coming up. Maple flowers fall all at once in front of the house, cover the car. Redbuds suddenly full bloom, apples too. Patch of watercress flowering along Grinnell. Black walnut trees leafing out early.

1988: Cherry tree full bloom today. First apple blossoms. First celandine opens. Lily of the valley: four inches. Lilacs early bloom in various places. Very first wild columbine. Wood betony and golden alexander have been out for several days at the Cascades. First bellwort, first wild geranium, some mock orange buds. Skippers seen. Jack-in-the-pulpit common, trillium early full bloom. Downtown, first pears drop their petals in a windy 80-degree afternoon.

1989: May apples are budding. First swamp buttercup seen, very first ragwort opens. Pussy willow leaves racing with the box elders, both about half size. Entire fields of yellow cress along the way to Fairborn. First water cress in flower, first garlic mustard, wild ginger. Toothwort and violet cress holding. Ruby-crowned kinglet female in the yard, singing and being answered. Green ash flowers. Around the lawn, blue eyes, chickweed, purple deadnettle, violets dandelions, spring beauties full bloom, comfrey leaves a foot long. Poplar leaves half an inch, some garlic mustard 12 to 18 inches. Mulberry buds greening.

1990: Middle Spring holding on: bluebells still full bloom, hepatica and spring beauties, toothwort, rue anemone, large-flowered trillium. Garlic mustard is growing up around them, though, and the canopy is thickening overhead. First bellwort, columbine, celandine. Last few Dutchman's britches. Early betony, early winter cress, golden alexander. Some phlox. In town, flowering crabs finally open wide. Ginkgo, locust and gum trees begin to leaf.

1991: Red-winged blackbirds mating, building nests, singing on fences all the way from Yellow Springs to Wisconsin.

1993: Winter cress budding at the golf course. Bleeding hearts have formed. Blue jays seem to become louder each day.

1995: In the east garden, bleeding hearts are well formed now, and Chris's dwarf iris is showing buds. The grape hyacinths planted with the daffodils last spring are in full bloom, Mrs. Hurie's blue speedwell has come into full bloom, along with the dead nettle which has spread and makes for rich color in the transition phase to the Late Spring flowers. The last scilla are bowed but hold.

Walking up the street to the triangle park, I see the pines have started their new growth, some trees having pushed out tiny cones, others with fresh green needles at the tips of their branches. In town, many pears have exchanged their flowers for leaves, and the forsythia in front of the house shows almost no gold at all. Red quince still full. Thyme-leafed speedwell found while mowing the lawn.

1996: The weather was cool until the 11th this year, then Middle Spring came in, and everything got out of hand. In the past week I've seen bats (three in the back yard last night). Pears opened completely. Redbuds started. Daffodils peaked, tulips came in and now are almost in full bloom. Bleeding hearts made hearts. Bird calls became even louder, more raucous in the mornings. Hosta came up. The west garden ferns came up. Jack-in-the-pulpit sent up its huge fat head. At the Cascades, rue anemone, toothwort and large-flowered trilliums were in full bloom, early meadow rue and ragwort and bellwort almost ready, wild phlox budding too. Ginger leaves have unfolded from the ground. Spring beauties filled Antioch lawn. Box elders suddenly flowered, some leafing. The west shrub line thickened with leaves, began to shut out the view of Dayton Street. The yard and all the grass in town took on the exciting vibrancy, intensity of April green, glowed with life, as though its usually invisible aura could no longer be contained and took on visible shape.

1998: Tadpoles have left the safety of their eggs now and have gone out one by one to explore the pond. My ginkgo leaves are an inch across outside the window. The ash are also an inch, and the sweet gum tree paces both. Some box elders have leafed, and the lower growth is almost complete. Silver olives are well developed along the freeway south.

1999: Madison, Wisconsin to Crookston, Minnesota near the Canadian border: At Madison, the trees well along, maybe half of Yellow Springs. Some green persists to Minneapolis, although the birches are really the only leafing trees past Eau Claire. In the hills, a clear tint of gold and red, like Kentucky or Tennessee in late march. Around the Twin Cities, forsythia and tulips. Minneapolis to Saint Cloud: flowers and leaves disappear. Roadsides grasses half brown. From St. John's at Collegeville north, the landscape is almost completely dull. At a rest stop near Alexandria, one lady bug in the sun, basal clusters of motherwort foliage, some purple buds on a viburnum. Near Fergus Falls, only poplars budding (but leafed in central Wisconsin). In northern Minnesota, farmers are working the great flat potato and beet fields. Crookston: large buds on the cottonwoods.

2003: First yellow swallowtail of the year seen at the Covered Bridge.

2004: Wood hyacinths and honeysuckles budded. Peach flowers gone. Pink quince coming in.

2006: Dianna Matthews called to report a cat running along with a bullfrog ("six to eight-inch legs!" she exclaimed) dangling from its mouth.

2008: In Wilmington, several crabapples seen in full bloom, and lots of garlic mustard seen open by the roadside south of Xenia. Redbuds full. Pears and forsythia still hold, but the flowers share their branches with new leaves. American toads were singing in the distance as I walked Bella after dark – the first time I've heard them this year.

2009: Wilmington pears are completely green now. White star hyacinths seen in bloom along Stafford Street.

2011: Rain continues, flooding in the area. Five cowbirds at the feeder this afternoon while I was talking to Tat, the first cowbirds in months. The new tulips are reaching full bloom, leaves thickening both high and low. Winter cress seen on the way to Dayton.

2012: Below-average temperatures may have stalled the precipitous advance of Middle Spring, shortening the span between the typical state of nature at this time of year and the accelerated state of this particular season. Still, I found the first locust flower on the side of the street today, locusts having moved up from Cincinnati in the past few days. From Goshen, Indiana, Judy wrote: "We were rewarded for venturing out on a cold and blustery day by being treated to acres of blooming trilliums--the huge ones, little nodding ones, and pink ones that I'd never seen before. We also saw a blooming May apple (not many with flowers out), false rue anemone, wood anemone, sweet cicely, and bouncing bet in addition to the usual henbit and common buttercup."

2013: A cardinal woke me up at 4:45 this morning, the day clear and chilly, frost on the grass. At South Glen this afternoon, ginger leaves were visible, but no flowers. Chickweed, pale, tall, full flowered, covered most of the woods floor, spreading up into the hills in glens of green. Bluebells, violets, toothwort, spring beauties, toad trillium, wild phlox, crowfoot. Buds on the ragwort, nodding trillium, winter cress, buckeyes. A few rockets and garlic mustard plants heading. Parsnips one to two feet. At home, Jeanie's white bleeding heart has opened up all the way, and Moya's pink bleeding heart is in full bloom.

2014: The serviceberry flowers are coming down now, should be gone in a day or two. In the yard, bluebells and lungwort continue in full bloom. Daffodils are declining. The Anna Belle and Indomitable Sprit hydrangeas have small, half-inch leaves now. Some ferns are up a few inches, but others haven't started, especially along the north wall. The east dooryard garden, all its snowdrops, crocus and aconites completed, waits for the hosta (just a couple of inches tall today) to cover them. Hops found creeping into the north gardens. I planted milkweed sprouts near the old wall. The pileated woodpecker continues to call; I've heard it for weeks. Around the village: the full bloom of dandelions in lawns and waysides; the first flowering of crab apples; catkins on river birches (but not Jeanie's in the yard); dogwood buds swelling; ginkgo and grape vine leaves both just coming out a little, pacing one another.

2015: Rose of Sharon starting to leaf at Moya's. Lily-of-the-valley budding. Maple seed wings falling to Stafford Street.

2016: Pink quince petals falling to the pond. The river birch has one-inch leaves. Weeds multiply throughout the garden in their late-spring surge. The allium stalks grow taller, their buds fatter. The viburnum on the north side of the house has its first white blossoms. Now the red crab apple petals have started to come down near the dooryard garden, and when Jill and I went north to Delaware, Ohio above Columbus, all the downtown streets were speckled with apple petals, the chilly wind spinning them around us. Several bright pink azaleas wide open at the university here.

2017: Spain: to Dumbria across valleys and mountains, lined with white, slowly spinning wind turbines, a drier habitat, hillsides covered with yellow ginestra and the prickly pea-flowered shrub. Eucalyptus and pine groves, blackberry hedges, brooks with the clearest water; some pasture, very little farmland. Plants included violets, the tall flowering plantains, a little mallow, periwinkle, buttercups, a foxglove-like plant in bloom (had been budding days before). In one stream near Olvieroa, white blossoms on a fine-leafed water plant reminiscent of watercress but much more delicate. Toward Dumbria, in a few shady corners, I found three-petaled white dayflowers. In town, late pink magnolias, full lavender lilacs and bright roseate azaleas, late flowering fruit trees. Ants seen migrating along one path. A row of black walnut trees just starting to leaf and flower. Hawthorn trees in bloom yesterday and today as we descended further north and west toward the coast and Muxia.

The moon was created for the counting of the days.

Hebrew Midrash Text

April 23rd
The 113th Day of the Year

For winter's rains and ruins are over,
And all the season of snows and sins;
The days dividing lover and lover,
The light that loves, the night that wins
And time remembered is grief forgotten,
And frosts are slain and flowers begotten,
And in green underwood and cover,
Blossom by blossom the spring begins.

Algernon Charles Swinburne

Sunrise/set: 5:46/7:21
Day's Length: 13 hours 35 minutes
Average High/Low: 65/44
Average Temperature: 54
Record High: 86 - 1960
Record Low: 28 - 1956

Weather
There is a 15 percent chance for a high in the 80s today and a 30 percent chance for 70s, making this the first day of the year on which the high rises above 70 forty-five percent of the time. Mild 60s occur another 45 percent of the days, with 50s coming five percent of the time, and 40s another five percent. Rain falls one day out of four, with odds for frost the same. The sun shines two days in three.

Natural Calendar
The transition week to Late Spring ushers in Jack-in-the-Pulpit Season, Miterwort Season, Wild Phlox Season, Celandine, Meadow Parsnip, Wood Betony, Wood Hyacinth, Fleabane, Spring Cress, Nodding Trillium, Larkspur and Bellwort Blooming Season. Garlic Mustard Season is here, covering the deep woods with white and green. It is Leafing Season for ginkgo, tree-of-heaven, oak, pecan, ash, locust, black walnut, and mulberry. Wild Cherry

187

Blossom Season spreads throughout the woodlots, along with Buckeye Blooming Season and Red Horse Chestnut Blooming Season. Clematis Season, Lily-of-the-Valley Season and Star of Bethlehem Season grace the garden. Mock Orange Season, Korean Lilac Season and Honeysuckle Season announce the most fragrant time of year.

Daybook

1982: Found trout lilies and wild phlox open today.

1985: More and more trees filling out this second week of heat. Black walnut, green ash, hackberry, sycamore, catalpa leafing. The white mulberry has green berries. Bridal wreath is blooming, snowball viburnum almost white. Some maples have near full-size leaves.

1986: Heavy frost hurts bleeding hearts, new pussy willow transplants, asparagus, ash, tree of heaven. Two quail ran across my path at South Glen.

1987: Bleeding hearts full bloom. Rose of Sharon leafing.

1988: Lilacs in early bloom at a few spots around town. More butterflies: skippers. Trillium grandiflorum early full at the Cascades. Downtown, pears drop their petals in a windy 80 degrees, then a thunderstorm with scattered hail. First celandine. Lily-of-the-valley is four inches high.

1989: Twinleaf and bloodroot seasons over. Bluebells still in full bloom, but being covered by garlic mustard, Lush undergrowth: every inch of the ground a wildflower of spring or summer. Fields of golden cress along the road to Fairborn.

1991: Petals of the pears washed into the street by the rain of the past few days. Leafing maybe half complete now in the high canopy. Crab apples full flower, as are dogwoods through town. Full bloom time of watercress and dandelions. Garlic mustard still early bloom. Hyacinth mostly gone. Peonies bushy and tall, full size. Only a few forsythia flowers left. Seeds, half an inch long, just forming from the flowers of a maple.

1992: Lilacs open all over town. Ginkgo leaves fully formed, but an eighth of their normal size. East daffodils are finished blooming except for the patch of giants.

1993: Quince opens along Limestone Street, lower canopy of box elders thickening. The tree line shades turn lighter, from red to orange to dapples of a glowing green. Rhubarb seed heads cut back; they were up about six inches, still tight. Lil's maple full bloom.

1998: First geranium opens in the dooryard. Tadpoles have doubled in size overnight. This is the center of apple and redbud and dogwood bloom. Daisies show their buds. Many high and medium trees are pale green with small leaves. I am estimating that today is approximately where I was in Montgomery, Alabama on the 23rd of March this year. Maybe the trees were a little fuller there.

1999: Crookston, Minnesota: Sun, 60 degrees: First early waves of dandelions, a mourning cloak butterfly. Joan and Jim Chandler say that grass is just starting to color in Thunder Bay, that snow only melted a week ago. They talked about the snowline in Canada in mid April, a line which moves north with spring. At the grave site of my uncle, as we stood praying in the sun, a lady bug flew to John, landed on his sleeve.

2000: John reports first crocus blooming on his farm in northern Minnesota, and peony stalks just pushing out of the ground. And Neysa reports an attack of ticks at her picnic here in Yellow Springs. Around the yard, star of Bethlehem and wood hyacinths are budding, first leafing begins on the rose of Sharon, peony buds are three-fourths of an inch across, some hosta leaves at least a foot high, late tulips still holding, and the apple trees, and the redbuds. There are small hearts on the bleeding hearts. Rhubarb plenty big enough for pie. Two days ago, the first (and only) asparagus spears cut from the garden for supper. Grape vines leafing now, sycamore leaves an inch long plus.

2002: Sycamore leaves just starting. The white oak at my window in Columbus has two-inch leaves. Throughout the landscape, leafing overcomes flowering: Late Spring.

2003: Appledorn tulips, pink azaleas, dead nettle, and bleeding hearts are in full bloom, parallel with the crab apples and redbuds. Forsythia has leafed, the pink quince budded. New bamboo in the south garden is six feet tall. Lungwort moves into its last flowers. The Great Blue and other large hostas are a foot high, as are the Asiatic lilies. Honeysuckle is budded and fully leafed. Leaves on Lil's maple are about two thirds full size.

2004: Red tulips coming in to complement the red crabapple flowers above them in the east garden.

2005: After three weeks of above-average temperatures, snow this morning, maybe two inches, fat wet flakes. Deep cold forecast for tonight. And Ruby Nicholson called about 11:30 this morning; she'd been out driving in Bryan Park, the most beautiful thing she ever saw, she told me, so beautiful she had to go back and drive through it all again. Then she started talking about how she hadn't seen cows switching their tails since last October, and how she'd been watching all winter and the cows hadn't switched their tails. On April 20th, she said, she had seen cows standing knee deep in mud, and she saw one of them switch its tail, but that was all, just once. She says she's got everyone she knows watching to see when the cows really start switching their tails. I'm supposed to watch, too. And so she also says that the next moon ought to be called the Cow Switching Tail Moon, and I'll name it that for her every spring from now on. Ruby will be 95 this spring, and Jeanie and I said that if we could be as happy at 95 as Ruby was this morning, we wouldn't mind at all getting old.

2006: To Cincinnati for the flower show: In Dayton and Yellow Springs, the high tree line was filling in lightly, something like the status of the foliage near Columbia in South Carolina during the last week of March. As we drove south toward the Ohio River, the canopy became fuller and fuller as though we were approaching

Charleston. All along the roadsides, silver olives were in bloom.

2008: Into South Glen at the Covered Bridge with Jeanie: Large patches of twinleaf foliage, all flowers gone. Fragments of Dutchman's britches and toothwort. Bluebells blooming but the blue hillsides are being swallowed up by garlic mustard heading up. Red bellied woodpecker in the Glen and at home in the back yard called throughout the morning. Grackles, sparrows, squirrels, red and gold finches, doves, a few cardinals have been feeding in the sun. Tree of heaven has swollen buds. Daffodils declining quickly, tulips still bright. Redbuds opening more now below the fringed box elder blossoms. At the Wegerzyn Gardens in Dayton, tulips, redbuds, dogwoods, crab apples were in full bloom, weigela open, nodding bluebells lining the entry road. Maples were in flower, ginkgo leafing out.

2009: Weeding in the northeast garden, Jeanie came upon an injured luna moth. Then late this afternoon, Jeanie heard bees; she looked up and there was a swarm over in the Lawson's yard, hanging from a branch high in the hackberry tree. Mock orange bushes have buds now. First garlic mustard is in bloom near the pond.

2010: Small copper butterfly seen as I was mowing the lawn, and a small, round, bright red spider (a velvet mite) in the dirt back by the shed.

2011: Heavy clouds this morning. The first grackle came to the feeder at 5:58. Cowbirds are back again today. Cardinals seen mating in the Osage trees. Rose of Sharon is leafing out.

2012: Viburnum and Korean lilac provide the most color in the north garden now. Honeysuckle flowers brighten the hedgerow around the yard, though, and the circle garden is full of violet wood hyacinths and lamium. Near the bird feeders, the first spiderwort opened last night, and the first sweet rockets bloomed in the Phillips Street alley. Sparrows and grackles and cardinals loud throughout the morning walk. Lots of robins hopping in the lawns. Throughout the Northeast today, heavy snows.

2013: To Beavercreek this morning: Dandelions thick on all the boulevards and in the fields, the peak of the Great Dandelion Bloom. A few apple blossoms opening. White star hyacinths found in bloom in the Phillips Street alley. On High Street, most of the star magnolia petals have fallen. Serviceberry trees hold their flowers while leafing now. All the silver maples still in bloom, forsythia flowers darkening slightly as they age. At Ellis Pond, two-inch leaves on the vernal witch hazel, Norwegian Maple in full flower (with flowers like Lil's maple), mountain ash with two-to-three-inch leaf clusters. Red maple setting seeds, elderberry bush with one-inch leaf clusters, buckeye leaves almost full size, bald Cyprus with half-inch foliage, silver maple one-inch leaves, pink magnolia and all the weeping cherries in full bloom.

2014: To the Covered Bridge with Jeff: Hillside after hillside of full-blooming bluebells, just like they were when I first saw them with Jeanie decades ago; along the path we found toad trilliums and wild phlox and toothwort; garlic mustard is growing tall, fully budded; clusters of green buds on the buckeyes. Shepherd's purse found at the end of its cycle, and a soft cress about two feet tall, either *arabis glabra*, tower mustard, or *brassica rapa*, field mustard/rape, a very soft-leafed plant with alternate, clasping leaves and yellow flowers of four petals.

2015: As I was digging the north east annual bed, I noticed that the first garlic mustard of the year was open. I marked off the goldenrod bed by the trellis, the foliage about three-inches long. I transplanted one peach sapling, a few Asiatic lilies, several stray purple coneflowers – also about three inches, and I completed the evening primrose (*oenothera*) bed behind the phlox. I uncovered the Joe Pye – two to three inches high -from the tangle of euonymous around it. At the Ellis Pond arboretum, red maple just barely leafing; *cornus florida*, a small-flowered dogwood was open; Japanese maples with one-inch leaves, wild plum in dense, full flower, fragrance rich and heavy; small leaf clusters on the Siberian elms; sassafras with pale green, lilac-like buds; first shiny buds on the sweet gum; one-inch leaf on the Katsura and hornbeam; blue ash in flower; columnar ginkgo with half-inch leaves; red horse chestnut and yellow buckeye both with two-inch leaves and flower spikes (not open); cyprus starting, half to a full inch of bristly foliage, a nearby larch about the same.

2016: Spreading fields of dandelions gone to seed at the south edge of town. The Great Violet Bloom continues unabated.

2017: Spain: North through more eucalyptus forest to Quintans, a prosperous small village on the way to Muxia,. A patch of Solomon's seal found along the path, but the variety of plants was small, included hemlock and maybe a few angelicas, one columbine, one mock orange, patches of white Asiatic dayflowers, wild foxgloves (that I thought of as a relative of snapdragons. Fields of hay not ready to be cut, some land being prepared for eucalyptus planting, and great mountain and valley vistas. Lots of butterflies, whites, sulphurs, a few blues, many gold-browns.

Wherever you are is home
And the earth is paradise:
Wherever you set your feet is holy land.

Wilfred Pelletier and Ted Poole

Bill Felker

April 24th
The 114th Day of the Year

Salve ver optatum,
amantibus gratum,
gaudiorum
fax multorum....

Hail, long desired spring,
boon to lovers,
shining torch of many joys....

MSS Benedictbeuern (bf)

Sunrise/set: 5:45/7:22
Day's Length: 13 hours 37 minutes
Average High/Low: 65/44
Average Temperature: 54
Record High: 88 - 1925
Record Low: 25 - 1910

Weather
Fine weather is the rule for April 24th: ten percent chance for a high in the 80s, fifteen percent for 70s, fifty-five percent for 60s, twenty percent for 50s. The sun shines 75 percent of the days, and rain comes just twice in a decade on this date. Frost occurs only once in a decade.

Natural Calendar
Azaleas blossom throughout the Lower Midwest in the warmest Aprils, just as field grasses and winter wheat become long enough to ripple in the wind. Chickweed has filled in the woodland floor. Silver and red maple seeds are an inch long. Flowering pears are passing their best, starting to get their leaves. Ferns are at least six inches tall in the new shade. The first yellow celandine blossoms in the alleys. Yellow-bellied sapsuckers mate as buckeyes come into bloom. Admiral butterflies hatch.

Daybook

1982: Winter cress and ragwort bloom begins, and Solomon's plume is ready. Wild strawberries flowering, hepatica done for the year, its new leaves coming out.

1984: Speckled bird egg found broken on the ground.

1986: Cherry blossoms mostly gone by today, a ten-day cycle of bloom in this warm April. Buckeye flowers are completely open now, dogwood in full bloom,

1988: Yellow-bellied sapsuckers seen mating beyond Sycamore Hole. Angelica coming up on the way to Middle Prairie. Most of the forsythia is gone at home. No more daffodils.

1989: Sparrows still building nests under the eaves. Yellow-bellied sapsuckers mating beyond my second fishing hole in the river.

1991: The box elder canopy is filling in, and from Clifton Road; the creek valley is touched with rounded pale green domes. At Aullwood, garlic mustard, winter cress, shepherd's purse, bluebells, large-flowered celandine in full bloom. In Yellow Springs the pears are leafing, cherry and buckeye trees full late bloom. Some maple flowers falling. First iris opens in front of the house, tulips full bloom, even the late daffodils slightly past their prime, lilacs coming in.

1993: Very first blossom on the pie cherry tree today. Buds have formed on peonies and red raspberries.

1995: In the cool afternoon, pear petals are falling throughout town as the apple and cherry blossoms are at their best. Silver maples start to leaf. Lil's sugar maple and ours in bloom. Ash buds are greening. First garlic mustard opened today. Celandine early full bloom now.

1998: Full celandine and purple speedwell. Some of the first apple petal fall. First clematis opens in the garden. End first wave of early dandelions. Last days of the fritillaria. Red and white bleeding hearts are in the center of their season. First wood hyacinth opens by the cherry tree stump. Lilacs on the downside of their blossoming, but still prominent. Garden asparagus has become too mature to eat.

1999: Madison to Yellow Springs, returning to late Middle Spring. Halfway between Rockford and Bloomington, the trees along are river are either in bloom or leafing. Twenty miles north of Bloomington, full dandelion flower. By Danville, grass is long enough to ripple in the wind. Redbuds and crabs in full bloom on the bright green hillsides. Spring beauties in Crawfordsville.

2000: Azaleas open in the east garden, and one star of Bethlehem unravels. One fritillaria left.

2001: Fleabane blooming in the protected microclimate at the south edge of house. Wheat is 12 to 18 inches on the road to Chillicothe, almost waving in the wind. Petalfall starts as Bradford pears collapse. Late tulips hold. Ferns to two feet. In the pond, loosestrife is two feet as well.

2002: First wisteria blossom today, first celandine flower, first star of Bethlehem. Beech just starting to leaf. Daisies budding. Wheat a foot tall.

2003: Some red oak leaves at Mills Lawn park are almost two inches long, other reds only a half an inch. First garlic mustard flowers opened today along the front sidewalk, and the first pink quince flower has unraveled.

2005: Beech leaf sheaths are extended, sharp, but not unraveling.

2006: Inventory: Full dead nettle, buds on wood hyacinth. Pink quince, apples, lilacs, redbuds, apple cherries, celandine, garlic mustard, dandelions, violets all full. Sage well leafed. Parsley big enough to pick. Bamboo three feet. Leafing rose of Sharon, monarda six to eight inches, earliest cress to seed. Three-fourth inch buds on the peonies, astilbe and waterleaf fully leafed, hosta half size, honeysuckles and mock orange budded. Late bluebells.

Lungwort still pink, oakleaf hydrangea leaves two inches, daisies budded, ferns to three feet, purple deadnettle aging, daylilies fully developed foliage, small viburnum in the north garden done blooming, but other viburnums are still full in town. White mulberry has one-inch leaves, side-flower hydrangea has three inch leaves, Asiatic lilies to two feet, heliopsis bushy, Canada thistle to two feet, mid-season tulips rapidly collapsing, still white daffodils, the first few star of Bethlehem and sweet rocket, Dutch iris two feet, lily of the valley has bells, white boneset to one foot, mint strong, first cressleaf groundsel opening, catmint bushy, rhubarb lush, first strawberry flower, catchweed tall and sticky, Queen Anne's lace a foot tall, bleeding hearts full, new apple tree full deep pink, Japanese knotweed to six feet, full pale azalea, first red azalea, first east garden late tulips, Virginia creeper fresh red shiny leaves, full forsythia leafed (all yellow gone), full honeysuckle leaf barrier, clematis tangled budded and leafing, wisteria leaf stems to three inches, Korean lilac keeps its tight buds, pears fully leafed in town, box elder leaves maybe half size, blue speedwell tall and full, red quince leafing, flowers holding. No locust or osage flowers or leaves yet. At the park, the small-flowered mock orange is opening.

2007: Red quince still in bloom. Dandelion peak throughout Dayton and the countryside, a little late. More dogwoods opening. Some lily of the valley tight and five inches; other patches have fully developed foliage. Lil's maple well leafed. The first azalea flowers are coming out in the east garden. Thyme-leafed speedwell noticed blooming as I cut the grass this afternoon.

2008: Another soft morning. The first lilac bud and the first azalea bud opened overnight. The early white, pale yellow, and the orange tulips are almost gone, scilla almost disappeared, daffodils further decayed. Leaves are coloring the forsythia, the serviceberries and the pears. Heavy petalfall on most of the large star and the pink magnolias, but Don's pink magnolia is just reaching its best. Red quince still full, dandelions still at their peak. John called from Lanesboro, Minnesota: the grass is just starting to green up, he said, and crocus were the only flowers in sight. Other bulbs were about three or four inches tall. Ruth Paige called to say she saw the first hummingbird at her viburnum today. The earliest in the Dayton Audubon Society book of birds lists April 20, 1964 as the earliest date observed for hummingbird arrival and May 5th the average date.

2009: The bee swarm is still in the hackberry tree early this morning as the temperature rises toward 80. The serviceberry flowers have shrivled, replaced by gray-green leave. At Moya's and at Don Beard's, the pointed-petal yellow tulips are in full bloom. At home, the first chives have budded. Celandine buds are getting ready to open. The fritillaria blossomed overnight. Chickweed is full under the Korean lilac. Standard lilacs, violet and white, are open. The cats were batting at the first wasps this morning at the east window. Pond cleaned this afternoon, one of the two-year-old dark fish seen. The bees left late in the morning. The mother cardinal is still on her nest in the bamboo.

2011: First garlic mustard open in the yard.

2012: No birds at 4:40, faint robins at 4:50, strong robin calls at 5:00, cardinal heard at 5:15, crows, grackles and doves by 6:00. The iris on Stafford Street are in full bloom, and the buckeye trees there are fully budded. Don's serviceberry trees have green eries, and Mateo's black walnut tree is leafing out now, ahead of the trees of heaven, which were burned back by frost weeks ago. Dogwoods are in decline. To the Koogler Reserve of the Beavercreek Wetlands this afternoon: Inventory of plants - only a few in bloom: blackberry, hemlock, fleabane, winter cress, common ragwort, agrimony, swamp buttercup, small-flowered buttercup, multiflora roses, purple violets, garlic mustard, jumpseed, honeysuckles, ironweed, sycamore, box elder, buckeye, small sedum, panicled dogwood, touch-me-nots, maples, corn salad, angelica, horse tail (glades full of it), spring cress, one magnificent cowslip, "May buttercup," golden Alexander, ground ivy, thin-leafed waterleaf, lilies, asters, dock (some in full bloom), Canadian thistles, a few wonderful patches of forget-me-nots, germander, hops, cattails, water willows, teasel and a number of current shrubs with yellowish flowers, certainly a *ribes*, and likely the wild black current, *ribes americium*. A beautiful habitat, contained, easy to walk, with many dramatic vistas and wonderful tall trees. Ruby called this morning, still had not seen any hummingbirds, even though she said she had put her feeder out in March.

2014: In Dayton, sycamores are starting to leaf. When I got home, I found a message from Ed Oxley: He had seen the first tiger swallowtail – just a few days later than the earliest sightings I've noted here. (But they were flying during many of our Early Spring trips south, the earliest tiger seen near the Georgia border on February 28 of 2012.) In the alley at home, the bittersweet is showing leaves.

2016: North to Delaware, Ohio today, cool and sun: We drove north back into the full bloom of dandelions and crabapples. At home, I found that the deer had eaten the tops off of the phlox. But lily-of-the-valley plants had their first flowers.

2017: Spain: To Muxia on the sea: Once more clear skies, but now with a little fog, perhaps from the sea nearby. We walked through hamlets and eucalyptus forests, up and down hills, now the most prominent wildflower being purple columbine. Many nasturtiums blooming in front of homes, and one field of golden swamp iris, ferns throughout, half emerged, one small patch of birds foot trefoil, two new yellow flowers with five petals about an inch across, tucked into the ground covers, reluctant to show their leaves to me. So as I walked, variety seemed to thin, and the beach habitat here, like others I have seen, less varied. Most butterflies, though, of all the walk.

There's an art of attending to weather, to the route you take, to the landmarks along the way, to how if you turn around you can see how different the journey back looks from the journey out, to reading the sun and moon and stars to orient yourself, to the direction of running water, to the thousand things that make the wild a text that can be read by the literate.

Rebecca Solnit

April 25th
The 115th Day of the Year

And the Spring arose on the garden fair,
Like the Sprit of Love felt everywhere;
And each flower and herb on Earth's dark breast
Rose from the dreams of its wintry rest.
The snowdrop and then the violet,
Arose from the ground with warm rain wet;

Percy Bysshe Shelly

Sunrise/set: 5:43/7:23
Day's Length: 13 hours 40 minutes
Average High/Low: 66/44
Average Temperature: 55
Record High: 89 - 1915
Record Low: 26 - 1919

Weather

Chances for highs in the 80s are the highest so far in the year - 25 percent, and 70s occur another 25 percent, 60s yet another 25 percent. Fifties come 20 percent, 40s five percent. The sun shines almost 70 percent of the days; rain falls 35 to 40 percent. Frost: 25 percent chance, the last time this spring that the chances are so high.

Natural Calendar

The season of Late Spring usually has five gentle cool fronts and stretches from the end of April until the end of May in the Lower Midwest and Middle Atlantic region (occurs at least a month earlier in the South). Most spring woodland flowers complete their bloom during this time, and almost all the trees leaf out. Frost season ends, and gardeners sow tender garden flowers and vegetables. Farmers put in all the corn and soybeans and prepare for the first cut of hay. The day's length grows until it surpasses fourteen hours along the 40th Parallel.

In Late Spring, the time of flowering fruit trees slowly

comes to a close, and the great dandelion bloom of Middle Spring turns to gray and fragile seeds just as dogwoods open. Bamboo stalks have reached at least three feet tall, and peony buds are as big around as pennies. All the gold disappears from Middle Spring's forsythia as daisies bud, and ferns unravel. The six-petaled white star of Bethlehem and the four-petaled pink and purple sweet rockets tell the time of year throughout the pastures.

Lilies of the valley have their bells, and the first bright yellow cressleaf groundsel is opening in wetlands. Rhubarb pies are growing everywhere as the first strawberry flowers, as Virginia creepers get their new shiny leaves, as azaleas brighten and as honeysuckle leaves turn the undergrowth deep May green. Earliest grasses go to seed.

Migrations of the white-throated sparrow, ruby-crowned kinglet, yellow-rumped warbler, black-and-white warbler, palm warbler, Nashville warbler, swamp sparrow, and hermit thrush reach as far north as Lake Erie.

Daybook

1980: The new cherry tree in the back yard has come into bloom.

1983: First robins heard at 4:17 a.m. Probably began earlier. Most forsythia flowers gone.

1984: Buds on bleeding heart. First pink magnolia blooms.

1986: First June bug on the front screen.

1987: Peach and cherry trees end their bloom cycle, apple still holds. Meadow parsnip and catchweed coming in.

1989: Crab apples in the village early full bloom. Pollen count is high from maples and oaks.

1990: Suddenly days in the 80s, garlic mustard comes into early full bloom. Apple and cherry are all open.

1991: Full bloom cherry, peach, apple, dogwoods, redbuds: the peak of all the flowering trees in Yellow Springs. At South Glen:

blue cohosh with green-gold flowers, wild geranium, spring cress, ragwort, phlox, white and yellow violets, toad trillium, *trillium grandiflorum* all full bloom. Wood thrush mating song heard, more elaborate than the cardinal's. Ash trees leaves about an inch long along Corey Street.

1992: Ferns a foot high now. Wisteria getting leaves.

1993: End of the east garden daffodils.

1994: I heard the high chant of the American toads coming from Grinnell pond, the first time this year.

1998: Confined to the chair by the side of the pond by a touch of pneumonia, the sun warming me, cardinals, doves, robins singing. Carpenter bees at work all along the south wall of the house. The first fleabane opened overnight. Daisy buds are stretching, showing white. One of last year's purple pansies is open. Wood hyacinth has opened around the cherry tree.

1999: While I was gone to Minnesota, the toad laid eggs, and the white lilac came into full bloom. The peonies are almost full size now. A few daisies show buds. Two cabbage butterflies play in the garden, and the apple tree blooms in the yard. The late maples in front of our house are finally blossoming, and everything is filling in except the osage and the locust. All the daffodils, except for the small double ones, are gone. Poppy foliage about a foot and a half, pacing the comfrey. Poplar leaves are the size of a squirrel's ear. Blue jay bell call common since mid April, cardinal sings all day, toad calling at 8:25 p.m. even though eggs have been laid. Dogwoods have opened now, following the pear-redbud-crabapple sequence.

2002: Rapid petal fall throughout the area, flowers engulfed now by leaves.

2003: Apple petal fall has begun, and redbuds are getting leaves. Silver olive buds pace the honeysuckle buds. At South Glen, ginger and May apples have buds, chickweed foliage turning pale with age. Buckeyes, late red magnolias, and lilacs remain in flower. Wisteria has come in along the highways. A volunteer pansy blossomed in the east garden.

2005: Creeping phlox common in Cedarville. Small Japanese maples seem fully leafed throughout. Full bloom dandelions, redbud, apple, red quince. Willow half leafed. Viburnum coming in at home.

2006: The yellow-bellied woodpecker continues its harsh call throughout the day – has been calling since February.

2007: Last night the wind blew hard across the village. I lay awake for a while and worried about the aging osage orange falling into the shed or crushing Jean's favorite redbud tree, maybe reaching the new porch and taking out the past summer's work.

This morning before sunrise I am sitting on that porch; we all survived the storm unscathed. The sky is clear deep blue, Jupiter still visible in the southwest. The robins have been singing for more than an hour; cardinals and doves just joined in a few minutes ago. Now the shiny grackles come through the high trees, gliding from their secret nests; cackling and clucking, they move down among the black branches.

When I first came outside, I looked for light frost on the grass, but the lawn was wet and dark. Now it reflects the glow in the east behind me over Glen Helen. The air is humid and still. Crows call to the west, and I hear the crows I hunted as a child in Wisconsin. They were wily, untouchable crows, and they watched me from high cottonwoods until I stepped within maybe a city block of them, and then up they went screaming.

I open the journal of Thomas Merton that I have been reading this past week, captured by his journey toward death. It is still too dark to make out the words. I think about one of the things Peter Matthiessen learned from the Tibetan Book of the Dead, that "a man's last thoughts will determine the quality of his reincarnation." I am coming to the last year of Merton's life. I want to see what he was like in those last days. I want to read his last thoughts. Of course, my own last days and thoughts are what really concern me.

When it is light enough to read, I am pulled in a different direction. I am captured by the sunlight spreading down the locust trees that line the far edge of the property. I close the journal, and I wait for cabbage butterflies and the first bees.

2008: South to Crossville, Tennessee: Departing Yellow Springs at the beginning of redbud and crabapple bloom, the peak of dandelion, pear and serviceberry bloom, the high canopy flushed but still dominated by the darkness of branches. The redbuds mark the highways all the way into Tennessee, lush and violet against the gathering greens. Dogwoods marked the woods, especially south of Lexington and though the mountains near Knoxville and west. All the hills had lost their March gray, were now clumped with every shade of gold and emerald. Along the Clinch River valley, the canopy seemed complete for miles at a time. Throughout Tennessee, bridal wreath, snowball viburnum, fleabane, azalea, wisteria, pussy toes, lilac, thyme-leafed speedwell, iris, fire pink, wild strawberry, bluets, mountain laurel, and buckeye were all in flower.

2011: Cardinal heard at 5:20 this morning, singing steadily in the rain. Flooding in the yard continues, gray skies all day. Some grackles paired up in the front yard today; they have been gradually thinning at the back feeder, like the starlings did about a month ago. Greg's lily-of-the-valley patch is showing a lot of white buds. Our front crab apple is starting to bloom, as are many more in town. The azalea is trying to match the apples but is a little behind. Dandelions still very strong throughout my walk, redbuds full bloom, most pears coming down, their white petals covering patches of the sidewalk along High Street. The fifty red tulips in the circle garden remain erect and bright. Robin vespers at 8:00 this evening, but no grackles heard.

2012: A considerable contrast with last year on this date: Our front crab apple has been done blooming for at least a week, our azalea has been in full bloom for at least that long. Redbuds are all gone to leaves, only a couple of scraggly tulips are left, pears having dropped their petals in March, dandelions and violets gone, lily-of-the- valley full bloom now. Late this afternoon, I walked at the

Siebenthaler Fen, a wetland habitat along Big Beaver Creek. Yellow roses seen on the way there. Inventory: Horsetail, current, tall and common ragwort, viburnum in bloom, maples, buckeyes, euonymus vines, sweet Cicely in full flower, ironweed maybe two feet, skunk cabbage with huge leaves, garlic mustard, ground ivy, cattails, water willow, box elders, winter cress full, teasel stalks, large aster leaves, curly dock, corn salad in flower, the scrawny budded dogwoods that I saw at the quarry and the Koogler wetlands, red-winged blackbirds nesting and singing, meadow rue (not budded yet), small-flowered buttercup, spring cress, cowslip, black raspberry, a mimosa plant, rushes of swamp iris, parsnip leaves, hemlock, common violets, multiflora roses, geese flying back and forth, several unidentified foliage clusters, along with what may be a swamp saxifrage.

2013: I went outside at 3:50 this morning, frost on the grass, full moon setting in the southwest, only a few robins twittering. Suddenly at 3:55, the chorus began throughout the neighborhood. At 4:02, the cardinals came in. When I went back outside at 4:20, the doves and song sparrows were singing.

2015: The sweet cherry blossoms are gone now, their season short like that of the serviceberries. Along the south and north borders, hackberries are in flower.

2016: Peter Hayes reports: "First hummingbird on the feeder right outside our kitchen window." This is just a day later than the one sighted by Ruth Paige in 2008 and three days before Rebecca Ramsey-Fenton's in 1986. The small bright red insect noticed as I worked the garden getting ready to plant zinnias. Joe Pye plants just emerging, a couple taller. Near Jeanie's fern garden: sweet Cicely underway. Honeysuckles budded. Leaving the house with Jill at about 7:00 this evening, I saw that the first wild geranium and the very first red azalea blossom had opened in the dooryard garden (some azaleas down the street completely covered with pink blossoms). Walking home at dusk, I heard robins and cardinals at vespers. When I arrived home, I found the first June bug under the porch light. Peter Hayes also reported his first June bug tonight. In 1981, I found the first June bug on the 26th.

2017: Muxia, Spain: Flowers tucked into the walls around the city, some sorrel, some speedwell, some clovers, a few smaller purple thistles with leaves of variegated color - cream and green, many sow thistles - as always, tall mallows, and many fields of wild calla lilies only a little past their prime. From Yellow Springs Jill sends a photo of the circle garden full of blossoming hyacinths.

A floating chronology is a sequence of events whose dates are all known in relation to one another, yet the time when the sequence as a whole occurred is unknown.

Martin Gorst

Bill Felker

April 26th
The 116th Day of the Year

Fair daffodils, we weep to see
You haste away so soon:
As yet the early-rising sun
Has not attained its noon. Stay, stay,
Until the hasting day
Has run
But to the evening;
And having prayed together, we
Will go with you along.
We have short time to stay as you;
We have as short a spring;
As quick a growth to meet decay
As you or anything.
We die
As your hours do, and dry
Away
Like to the summer's rain;
Or as the pearls of morning's dew,
Ne'er to be found again.

Robert Herrick

Sunrise/set: 5:42/7:24
Day's Length: 13 hours 42 minutes
Average High/Low: 66/45
Average Temperature: 55
Record High: 88 - 1986
Record Low: 30 - 1919

Weather
Today brings some of the best odds for sun and warmth so far this spring. Highs rise to the 80s on 30 percent of the afternoons, to the 70s on 35 percent, making April 26th the day most likely to be warm in the first four months of the year. Sixties occur 15 percent of the time, and cooler 50s the remaining 20

percent. Skies are clear to partly cloudy 70 percent of the days, and rain occurs just one year out of five. This is one of two April days on which frost almost never strikes (the 30th is the other day).

Natural Calendar

Late Spring arrives when the antlers of deer begin to grow, when the first parsnips bloom, the first indigo bunting arrives, the last daffodils disappear, and bumble bees come out for pollen. The first blue jay is born in the first days of Late Spring, and all the garden weeds are sprouting. In the woods, wild phlox, wild geranium, wild ginger, celandine, spring cress, sedum, golden Alexander, thyme-leafed speedwell, garlic mustard and common fleabane are budding and blooming.

Black tadpoles swim in the backwaters. Bass move to the shallows. Great brown "June" bugs *phyllophaga)* begin their evening flights. Allergy season intensifies with Late Spring, the time when trees are in full flower throughout the Great Plains, the Northeast, the Northwest and the Rocky Mountains. And in the Southeast, all the grasses are coming into bloom.

Daybook

1981: First at the screen door.

1982: First pie cherry blooms in the back yard.

1983: Covered Bridge: Wild phlox is strong now, purple and blue, white violets common, first ragwort at the swamp, first white trout lily, lots of toad trillium, small flowered buttercups, bluebells. Only a few violet cress in bloom, one last twinleaf, no bloodroot.

1984: Cascades: First day in the 80s. Toothwort full, some Solomon's seal open, bellwort budding. Rue anemone, trillium grandiflorum, yellow trout lily, hepatica, bloodroot, violet cress, toad trillium, bluebells, cowslip, meadow rue all open and still in the middle of Middle Spring. Jack-in-the-pulpit up but not fully formed.

1985: Fleabane blooms in the lawn. Trip to Washington, DC: From Springfield east, the canopy is green, thick and young, not completely full. Some May sweet rocket in bloom by Zanesville. Dogwoods are open on the hillsides, coltsfoot all gone to seed in the Pennsylvania mountains, probably in full bloom two weeks ago. North Maryland is lush with viburnum, redbuds, and bridal wreath, apple orchards full bloom, dogwood scattered through the hills, low mountains yellow-green with trees in flower. Roadside staghorn sumacs are getting leaves, sycamores and maples with half-size leaves. In Washington, everything is in full bloom, azaleas prominent. Yellow poplar leaves are completely formed, and Virginia creeper. Garlic mustard almost gone.

1988: Ginkgo and sugar gum leafing, tree line has a full green tint, but the oaks are still bare, open branches still predominate in North Glen (like between Columbia, South Carolina up the mountains into Asheville this March 28th). Garlic mustard very early bloom now,. Raspberries budding. Connie writes: "On Tuesday (the 26th) there was a circus of shad spawning, which had the community in an uproar. People came from all over (I saw a car from Greene County) to check it out. The kids were trying to snag them with bare hooks - they were that thick."

1989: Rhubarb has huge seed heads, and the stalks are big enough for pie. Middle Spring is ending, garlic mustard early bloom. From Clifton Road, looking into the creek valley, the tree line finally has major patches of pale green. Redbuds full bloom. Library crab apples just beginning. At home, the apple and cherry are fully open, dogwoods in town pacing them. Cactus cress full bloom South Glen.

1990: Viburnum in full bloom at Wilberforce. Saw two squirrels mating in the back trees.

1991: Common fleabane has been out for a few days. Raspberries full bloom. Apple petal fall starts today, honeysuckles budding, plums and cherries still hold all their flowers.

1992: Dandelion fields have gone to seed.

1993: First mosquito in the house this morning. Bleeding hearts full bloom. Early daffodils in the south garden fade, middle varieties still strong, some just opening. Redbuds brighter, just beginning to open. Spring beauties full bloom in village lawns. Purple magnolia dropping petals. Foliage coming out on the forsythia, some bushes half yellow, half green. Blue jays very loud and aggressive. Some of the Japanese knotweed comes up to my chest. Asiatic lilies a foot or more, daylilies a little taller. First winter cress seen on the way to Wilberforce. Garlic mustard has shot up in the last two days, is budding now. First forget-me-nots in the east garden.

1995: Winter cress seen in full bloom on the way to Wilberforce. Tulips have peaked. Ranunculus/buttercup is budding in the south garden. First wild ranunculus opens in the lawn. The witch hazel along Dayton Street and the red oak at the school yard have just started to leaf; the lindens in the triangle park are a little ahead of them. Box elder leaves are getting big now, maybe a third of their full size. Brunera flowered for the first time this afternoon. Silver maples are leafing everywhere, filling out lush with seeds and new foliage. Red maples are red-orange with large new seedpods. Honeysuckles and peonies are budding.

1998: Bluebells about gone in the yard, only a few blossoms hold. First azalea petals spread out this morning, they have seemed ready to open for days now. In the pond, another fish has disappeared: Flash, who was orange with white markings. Goldie, the most skittish and spacey of the coy, was taken by some predator at the end of March. She had been our favorite fish, unusual in her yellow and black markings, and quite excitable. When we fed the school, the others would come to the surface and feed right away, but Goldie would race back and forth along the bottom until she calmed down and finally came to the top to get the last pieces. I remember reading something in Isaac Walton about a frog that leapt on the back of a giant pickerel and hung on until the fish was exhausted and finally expired. And several years ago, Mrs. Bletzinger told me how she had witnessed a frog jump on the back of one of her pond carp and cling to it until they both disappeared beneath the water. In the case of Goldie, I suspect her killer might be Jacques, the green frog which came to the pond last fall. I imagine him crouching under one of the flat stones of the waterfall at the west end of the pond. As the fish come to feed in the algae by the running water, he leaps out in ambush, rides his prey to his lair under the falls where he holds it in the dark until it expires.

2000: Money plants are full blue, and bleeding hearts now have large red and white hearts in the east gardens; the first wild strawberry flowers in the back lawn. Bluebells in the yard are holding. Azaleas full bloom. Along the path north toward Springfield, pink and white honeysuckles are in early bloom on a few bushes. Cressleaf groundsel, like huge sensuous winter cress, is budding in the wet ditches. Garlic mustard is in full flower. The first sweet rocket is open. Cardinals still fly back and forth across the path, but the grackles from earlier this month have disappeared or grown silent, guarding their nests.

2001: Pink quince, star of Bethlehem, and celandine open today as redbuds turn pale and get their leaves. Dandelions still at their peak. Strawberries full bloom, rhubarb ready for pie. Amy says she found a box turtle on April 21st. She also told me that morels emerge when May apples are completely out of the ground.

2004: Hostas half size, astilbes well developed. The tree line along the highway are pale green. Violets, pale pink azaleas, dead nettle, one bluebell, and lilacs full bloom. Early to middle petal-fall of apples about town, but our redbud, the new red crabapple, and the red tulips below it are in full bloom. Celandine has been open for two days. All daffodils dead-headed. Oak-leaf hydrangea leaves are about two inches long. Asiatic and Oriental lilies are one to two feet tall. Red quince has finished its cycle.

2005: Robins begin their chorus at 3:55 a.m. EST, cardinal at 4:15.

2006: Neysa reports red termites swarming in her apartment in Miami Beach.

2007: The first star of Bethlehem has opened in the north garden. First garlic mustard flowers seen in the boulevard in front of our house. Two viburnum shrubs from North Carolina and most of our forsythia very slow coming back, may be seriously damaged. The bamboo leaves have been shedding more rapidly as new growth has begun on its branches. Peonies and lily of the valley have very small buds, and many ferns are over a foot tall. Bittersweet buds showing some green.

2008: At the Daniel Boone State Park near Richmond, Kentucky, we found a woods full of Miami Mist, wild blue phlox, larkspur and white violets. Dogwoods and redbuds here, the tremendous varieties of luminescent greens, the same as through the mountains to the south, mark this time of the year the very best for driving the Border States.

2009: Sleeping with the windows open, we heard the robin chorus start about 5:00 a.m. First cardinals and doves noticed at 5:20. Nine-bark leaves are losing their yellow newborn color. White and red mulberry trees are budding now.

2011: Celandine seen in bloom this morning as we walked around the yard, and redbud flowers are falling. Dogwoods are open now around the neighborhood, a nice one at the Catholic church – their Japanese maple fully leafed, and blue speedwells in the lawns, white daffodils at Don's (his cherry tree still in bloom). Our crab apple has begun to bloom. Bleeding hearts in full flower in the alley, and knotweed has grown up to six feet. Violets, dandelions, lilacs, creeping Charlie and deadnettle at their best, red quince dwindling, honeysuckles deeply budded. Clouds gave way a little to sun this afternoon, but tornadoes ravaged Arkansas last night. April has seen the most tornadoes in April history. Tonight, vespers of robins, cardinals and sparrows. From Vermont, Cathy writes: "Spring has sprung here - daffodils are up and blooming. The vole has become bold and runs through the room with us in it. He just ran past me, not 4 feet away. I can hear him (or her) in the kitchen rummaging around. Maybe it's time to set the live trap. I'll miss its company."

2012: The first purple clematis opened on the trellis today, many more seen throughout town. Black walnuts pace the American beech trees leafing out, leaves about a fourth of their full size. And

I wonder at the beauty and wisdom in this repetition, accumulation, rhythm, the song, the adventure of the recurring path: so that each fragment is blessed with such a history and promise that summary is impossible, that only enumeration can quiet the hunger for understanding.

2013: The robins and cardinals were in full song when I went out this morning at 4:45. Middle Spring quickly bringing down pear petals and serviceberry petals. Forsythia darkening and losing its flowers, filling in with leaves – so that the hedge in front of the house offers complete privacy now. Honeysuckles are well leafed now and developing buds. The latest daffodils hold, and tulips are still prominent. Paulownia buds continuing to expand, but not leafing yet. Peonies with prominent small buds. Rhubarb bushy. If I had a larger patch, the stalks would provide a pie. At the quarry, redbuds, pears planted by birds were in full flower, a very early weigela was open.

2014: Don's pie cherry tree is in bloom, as are all the pears and redbuds, crab apples coming in a little late, off schedule. Star magnolia leaves pace the dusky leaves of the serviceberry trees. Red quince still full along the northeast fence. At the south entrance to the North Glen, Jack-in-the-pulpits, toad trilliums, nodding trilliums. At home, the first small fritillary, the first cabbage white, and the first sulphur – the first butterflies of the year in the yard. Vicki sent a message: the robin eggs that she had been watching all week hatched today.

2015: Hosta transplanting time: almost all the plants are up a little, many a foot or so. In the triangle park, all the crab apples are in full flower. First celandine found in bloom by the south wall, and the struggling white bleeding heart that Jeanie planted has blossoms. Four cabbage whites whirl in spring randori through the back yard, the first time I've seen more than one at time. Allium well budded. On the college lawn, masses of spring beauties, violets, dandelions. Throughout the village, crab apples full and coming in, some pears leafing. Rachel's ginkgo has foliage half an inch long.

From Goshen, Indiana, Judy lists the following plants

found on her walk today, confirming her season about ten days behind the Yellow Springs season: "purple (deep purple and blue) and yellow violets, spring beauty, wood anemone, false rue anemone, cut-leaf toothwort, trout lily, Dutchman's britches, wild blue phlox, bloodroot, nodding trillium and two-leafed toothwort. And of course garlic mustard, just budding. I always want to yank it up. The big trilliums aren't out yet. This weekend we'll go to the park in Benton and see Solomon's seal, huge fields of big trilliums and spring beauty, toad trilliums and more. May apples are up but of course not budding yet."

2016: The wood hyacinths are in full bloom now, and the first Indian hyacinth started to flower overnight. A few late daffodils hold on to highlight the violets of the hyacinths. Some tulips still keep their petals, but they are getting raggedy and disheveled. Near the porch, the blue windflowers still keep their blossoms, but the glory-of-the-snow is down to maybe a fourth of its earlier glory. The orange trumpet creeper at the southwest corner of the patio is just starting to send out its leaf buds. The bluebells by the annex-shed are weakening now, stalks long and gangly like on this day in 1998. I planted the northwest zinnia plot this morning, moved some goldenrod put in two small dogwoods one on either side of the north trellis. First honeysuckle blossom seen along Limestone Street. An entire row of full blooming, purple iris seen near Greene Street.

Can trouble live with April days,
Or Sadness with the summer moons?

Alfred , Lord Tennyson

April 27th
The 117th Day of the Year

We praise now this renewal of the year:
Happy are they
who find their love therein,
their heart's desire.

Manuscript of Benedictbeuren
(bf)

Sunrise/set: 5:41/7:25
Day's Length: 13 hours 44 minutes
Average High/Low: 66/45
Average Temperature: 55
Record High: 90 - 1986
Record Low: 28 - 1907

Weather

Now a day in the 90s becomes possible; and there is a 30 percent chance of a high in the 80s, and a 25 percent chance for 70s. Highs in the cooler 60s occur on another 25 percent of the afternoons; chilly 50s come 15 percent of the years, and 40s once in a decade. Skies are mostly clear seven years in ten, and rain falls just three years in ten. There is a fifteen percent chance for frost.

Natural Calendar

The garlic mustard of Late Spring comes into bloom when the first indigo bunting reaches the Ohio Valley. Crocus and purple deadnettle leaves turn yellow in the grass as the growing canopy turns the hillsides green. Cobwebs appear overnight, glisten with morning dew. Most dandelions have gone to seed, and ruby-throated hummingbirds arrive at their northern feeders. There are buds on the black raspberries, mock orange, and mulberries. Star of Bethlehem and wood hyacinths have come up in the garden. Nettles are waist high along the fencerows.

Daybook

1979: The apple and cherry trees are have started blooming today.

1983: Crocus leaves turning yellow. Tulips in the yard are at their peak, first cherry and apple blossoms in the yard, magnolias holding throughout town.

1984: Ginger blooming. First white violet seen. Bloodroot finished for the year, wing-like leaves growing huge. Twinleaf gone, Dutchman's britches mostly gone. One white trout lily seen. Skunk cabbage leaves have grown to two feet. Water cress, swamp buttercup full bloom. Kingfisher seen nesting near the Covered Bridge. At home, first small flowers on the bleeding hearts.

1986: Clifton Gorge, 7:00 a.m. Most of the upper canopy still bare. First honeysuckle flower, first catchweed, first Solomon's plume, first garlic mustard, first star of Bethlehem. Geese fly over. Herd of ten deer seen, all does. Patches of dewy cobwebs on the grass. Small-flowered buttercup going to seed. Spring beauties, closed before sunrise, start to open at 7:30, are completely out by 8:15. Sweet Cicely low and young. Rich sweet pollen scent in the air. Ragwort, trillium grandiflorum, phlox, miterwort full bloom. Bluets discovered, full bloom. First Virginia creeper leaves. Mint a foot tall. Poison ivy vines three inches. First ladybug. First wild geranium. First goslings of the year, yellow and fuzzy, maybe a week or ten days old. In the village, first iris opens.

1987: First major crop of dandelions goes to seed.

1989: Yard and South Glen: Green stink bug found in the garden. First tick got in my hair. Peonies bushy and tall now, normal size. Ash leafs now, poplar leaves half size. First celandine flowers. Buds on the sweet Cicely. Violets, dandelions, winter cress, toad trillium, toothwort, bluebells, spring beauties, meadow rue, Jack-in-the-pulpit, thyme-leafed speedwell full bloom, shepherd's purse late. Nettles: some past my ankles. Early full bloom of the garlic mustard. Wild lettuce is bushy, paces the field thistles, the angelica and nettles, has maybe ten-inch leaves. Honey locust budding. Swallows on the river, and a female scarlet tanager in the bushes by the river bank. In the village, tulips full bloom. Honeysuckles bud as grapes leaf out.

1991: Major petal fall season begins with pears, spreads to the apples. Wind throughout the day, cherries begin to lose hold in the afternoon. In the lawn, purple deadnettle is yellowing. First star of Bethlehem opens at the garden gate. First horseradish blossoms in the garden, first patches of yellow ranunculus at the south wall. First pyrethrums budding. All daffodils, hyacinth, and all the Early Spring bulbs gone, the east garden full of dandelions and violets now. First honeysuckles bloom.

1993: Half of my tomato sprouts killed by frost this morning. First celandine flowers found in the east garden. First bat seen around 9:00 p.m. Some house finches brighter red.

1994: Celandine and garlic mustard opened yesterday or this morning in the east garden. Most of the small, late daffodils are still blooming there. Tulips full in the north wall garden, ferns just starting to come up along the house, a foot high in the back bed. Asiatic lilies lush, some a foot high. Rhubarb seed heads fully developed, two and a half feet tall. Lilacs suddenly in bloom all over town, and crab apples and buckeyes, too. Cherries and redbuds hold. Wild hyacinth found at the Covered Bridge. Water cress and wild phlox full bloom along Grinnell, wild ginger open, first Jacob's ladder. Wild geranium and ragwort well underway.

1996: The white lilacs are blooming - actually a little ahead of schedule in spite of the bitter cold.

1998: Late bloom of all the lilacs. Sun and cool today, greenhouse windows steamed from the contrast with the warm and humid indoor air. In the south garden, sweet Cecily is about eight or nine inches high and fully budded. The pink quince has long buds, almost twice as long as our azalea buds and ready to open. The largest tadpoles have spots or speckles today. Purple loosestrife in the pond is well along, maybe eighteen inches high. The pickerel plant is four to five, the lake rushes two feet plus. The water lily plant has sent up five leaves, but they are small, maybe two or three inches in diameter. Yesterday Jeanie brought home watercress and water hyacinths and duck plant, a small algae like plant that spreads across the top of the water. Things are looking like May.

1999: First garlic mustard and celandine seen. Cowslip still strong, and ragwort. First water lily leaf reaches the top of the pond, first major dandelion seeding throughout the countryside.

2000: North Glen: Solomon's plume and seal, full trillium grandiflorum, colombo (*frasera caroliniensis*) still holding at basal leaves, early wild geraniums, full wild phlox, some ragwort, a few toad trillium, May apples and ginger budding, Jack-in-the-pulpit, full miterwort, late periwinkles, violets declining, the canopy above still open. In town, apple petalfall almost complete, a few redbuds leafing.

2001: Buds on the silver olives, the first honeysuckles, and the blackberries at Middle Prairie. One yellow swallowtail seen, two admirals, one small black butterfly with prominent white bars on its wings.

2002: First buttercup in the south garden. Rose of Sharon starting to leaf. Wild grape and Virginia creeper leaves are half size. Cressleaf groundsel is tall and full bloom everywhere. North garden ferns are two feet, hops six feet and reaching for the upper branches of the budding honeysuckles. Rhubarb ready for pie. First two red azalea flowers appear in the front yard.

2005: Cowslip has disappeared, but ragwort is in full bloom across from the Covered Bridge. The first dandelion patches are going to seed.

2006: Thyme-leaved speedwell noticed blooming along Dayton Street this morning.

2007: One patch of dandelions near the freeway completely gone to seed. Doves are nesting in the trellis by our front sidewalk. Winter cress in full bloom at Peggy's, one cressleaf groundsel plant open beside the sewer drain. Some lilacs have a few blooms, single purple flowers, some raggedy white clusters. I noticed that the first wood hyacinth had budded in the apple tree garden.

2008: Returning home from Tennessee, we watched the canopy thin as leaves ceded to buds. The dandelions that had all gone to seed in Kentucky reappeared and had taken over our lawn. The first wood hyacinth was budding in the circle garden, the star of Bethlehem was budding, lilacs were about a fourth out, peonies full of round buds, thyme-leafed speedwell had bloomed. Peach flowers were almost gone, much of the forsythia had gone to leaves, but the pink azalea was open, the red azalea with colorful buds, all of the apples and redbuds were in full bloom. In the pond, the head of our white and black koi, Emmett, had turned a solid pink while we were gone. Before supper, we went out with machete and shovel to cut off the bamboo sprouts that had taken over the south yard. Some of the shoots were more than a couple of feet tall.

2011: Rain continues much of the day here, with more tornadoes in the South. Outside the shop where I work, creeping phlox full bloom. Across from the Covered Bridge, the cowslip is still in flower. Throughout town, lilacs and crab apples are full, pears leafing or leafed, pink magnolias shedding. Rachel's ginkgo's leaves are about a third developed. The first large patch of dandelions along Limestone Street has gone to seed.

2012: In Peggy's garden, violet iris and geraniums together. At home, the pink azalea blazes in the sun, and all the purple wood hyacinths are still in bloom. Lilacs are decaying quickly in the yard, but full in many other places. Another trip to the quarry: Two fingerling bluegills rescued from a drying pond area, brought over to a deeper pool. Many tadpoles found there. Locusts in full bloom all around, dogbane about a foot high, daisies flowering by the side of the road. Remnants of small white asters in one large field. Winter wheat deep green, maybe a foot or two high, and waving in the wind.

And Judy writes from Goshen, Indiana (200 miles northwest of Yellow Springs): "We slogged through the aptly-named Parson's Swamp Woods on Wednesday and saw marsh buttercup, Jack-in-the-pulpit, trillium, paw-paw blossoms, fleabane, sweet cicely, blossoming May apple, violets of all kinds, wild ginger and wild geraniums. Today we drove for about an hour to a nature preserve on the edge of a moraine. Much upping and downing over lovely woods, rife with large trillium, some pollinated; blue-eyed Mary, Canada waterleaf, false Solomon's seal and hairy Solomon's seal, cleavers, wood poppy, nodding trillium, bishop's cap, Canada violet, more Jack-in-the-pulpit and acres of blue phlox and wild geranium, along with ramps, hepatica leaves, and bloodroot leaves with flower pods for next year. Also one odd plant: puttyroot, a member (although a really unspectacular one, I must say) of the orchid family. We saw all three stages: leaf, shoot, and old flowers on a stalk."

2013: First garlic mustard blossoms seen, and first speedwell. Don's cherry and our sweet cherry keep their petals, the flowering of apple trees spreading through the village. Viburnums with multicolored flower clusters in bloom. Ferns up one to two feet. Alliums, Indian hyacinths and wood hyacinths are budded. Hostas offer color now in the some yards.

2014: Moya showed me another praying mantis ootheca in her yard yesterday, this one attached to a raspberry bush. Her bleeding heart did not come back this year, but she has a new abundance of Mrs. Lawson's yellow heirloom tulips (with pointed petals).

2015: Still and chilly in the middle 30s, sky clear. First robins twittering at 4:22 a.m. EST, no birds earlier when I walked Bella around the block. Perennial salvia and two rhododendron shrubs planted. Bur oak leaves one inch across from the Antioch gym. I jogged to Ellis Pond for the first time in decades: Scarlet oaks and ashes budding with some flowers; white oak with very small leaves; sycamore leaves at least an inch long.

2016: Cold today after a nice warm spell and thunderstorms (tornadoes in the Central Plains. At Jill's honeysuckles and the first burning bush flowering, blue speedwell in patches of her lawn. Deep into North Glen away from the river toward the Pine Forest area: bluebells wearing down, lanky chickweed flowering all across the forest floor, occasional Jack-in-the pulpits, large-flowered trilliums, spring cress, abundant garlic mustard and wild geraniums, common ragwort, tall ragwort, buttercups, white violets.

From the moist meadow to the wither'd hill,
Led by the breeze, the vivid verdure runs,
And swells and deepens, to the cherish'd eye.

James Thomson

Bill Felker

April 28th
The 118th Day of the Year

Late Spring,
Wild Phlox,
Sedum, Ginger,
Miterwort, Mustard,
Bellwort, Celandine,
Poppies, Buttercups,
Catchweed, Larkspur,
Peonies, Rue.

Hepatica Sun

Sunrise/set: 5:39/7:26
Day's Length: 13 hours 47 minutes
Average High/Low: 67/45
Average Temperature: 56
Record High: 85 - 1894
Record Low: 29 - 1934

Weather
The 28th is one of the cloudier days in late April, overcast more than half the time, rain falling 45 percent of the years. The high temperature distribution: five percent chance for 80s, fifty-five percent for 70s, ten percent for 60s, twenty-five percent for 50s, five percent for 40s. Frost: one morning in ten.

Natural Calendar
Garden chives bloom when the first tall grass heads up at the approach of Late Spring. Black walnut trees leaf out and the green ash trees blossom while the maple flowers collapse all at once. Pussy willow leaves are racing with the box elders, both about half size. Poplar leaves are half an inch, some garlic mustard 12 to 18 inches. Mulberry buds are greening.

The Stars
Before sunrise, Hercules has moved to near the center of

the sky. The Summer Triangle, which includes Vega, Altair, and Deneb, is just a little east of Hercules. The Milky Way passes through the Triangle, separating it from autumn's Pegasus rising on the eastern horizon. The Corona Borealis has shifted into the western half of the heavens, and the pointers of the Big Dipper point almost exactly east-west.

Daybook

1981: Frist dogwood seen in bloom.

1982: Cascades habitat: Hepatica declining now. Honeysuckle ready to bloom. Early meadow rue opening.

1983: Cascades: Very first garlic mustard blooms, first bellwort. One columbine ready to open. Some Dutchman's britches and hepatica holding on here. Some miterwort and ragwort open. Three or four blue jays fly around the yard, noisy. Cardinal nesting in the rose bush by the apple tree. Viburnum at Wilberforce with tight green flower clusters.

1984: To Washington, DC: Foliage from Yellow Springs to Hagerstown, Pennsylvania consistent; the Greene County climate holding three hundred miles east through the Appalachians. Coltsfoot full bloom in the mountains. Down toward Washington, everything comes into bloom.

1985: Sweet rocket in bloom. Osage flowers barely open as the last apple blossom fades.

1986: First hummingbird reported by Rebecca Ramsey, a week before the average date for their arrival. Baby blue jays seen just out of the nest. Black walnuts leafing, late maples just starting to leaf. Snowball viburnum starting as the late maples start to leaf. Bridal wreath opens along Short Street. Starlings seen building nest.

1987: First baby robin found, blown from its nest in last night's storm. Viburnum full bloom, parallel with the late flowering crabs. Full time of winter cress, some pastures completely golden, tree line yellow-green. Pokeweed is emerging now. South Glen: Starling nesting at Sycamore Hole, the big sycamore has small leaves now. Jack-in-the-pulpit is out, wild ginger flowering. Waterleaf is budding. Hepatica done blooming. The undergrowth is ankle high, solid with catchweed, waterleaf. Garlic mustard is up to my thighs in early bloom.

1988: Connie's letter: "Then on Thursday (the 28th) – a chilly, nasty day – I saw our first set of seven ducklings. There were blossoms on the wild strawberries and everything seemed all right with the world."

1989: Osage and tree of heaven start to leaf together

1990: Apples late full, petals falling in the wind, cherry too, tulips late, most gone. Lily-of-the valley early bloom. Now the blue speedwell is completely open, the ranunculus came in two days ago, the last hyacinth fading. Sweet rockets budding, garlic mustard early full, strawberries heavy with full bloom, rhubarb more than ready, garlic knee high and strong, knotweed waist high, blue jays building nest in the apple tree. Purple lilacs have all emerged in the last week of 80 degree highs. Honeysuckles budding. Peonies budding, goosefoot sprouting. Hosta six inches, some ferns a foot and a half high. Pines have new growth. Buds on the pyrethrums. Now the whole landscape is greening except for the highest canopy.

1993: Very first garlic mustard seen. Harlan reports that the cherry trees in Washington DC were in full bloom the first week of April. Yellow Springs cherries are full now, one or two apples in bloom, the rest budding. This has been such a cold, Late Spring. Lilacs ready to open in some places. Cabbage butterflies seen mating at Grinnell Pond.

1995: At Grinnell Pond: Middle Spring is through. Only an occasional toothwort remains from that season. Hepatica, Dutchman's britches, twinleaf, bloodroot gone. Ginger is tall and wide open. The first wild phlox is blooming, and the first bed of wild geraniums. Delicate miterwort stands straight up full bloom from the green rocks. Jack-in-the-pulpit completely developed. Solomon's seal and plume budded, near full size. The undergrowth rises quickly now, swelling to reach its peak before the canopy closes in May.

1996: To Chicago for Luke's birthday and high-school graduation party. The landscape appeared stable with little change as we drove north, the roadside grasses bright green, trees in flower. In Chicago, though, the magnolias were in full bloom, whereas they had been almost all down in Yellow Springs. Early and middle daffodils were in full bloom, but in Yellow Springs they were almost gone. Redbuds were full both places. On the return trip, it seemed easier to see the difference in the trees. In Chicago, there was intense movement, buds unraveling, flowering; into Ohio, the flowers were peaking, and the season of leafing was dominant.

1998: The very first sweet rocket of the year flowered this morning at the east end of the south wall garden, the same day as in warm 1985. Across from the Covered Bridge, the ragwort is huge, replacing the brightness of the wilted cowslip. Around the house the forsythia leaves have created a full barrier now, and the honeysuckles have done the same thing along the north and west sides of the yard. The pruned red mulberry trees on the north border are sprouting leaves. Snowball viburnum seen along Elm Street, green-white, early bloom. The year slipping deeper and deeper into Late Spring.

1999: Toad sings off and on all day and night in the rain. Second leaf on the water lily.

2000: First buttercup in the south garden.

2001: First rhubarb pie from the garden patch.

2002: The robin chorus gets underway after a thunderstorm this morning: 4:33 a.m. Cardinal heard at 5:10.

2003: First web by a long-jawed orbweaver spun across the pond last night. I collected the first pink quince petals from the water.

2004: I was digging in the garden, had worked up a sweat and was resting in the shade of the back porch, sipping a glass of iced tea. Sparrows were chirping steadily in the full-blooming honeysuckle bushes nearby. The sky was clear blue, and a light west wind was moving the high trees.

My pulse was up from the garden work, and as I rested, I checked my heartbeat with the second hand of my wristwatch: 75 beats a minute. I rested a little more, looking out over the purple lilacs, and listening to the birds.
The sparrows were so loud, and so steady, and then I realized that they were chirping at about the same rate as my heart was beating.

I checked my watch and I timed their song. Their vocalizations were a metronome matched to the beating of my heart. That evening, I was walking my dog through the neighborhood and I noticed robins chirping their familiar, up-and-down singsong call, and again I timed my rhythm and the birds' rhythm and found they blended almost perfectly.

Since then, I've found the correspondence between my pulse and birdsong to be a little less consistent than I first discovered, but I wonder still about how many other rhythms I may be part of -- and there must be so many more -- rhythms of which I have no awareness but with which I am doubtlessly in sync, rhythms which not only measure out and pace my life, but which also give it context and even its most fundamental meaning.

2005: A mother cardinal has been nesting in the bamboo along the south wall since about the middle of the month. Red-bellied woodpecker must be nesting nearby, has been calling throughout the month, continues now.

2006: Toad trillium, wild phlox, one buttercup, sweet Cicely, a few trillium grandiflorum and plenty of garlic mustard seen on a walk this morning. The sycamores here are bare, but the ones along Corey Street have small, pale leaves. At home, a few small, red water lily leaves are moving toward the top of the pond.

2007: Two red oaks at the school park have leaves the size of a squirrel's ear. One oak's leaves are about an inch long. Black walnut trees and ashes have small leaves, one half to one inch, and tree of heaven branches are sprouting again after having been burned back by frost early in the month.

2008: Rain and sleet today, tomorrow night frost predicted. In the South Glen, summer rising: wood nettle, ironweed stalks.

2009: One cardinal call at 4:23 a.m., the rest of the cardinals, along with a blue jay, steady from 5:13.

2011: Continued rain this morning as tornadoes kill hundreds in the South. On Limestone Street, a few small, pale violet iris in bloom, all the pears have fully developed leaves. Near the Catholic Church, holly is starting to flower. Dogwoods are full everywhere in town. A quieter evening walk, cardinals singing, but no grackles clucking. Peggy's wild geraniums opened a couple of days ago; Mrs. Timberlake's are early full in the alley. On the south side of the house, the witch hazel is starting to put out leaves. A few wild strawberry flowers seen. Tree of heaven leaves-branches are a little more than an inch long now, the paulownia trees just a bit behind them, their swelling buds soft, layered, sensuous. The very first red azalea in the east garden bloomed in the rain this afternoon.

2012: Tall alliums are open in the circle garden and at Liz's on Stafford Street. Her early yellow rose has numerous flowers this morning, and she has one poppy in bloom.

2014: Pear petals coming down in the rain and wind. Deadly tornadoes yesterday and today across the nation's midsection and the South.

2015: Grackles continue to feed throughout the day – as they have for weeks. The first polygonia butterfly came to the yard, rested on one of the stone garden dividers. Mulberry leaves are half an inch long. The Danielsons' maple is in full flower. Lil's and Mrs. Timberlake's are leafing.

2016: Now the glory-of-the-snow patch is done for the year, but the windflower area is still filled with flowers. Bluebells almost gone. A few ranunculus in bloom along the southeast side of the house, their foliage finally spreading some. Scott told me about noticing Baltimore Orioles gobbling webworms. The webs appear just a little before the Orioles. Perhaps the birds follow the webs all the way up from the South, waiting to eat the hatching worms before they move on. Purple iris in full bloom throughout the village now, bridal wreath early full, the north-side viburnum in full flower, some snowball viburnum whitening.

2017: Finisterre, Spain: A beach habitat with mallow, ginestra, sow thistles, golden swamp iris, buttercups, Angelica (or hemlock), dark purple vetch, yellow daisies, speckled (pink and white) clover, English plantain and what appears to be a variety of black medic clover. It appears some hydrangeas (similar to Endless Summer variety) are starting to flower. Occasional viburnum/hydrangea bushes in bloom. The walk to the "end of the world" lighthouse was lined with blackberry brambles, white daisies, some nasturtiums, ferns and bushy fennel, yellow sweet clover, a few tall bushy plantains in bloom, a morning glory related low flower in the sand, elderberry bushes in flower along the roads and what appears to be a bridal wreath-like shrub. Only a couple of calla lilies noticed in the Finnisterre habitat.

A path comes into existence only when you observe it.

Werner Heisenberg

Bill Felker

April 29th
The 119th Day of the Year

The moon will never be
And never I so radiant.
Flowers only glow,
And time makes only darkness:
Nothing like the sun.

Neysa Jin (age 9)

Sunrise/set: 5:38/7:27
Day's Length: 13 hours 49 minutes
Average High/Low: 67/46
Average Temperature: 56
Record High: 87 - 1899
Record Low: 30 - 1977

Weather

An average April 29 brings rain five years in ten, with totally overcast conditions in the same proportion. Temperatures in the 80s or 90s are rarely recorded today, but highs in the 70s come 45 percent of the afternoons, with 60s occurring on another 45 percent. The remaining ten percent are in the 50s. Frost occurs one morning in five.

Natural Calendar

Rue anemone, Jack-in-the-pulpit, toothwort and large-flowered trilliums are in full bloom, early meadow rue and ragwort and bellwort almost ready, wild phlox budding too. May apples are budding. Ginger leaves have unfolded from the ground. Spring beauties fill the lawn at Antioch College. The all the grass in town and country take on the exciting vibrancy, intensity of April green, glow with life, as though its usually invisible aura could no longer be contained and took to shining.

Daybook

1983: Cardinal's nest in the wild rose bush has three tan, speckled eggs. Peony stalks flesh out with leaves, have tiny flower buds.

1984: Our pie cherry tree finally comes into bloom.

1985: Honeysuckle blooms.

1986: Very first raspberry flowers. In the greenhouse, one aloe flower spike is almost a foot and a half long.

1987: At Sycamore Hole, one shiner caught with scales turned pink and his snout bristly, far from the mid-year's normal pale silver and smooth surface. Above us, the canopy of leaves was closing in.

1988: Josh brought over a baby rabbit, maybe six inches long.

1989: Leafcup a foot and a half tall. Buckeyes flowering, parallel to the redbuds. Silver olive is half leafed. Tree line greening. North High Street canopy is closing with a combination of flowers and leaves. At John Bryan Park, the pasture grass is past my ankles now, the spring walks becoming wetter and a little slower. Maggie called from Madison, reports forsythia and daffodils, some tulips. It is April 12th there, Yellow Springs Time.

1990: Honeysuckle blooms. Dogwood full. At Clifton Gorge, miterwort, Solomon's plume, wild strawberry, sedum, sweet Cicely blossoming. Dock is budding. Most cherry and apple petals in the yard fell today. Last summer's catalpa seedpods suddenly falling now.

1991: Strawberries full bloom. Leafing intensifying in the second tier of the canopy, the oaks in bloom. Flower clusters falling from the sweet gum. Petal fall for flowering crabs has peaked. White fields of dandelions gone to seed. Iris just starting to bud at home, but Chris says her first one has opened. Purple loosestrife along the Ohio River is a foot tall.

1993: At South Glen: toothwort still holds, early trillium grandiflorum in bloom, early phlox, meadow rue. Toad trillium lush. Among the spring flowers, July's wood nettle has come up about six inches, leaves an inch long. Flickers noisy through the afternoon. In the yard, honeysuckle foliage begins to form a barrier against the street. Forsythia filling in too, half flowers, half green. Squirrels chasing each other in wild dramatic games through the tall locusts. Dandelions in full bloom, dense throughout. Viburnum now mostly full in the village. Purple loosestrife has come up the last day or so, it's a couple of inches tall this afternoon. Redbuds full.

1995: First wild cherry tree blooming. First daisy buds in the south garden. Spring beauties still hold on the Antioch green. Field penny cress grows lanky, pacing the winter cress. May apples are budding.

1998: The sweet Cicely is open along the south wall of the old house, the same day noticed as in 1990. Around the new blooms, dense bright sprouts of August's clearweed hide the ground. Star of Bethlehem seen at the corner of Grinnell and Wilberforce Clifton Roads. Full bloom of the early honeysuckle along Grinnell. Early bridal wreath along south Limestone. First leaves on the red buds. Full decay of dandelions. High canopy greening more. The seventh water lily leaf reached the surface of the pond over night. Fat pink buds of the late quince start to open in the morning. First horseradish flowers by noon. Comfrey waist high. The tallest knotweed is six feet.

2000: Cascades and high ridge: cowslips hold in the swampy areas; one patch of purple larkspur is in dramatic full bloom. Solomon's seal and Solomon's plume early opening. Shooting star, nodding trillium, blue cohosh in flower. One last trout lily, one last Dutchman's britches, fragments of the last toothworts, late bluebells being overgrown by garlic mustard. Small-flowered buttercup still here. Around town, the iris and poppies are budding and large-flowered celandine open.

2001: First blossoms on the wisteria at home – the first bloom after years of waiting. Ranunculus started yesterday, iris in Dayton on the 27th. Pyrethrums and daisies budding. Lilacs hold full. Poison ivy leaves start to show up in the north garden.

2002: Bridal wreath starts at Susi's.

2003: Cressleaf groundsel is about a foot high in the north garden, its first yellow flowers opening today. First blossoms noticed on the wisteria.

2005: Very first cressleaf groundsel bud unravels, first sweet Cicely seen. Pink quince opening, bamboo now seven feet tall. Catmint full and bushy. Bluebells hold. Forsythia and honeysuckle all leafed out. Green frog still here.

2006: First pink quince petals falling. In just the last day or two, green flower clusters have appeared at the north-garden viburnum. Very first wood hyacinth opens. Star of Bethlehem now in full early bloom. Late-season tulips are now blossoming. Buds noticed on the new wisteria (two years old). Dandelion bloom is done in the yard and around town.

2007: Garden dug for lettuce and spinach. Stella d'oro lilies transplanted. Several wood hyacinth buds getting ready to open. Dandelions still beautiful throughout the lawn. Wisteria buds are lengthening. Rose of Sharon buds greening. More strawberries blooming. Celandine noticed flowering. Pink flowering buckeye fully budded at the school park.

2008: The tree line that looked so bare when we returned from Tennessee a few days ago continues to fill in quickly. The honeysuckles around the yard have provided a complete barrier now. Rose of Sharon is leafing, as are the river birches near Fairborn. The serviceberry trees that were blooming on the 25th have leafed out so quickly. Pears still have flowers, but leaves predominate. Don's late pink magnolia is aging, his pie cherry full late bloom. All the crab apple trees in town are lush and fragrant. The red quince flowers are starting to be overrun by leaves. Late-season tulips and the white daffodils are at their best, mid-season varieties losing petals. Jerusalem artichoke foliage has emerged, leaves about two inches long. Cressleaf groundsel seems ready to flower – the smaller variety already open near the fading cowslips at the Covered Bridge. Garlic mustard is in full bloom all over the area. The evening robin mating chorus seems to have stopped, although robins and doves still call.

2009: The blue jay was calling again this morning a little after 5:00. He has been present for almost a week now, adding a new rhythm to the early birdsong. In the alley today, Mrs. Timberlake's bridal-wreath spirea is just starting to bloom. Don's pie cherry is done blooming, and the service berry leaves are summer green and about full size. Black walnut flowers are all over the sidewalk in front of the Lawsons'. Red quince flowers are being pushed out by leaves. Cressleaf groundsel opened in a few places yesterday. Bamboo stalks are up to seven feet tall. In Wilmington, the Judd viburnum along the highway has lost all its petals. From Xenia south, the dandelion bloom is over and winter cress is in full flower across the pastures. A large patch of iris in bloom seen outside of Xenia. Walking Bella tonight, I saw the end of dandelions near Lawson Place.

2010: Buds on the oakleaf hydrangea, first purple flower on the perennial salvia, first raspberry flower in the garden, Liz's allium opening.

2011: Oakleaf hydrangea leaves are small but well formed. Bridal wreath is budding in the alley, and the first wisteria is open on the garden trellis. Witch hazel and trumpet vine finally pushing out a few leaves. Box elder bugs mating. One of the middle summer myrtles has put out a small red sprout. Mrs. Lawson's yellow tulips have all faded, but some of the late varieties at home are still strong. Bamboo is past six feet now, Jerusalem artichokes up a few inches. Don's pie cherry is just starting to lose its flower petals, as are some of the crab apples in the Bill Duncan park. Cardinals and a red-bellied woodpecker at dusk.

2012: The crepe myrtles developed numerous small red leaves throughout April this year. Jeni reports from Portland, Oregon: The tulips are in late full bloom at the tulip festival there.

2013: Lilacs and crab apples full throughout the village (but our apple still holding back), bridal wreath spirea with small buds, pacing the honeysuckles. A few petals falling from Don's cherry, the leaves on his serviceberry trees about an inch long. The silver maple seeds in front of Rachel's old house are heavy and fat, an inch or two, curved. Celandine and garlic mustard gathering momentum. The taxus shrubs along Union Street have new half-inch growth. A red-bellied woodpecker and very insistent blue jay calling when I walked Bella a little before 8:00 this morning. At Ellis Pond, the yellow poplar leaves are getting fatter, some up to two inches, and the sugar maples are matching them. All the oaks are leafing a little, except the swamp chestnut oak, which is still just budded. The hickory has small round bud clusters, and some are getting ready to flower. The ashes are leafing now, small palmeates, the leaves half to a full inch. Along the south wall of the house, the tallest bamboo stalk is up to my waist. In the north garden, all the grape hyacinths are gone.

2014: More tornadoes in the South. Hail and thunder here an hour before sundown after a warm day in the 70s. The first wild strawberry flower noticed by the back porch.

2015: To Xenia and back: Full crab apple, snowball viburnums and dandelion bloom all along the road. At home, a few buds of our red-flowered crab started to open, the old azalea straining, will certainly blossom in a day or two. The white star hyacinths are still blooming in the alley, and red quince flowers hold along High Street – even though leaves are growing all around them. Planted a bed of red, plumed amaranth.

2016: Now the circle garden hyacinths dominate the backyard color, and the tall alliums are pushing out just a little just as the first of the hyacinths browns. The Kentucky coffee tree has slender, pale leaves, the Zelcova with wider leaves, both trees in adolescent leafing. From Springfield, Marianne Mitchell writes, " We have our first oriole of the year building his nest in our back yard. Very exciting." That is the earliest sighting I have recorded so far; other reports have come in from the first week of May.

The first in time and the first in importance of the influences upon the mind is that of nature. Every day, the sun; and, after sunset, Night and her stars. Ever the winds blow; ever the grass grows.

Ralph Waldo Emerson

Bill Felker

April 30th
The 120th Day of the Year

And so vast is Spring you can't set it down,
Say burgeoning bluebells, and besides
It's coming up as the rain falls.
Plants riding the rising thermal gradient
Like Hawaiian surfers wearing flowered
Bathing suits and the spray from the
Breaking wave is cherry blossom spume
Blown from dark craggy trunks.

Robert Paschell

Sunrise/set: 5:37/7:28
Day's Length: 13 hours 51 minutes
Average High/Low: 67/46
Average Temperature: 56
Record High: 90 - 1899
Record Low: 30 - 1892

Weather
Today's high temperature distribution: 15 percent chance for 80s, forty percent for 70s, forty-five percent for 60s – and this is the first time in the year on which a high below 60 degrees is unlikely. Chances for rain are 50 percent, but the clouds give way to sun 80 percent of the days. Today's record high of 90 degrees is the first record so warm in the year, and the first high above 90 since October 5th.

Natural Calendar
Many pines have new growth, some trees having pushed out tiny cones, others with fresh green needles at the tips of their branches. In town, many decorative pears have exchanged their flowers for leaves, and the forsythia shows almost no gold at all. Some orchard grass and rye are ready to harvest. Bluegrass can be budding

Bill Felker

The Stars

The stars at bedtime tell that the danger of frost is almost past. June's Arcturus still hangs a little to the east of the center of the sky, and that means a light freeze can happen one year in ten. But as that star shifts into the west, it pushes away the chances for freezing mornings with it. When Arcturus is well into the west at bedtime, any tender vegetable or flower can be planted without risk.

Daybook

1983: Field mustard blooming now. Pears leafing downtown; only a few crab apples keep their blossoms. Buckeye leaves fully developed.

1984: Leaves starting on my gingko and white mulberry.

1986: First wood sorrel seen today. First blooms on the lily-of-the-valley, sycamore leaves emerging.

1988: Cherry petals falling in the breeze. Daisies budded, half an inch across. Redbuds still in full bloom, apples and crabs too. Half the maples are leafing. Front maples just flowered, Lil's a fourth size. Peak of bleeding heart bloom and foliage. Full green tint to the woods; oaks have begun.

1990: Redbud is leafing now. Fields of dandelions go to seed throughout the county. Cowslip gone about five days ago. Dove building a nest by my window, blue jay building in the apple tree. Dayflower foliage came up a couple of days ago. Buckeyes still in full bloom. Some maples completely leafed out, others just starting. Grape vines leafing. Purple deadnettle yellowing in the yard around the aging dandelions.

1991: First purple sweet rockets opened today. Some sycamore leaves are half size now. Lily-of-the-valley just starting to bloom along Dayton Street and in the pussy willow garden.

1993: In this cool spring, most apples, dogwoods, and cherries remain in full bloom. Pears are leafing, even though many still

242

have flowers. The tree line into the North Glen valley is completely alive now either with new pale leaves or orange buds or golden flowers.

1995: Lilies-of-the-valley budded, and are almost open. There are buds too on the hawthorn trees. The first white lilacs found today. Petal fall begins in the back yard, and on scattered crab apple trees about town. The first level of the canopy, box elders and maples, pussy willows, honeysuckle, apples starts to close in. The center of dandelion bloom has passed – great fields of seeds now.

1996: Cowslip declining today across from the Covered Bridge.

1998: Oak leaves are two to three inches long by the Antioch sculpture studio, quite a bit larger than the "squirrel's ear" size I said in the newspaper. Sycamores are two inches. Juniper has one to two inches of bright, pale green new growth.

2000: Very first flax and sweet William today. Thyme has been blooming in the garden for maybe two or three days. The first horseradish flowered yesterday or the day before. Poplar almost fully leafed, the front maple leaves half size, providing shade. Clematis fully budded. Ferns up two feet in places, the big blue hosta almost that high. The blue and white wood hyacinths in the south garden are in early bloom, and the small red dwarf tulips have come in over the past week.

2001: First spiderweb seen across the pond, woven by a small long-bodied orbweaver. Wood sorrel suddenly opens in the berry patch, bright yellow in the white strawberry blossoms. The bright pink azalea opens in the east garden. First sweet rocket along Grinnell Road.

2002: Very first Korean lilac flower by my office in Columbus.

2003: Wood hyacinths are just starting to open by the west wall, purples and whites. Along the freeways, the dandelion bloom has come to an end. Viburnums are in full bloom, redbuds and crabs losing their color, petals falling. First star of Bethlehem opened yesterday in the north garden. Two new redbud trees planted.

2006: Apple blossoms gone on many trees, but many still full bloom. Redbuds and the new apple in the east garden hold well.

2007: Robins, cardinals, sparrows, finches and grackles feeding and doves mating in the back yard this morning. Blue jays calling toward Dayton Street.

2008: White boneset is bushy now, about six inches tall. Three coleus planted in the east garden. The evenings so much quieter now. Redbuds and apples still full. Chives and allium have been budded for at least a week. Clematis, trumpet vine, wisteria leafing. White bleeding hearts have been open along the east fence for a few days.

2010: Dogwoods still full, but apples and redbuds are gone. Iris are coming in now, along with allium and honeysuckles. Grackles less frequent at the feeders, red-bellied woodpeckers more insistent.

2011: First star of Bethlehem opened today. Red-bellied woodpecker steady in the morning. Blue jays very active, feeding. Small toads hopping in the lawn and south garden. Indian and wood hyacinths showing violet on their buds, pink quince early opening, buckeyes starting to flower. The first yellow swallowtail of the year passed through the yard this afternoon, another seen as I drove back from the store.

2012: Black swallowtail and a zebra swallowtail seen at lunch. Yellow warbler in the faded lilacs at 1:40 this afternoon, and the first monarch butterfly as I worked in the north garden planting roses. Hyacinths, sweet Cicely, lamium, sweet rockets, honeysuckle, lily-of-the-valley, garlic mustard, perennial salvia, early spiderwort, dominate the yard. The dooryard azalea continues to hold on so bright pink, and the Korean lilac is still full.

2013: Ellis Pond: Hemlock past knee high. Toads in the distance. Norwegian maple with two-inch leaves, maackia tree just starting to leaf. Redbuds and pink magnolia hold full. pawpaw with droplet-like leaf clusters. Sycamore leaves one to two inches. Half-inch cones starting on the spruce. At home, most of the daffodils and tulips are gone, will need to plant many more clusters for next Late Spring. The red crab apple is coming in strong, all the perennial foliage taking over throughout the gardens. Paulownia and tree of heaven are finally starting to leaf.

2014: Ellis Pond: American chestnut, pecan and European beech with straining buds, wild plum full late bloom, bur oak leaves, ginkgo and black cherry at about an inch, pear almost completely leafed, full late pink magnolia, Persian parrotia with three-inch leaves, no life on the pawpaw, lacebark elm barely leafing, mountain ash and yellow buckeye with flower buds and leaf clusters. Toads in the distance. At home, the red crab apple is in full bloom, the daffodils and tulips almost gone. The azalea has two flowers, the rest of the bush hurt very severely by the cold winter.

2015: Planted tall kale, a few more pumpkins; transplanted three Lenten rose plants to the front garden, cut back more bamboo. In the front yard, our red crab apple is in early bloom and the very first wild geranium. The first lilly-of-the-valley is just opening. Jogging through the village, I saw forget-me-nots full, wild cherry trees and crab apple trees full, a birch with dangling catkins, tree-of-heaven with short bristles of leaves, Paulownia buds barely showing, red quince holding, sweet gums just barely leafing, a few sizeable patches of tulips (and Moya's vintage yellow tulips full bloom), aging but strong redbuds and snowball viburnums everywhere.

2016: Cold and rain: First catchweed found blooming, forget-me-nots late, behind the store downtown. The red crabapple in front of our house has dropped all its petals, wild geraniums full, ranunculus coming in the southeast garden.

Waiting for spring can be like trying to go to sleep when I have insomnia. Sometimes the best thing to do is to count. Counting is a simple measure of time, limits passage to individual pieces, takes away its mystery and emptiness. Counting is an act of will, forces focus, contributes to a sense of control, works against discouragement, places the counter in opposition to the psychology and physiology of sleeplessness.

Numbers are infinite, and so are the pieces of winter. Counting in sequence creates apparent progress and finite limits. Even though awareness of winter's events seems to produce few results, seems to have no sum or substance, observations can be like digits in a sprawling but promising nighttime equation, the fruit of persistence and dogged hope.

Like counting sheep or breaths or numerals, counting dimensions of the interval between autumn and April requires no rules or ethics, is not competitive, does not require special study or skill. Like counting sheep or breaths or numerals, the choice of things to be counted is arbitrary, has no necessary socially redeeming value, does not end poverty or bring peace, has no theology.

This is the anarchy, the freedom that looses the mind's eye to rhythm or accumulation or listing or repetition or the emptiness of any single object until something new suddenly occurs without our creating it and we fall asleep and dream or discover spring.

bf

Bill Felker

Bill Felker has been writing *Poor Will's Almanack* for newspapers and magazines since 1984, and he has published annual almanacs since 2003. His radio version of *Poor Will* is broadcast weekly on NPR station WYSO and is available on podcast at **www.wyso.org.** His first book of essays, *Home is the Prime Meridian: Essays in Search of Time and Place and Spirit,* was published in 2017 and is available on Amazon. A second collection of essays and the entire twelve volumes of *A Daybook for the Year in Yellow Springs, Ohio* are expected to be available by early 2019.

For more information, visit Bill Felker's website at **www.poorwillsalmanack.com**

Bill Felker

—

A Daybook for April

Made in the USA
Columbia, SC
18 March 2018